REBEL RAIDER

ADMIRAL SEMMES
The first great commerce raider of the days of steam.

REBEL RAIDER

BEING AN ACCOUNT OF
Raphael Semmes's
Cruise in the C. S. S. Sumter

COMPOSED IN LARGE PART OF EXTRACTS FROM SEMMES'S

MEMOIRS OF SERVICE AFLOAT

WRITTEN IN THE YEAR 1869

SELECTED AND SUPPLEMENTED BY

HARPUR ALLEN GOSNELL

LIEUTENANT COMMANDER, U.S.N.R.

Chapel Hill
THE UNIVERSITY OF NORTH CAROLINA PRESS
1948

COPYRIGHT, 1948, BY
THE UNIVERSITY OF NORTH CAROLINA PRESS
MANUFACTURED IN THE UNITED STATES OF AMERICA

BY THE WILLIAM BYRD PRESS, INC.
RICHMOND, VIRGINIA

THIS BOOK WAS DIGITALLY PRINTED

PREFACE

COMMANDER RAPHAEL SEMMES OF THE CONFEDerate States Navy made a cruise in the *Sumter* which rivalled in importance and perhaps exceeded in interest his better known cruise in the *Alabama*. This volume takes the narrative of the *Sumter's* career out of Semmes's *Memoirs of Service Afloat* and presents it just as written, with one very comprehensive exception. The narrative alone is reprinted here; all of the extraneous material with which it is so profusely interspersed and surrounded has been eliminated, since that has little or no bearing upon the ship and her people, or their adventures. As an example, the original *Memoirs* get under way with a cool 25,000 words on the legal pros and cons of secession.

The international law of war and neutrality is touched upon often by Commander Semmes. He was anxious that all the niceties should be observed by himself and his ship in order that nothing should reflect upon his new homeland in the eyes of the world. Since World War I the average person has the idea that international law in time of war has little force. This is a terribly mistaken notion. He who holds it overlooks the hundreds of occasions on which a law is obeyed, as contrasted with the isolated notorious instances of its violation; similarly he forgets the dozens of laws that are observed every time without exception. And of course there are reasons why the international law of war is observed—wholly apart from the fact that so many States and persons are prone to do the decent thing instinctively. The great deterrent is fear of reprisal. Such reprisals in different instances may cover an extremely wide range. They may vary from some minor immediate retaliation in kind carried out by the offended individual, all the way to the declaration of war by a strong neutral State. This latter may cause the offending belligerent to lose his war instead of win it—a slight difference.

It is realized that the reader is not desirous of making any great study of international law in this book. Therefore no comment will be made by the present writer about any point that comes up *unless the action taken was incorrect.* This was not true on many occasions. For instance, for a particular occurrence, there were often Semmes's contention, the Federal contention, and neutral action. The neutral action was usually correct. And in many more instances Semmes voiced his contention and acted accordingly. And he was usually correct too. In all such episodes no comment is appended to the original text, and the reader can assume that the procedure was in accordance with the law. Where bad law was imposed in a number of similar cases the infraction will ordinarily be pointed out in the first instance only. In one or two places where extended comments are called for, they are inserted a page or so after the event in order that the continuity of the narrative may not be impaired.

Much of the editing that appears in a volume such as this one is necessarily of the kind that takes the opposite side of the question from that held by the original author. Accordingly some readers may feel that some lack of generosity is being shown. The present editor hopes that such feeling will not arise; and in any case he is confident that anyone who reads the original edition will agree that the venerated Admiral does not appear at a disadvantage in this later work.

As each question of law will be covered pretty fully as it comes up in the following pages no discussion of details will be presented here. Two very important general points will be mentioned, however, in order that the readers may better comprehend things from the outset: The Confederacy was never recognized *de jure* as an independent nation. However, owing to its military strength and the magnitude of the war which resulted from secession, the Confederacy was early recognized as a *de facto* government—as a "belligerent." "Belligerent rights" were accorded by neutral States and conceded by the Union government. This means that, even with no "recognition of independence," the Southern armed forces and government agents received all the rights and were under all the obligations under the international law of war and neutrality that are enjoined upon the subjects of any State that is at war. The details of all these rights and obligations are another matter. The fundamental principle underlying a great many of them, however, may be understood if one remembers the precept expressed so admirably by A. Pearce Higgins, the eminent English authority: "International law will not allow neutrals to do for one belligerent that which the success of his adversary's navy prevents his doing for himself."

Neither the text nor this Preface will undertake to clear up for the reader many of the host of tiny points of sea lore and terminology. There are, however, two oft-recurring questions which will confuse many, and they will be covered here in a few lines. It will be observed that Semmes speaks often of "knots per hour" which expression we are now taught to abjure. For some time now a knot has been a unit of velocity only, and means a "nautical mile *per hour.*" (A sea mile equals approximately 1.15 land miles.) Seventy-five years ago it was not incorrect to use the word "knot" interchangeably as a unit of distance also, (equalling one sea mile). Thus Semmes on different occasions wrote, for instance, "8 knots" or "8 knots per hour," meaning in each case eight sea miles per hour.

Then there is the use of the term "ship." Semmes's use of it does not differ from the correct usage of today. But there are two fundamentally different kinds of "ships". One kind is a three-masted sailing vessel with square sails on all masts, as distinguished, for instance, from schooners, brigs, etc. Then again, "ship" is the broad term used for any seagoing vessel and thus *includes* all of the first kind of ships. *Neither one is ever a "boat."*

CONTENTS

		PAGE
	Preface	v
I.	North and South	3
II.	The *Sumter* Runs the Gantlet	11
III.	Cienfuegos, "The Land of a Hundred Fires"	33
IV.	On the Spanish Main	54
V.	The English, the French, and the Dutch	79
VI.	The Birds Have Flown	101
VII.	In the Shadow of Mont Pelée	121
VIII.	"Stand By to Cut!"	136
IX.	The North Atlantic in December	147
X.	Battling the Don	160
XI.	"The Rock"	175
XII.	The Sand is Running Out	190
XIII.	The *Alabama* and After	195

APPENDICES

A.	Chronology of the C. S. S. *Sumter*	207
B.	Northern Vessels Captured	209
C.	Neutral Vessels Overhauled	210
	Index	213

ILLUSTRATIONS

Raphael Semmes, the First Great Commerce
    Raider of the Days of Steam   *Frontispiece*

                                                        FACING PAGE

The Confederate Cruiser *Sumter* leaving New Orleans,
    June 18, 1861. From a sketch made at the time   20
The U. S. Steam Sloop-of-War *Brooklyn*   21
The U. S. Sidewheel Sloop-of-War *Powhatan*   21
The *Sumter* running the blockade of Pass à L'Outre, by the
    enemy's ship *Brooklyn*, on the 30th June, 1861   36
Captain Charles H. Poor, of the U. S. S. *Brooklyn*   37
Track of the C. S. S. *Sumter* in the year 1861   52
Officers of the C. S. S. *Sumter:* Lieutenants W. E. Evans, R. T.
    Chapman, J. M. Kell, J. M. Stribling; Engineer M. J.
    Freeman; Surgeon F. Galt; and Paymaster H. Myers   53
Lieutenant John McIntosh Kell, C. S. N., First Lieutenant of
    both the *Sumter* and the *Alabama*   68
The U. S. Steam Sloop-of-War *Iroquois*   69
The Burning of the Clipper Ship *Harvey Birch* in the English
    Channel by the C. S. S. *Nashville,* November 19, 1861 69
The *Sumter* running the blockade of St. Pierre, Martinique,
    by the enemy's ship *Iroquois* on the 23d November, 1861 132
Captain J. S. Palmer of the U. S. S. *Iroquois*   133
Gibraltar and Vicinity   148
The U. S. Steam Sloop-of-War *Tuscarora*   149
Semmes's Nemesis, the U. S. S. *Kearsarge*   149

REBEL RAIDER

CHAPTER I

North and South

RAPHAEL SEMMES WAS BORN IN CHARLES County, Maryland, on September 27, 1809. Of English-French stock he came from forebears who had been in this country for many generations, one of his ancestors having been a signer of the Declaration of Independence. His education was marked in general by two features: first, the small amount of any formal schooling; and secondly, his careful application to the study of law, which interest began at an early age and ran through his entire life. It started when he was a boy in Georgetown, D. C., where he, an orphan, was brought up by an uncle and aunt. It would be unjust ever to refer to Semmes as a "sea lawyer," because of the unfortunate connotations so often implied in that phrase. He did become learned in most of the important branches of the law, including admiralty and international law. We shall find him many times contending for the justice and correctness of his side of the case, whether it was connected with international law or other rights and privileges, and whether he was involved with opponents in or outside his ship. He was not the "sea lawyer" type, moreover, because his contentions were always in order and properly made, and were almost always correct.

Semmes's long naval career began in 1826 when he was appointed midshipman. There was no Naval Academy in those days and the midshipmen were sent to sea, there to receive their training and the greater part, if not all, of their meagre schooling. His first ship was the *Lexington,* and his cruise in her was notable for a voyage to Trinidad. The mission was the return to this country of the remains of Commodore Oliver Hazard Perry; he, at the age of 28, had made himself immortal by his victory in 1813 over the British fleet in the Battle of Lake Erie—"We have met the enemy and they are ours,—two ships, two brigs, one schooner and one sloop."

With cruises in the *Erie* and *Brandywine,* Semmes completed his midshipman's training in 1832, becoming thus a Passed Midshipman. He graduated first in his class. Then came the first of several instances in his naval career when Semmes seems to have been more or less laid on the shelf. For a year he did duty at Norfolk consisting primarily of care of and supervision over the Navy's chronometers. Interludes such as this one came about, no doubt, as a result of his superiors having noted his studious nature, his academic attainments, and his somewhat retiring disposition. After the time with the chronometers, he had to wait for two years before receiving his first real assignment. In the interval he was able to concentrate seriously on his law, and he was admitted to the bar.

In 1835 Semmes was ordered to the U. S. Frigate *Constellation* for his first tour of active sea duty as an officer. This famous vessel, now 150 years old, is still on the Navy List, having been dry-docked for repairs in August, 1946, after an adventurous "voyage" from Newport to Boston at the end of a tow rope. Early in 1837, Passed Midshipman Semmes became Lieutenant Semmes and shortly thereafter he was married. His bride was Anne Elizabeth Spencer of New Jersey. She, the daughter of a Protestant missionary, became a Catholic in conformity with the religion of her husband.

Apart from a brief period on the Receiving Ship at Norfolk in 1840, Lieutenant Semmes was inactive virtually for all of the interval from the end of his cruise in the *Constellation* until 1841. In this year he received orders to shore duty at the Navy Yard at Pensacola, Florida. He moved his home close to Pensacola, occupying a house in an adjacent spot in Alabama where, even now, few communities exist. He changed his citizenship from Maryland to Alabama. In those days one's citizenship of a State was a not unimportant matter, though no "oath of allegiance" was involved.

The tour of navy yard duty, which lasted two years, was followed by more than five years of sea service including the years of the Mexican War. These five years commenced auspiciously when Semmes received his first command. It was a vessel of only 250 tons, the *Poinsett,* but she was a steamer, one of the very few in the Navy at that time. She was one of three which the Army had acquired for the prosecution of the Seminole Indian War in Florida. This ended in 1842 and the Navy took over the steamers. More than likely because of the fact that she was a steamer, the *Poinsett* was selected, in 1844, to carry to Vera Cruz a representative of the State Department who was then to proceed to Mexico City. Semmes wangled permission to accompany his passenger on the overland journey and thus made the first of his several worthwhile visits to Mexico. Semmes had the *Poinsett* for a year and a half, after which she was sold (in 1845) for the princely sum of $5,000.

Back to sail again and there were brief tours of duty in the *Consort, Warren, Porpoise,* and then the *Somers* of ill-fated memory. This last vessel, a brig, was under a cloud as a result of the incipient mutiny on the high seas which had been nipped in the bud on board her in 1842. The culprits were tried and three of them were hanged in short order, two of them having meanwhile confessed. The noteworthy feature was the fact that one of the two, an acting midshipman, was the son of the Secretary of War. It is not difficult to imagine that his punishment would not have been consummated if the proceedings had been allowed to drag on until and after the ship had reached a home port. He was a thoroughly bad egg who had escaped punishment on several earlier occasions only through political influence.

Semmes got command of the *Somers* in 1846 and by this time hostilities with Mexico had commenced. In his few brief weeks in her, he acquired a high reputation for seamanship and energy on the blockade duty to which the *Somers* was assigned. The station was the vicinity of Vera Cruz, and one very interesting incident occurred shortly after Semmes took over. A vessel had slipped through the blockade—in another ship's sector—and there she lay at anchor under the enemy's fortifications. Semmes determined to move in and destroy her. In daring style, one dark night, he took his ship in as close as practicable and fitted out a boat's crew. This boat and its crew from the *Somers* stole in, boarded the blockade-runner, burned her, and returned to their ship. All in the manner of Decatur's gallant destruction of the captured *Philadelphia* in the harbor of Tripoli in 1804.

Sad to relate, this "blockade-runner" had been deliberately allowed to pierce the blockade; she had actually been *sent* in for purposes of espionage. Word of this had not been passed, for no one had imagined that a project such as the one which Semmes actually carried out would even be contemplated. This outcome, in turn, is reminiscent of the 1918 affair in which an Italian officer in a one-man mobile raft penetrated the defenses of Pola harbor, and mined and sank an Austrian battleship. For, in this latter instance, it had not yet been learned that the battleship had earlier gone over to the newly organized Jugoslavs.

Shortly after the "blockade-runner" incident, the *Somers* ended her turbulent career. She turned over in a light squall and went down in ten minutes with half her crew. Semmes got out of this one cleanly, as he was acquitted by the subsequent Court of Inquiry and was given two commands afterwards. This would appear to have been rather lucky, as Semmes himself admits that his ship was almost completely unballasted—"scarcely any water or provisions, and but 6 tons of ballast on board." Thus she was not prepared to encounter even the lightest of squalls while carrying more than the shortest sail. Yet the *Somers* (according to Semmes) was carrying topsails, courses, jib and spanker. When Semmes's attention was called to the approaching squall, he ordered the mainsail and spanker furled. When the squall struck, the mainsail was off her and the spanker half furled. No other incident is at hand where Semmes's seamanship has been in question.

After the *Somers* was lost Semmes served as flag lieutenant to Commodore Conner who commanded the blockading squadron. During the siege of Vera Cruz, some of the American guns ashore were Navy ordnance. Semmes commanded one of the batteries of these pieces. After the surrender of the city, it will be remembered, General Winfield Scott's army set out on its victorious march to and into Mexico City. In the course of this expedition, word was received at base headquarters that certain U. S. officers who had been captured were not receiving proper treatment at the hands of the Mexicans. Semmes was chosen to proceed to the front, pass into the enemy lines, and make representations on the subject. He was undoubtedly selected because of his earlier journey from Vera Cruz to Mexico City. By the time he reached the American advanced forces, the prisoners in question had escaped. Thereupon another fortunate break developed for Semmes. It was deemed impracticable for him to travel back to the coast at this time. Accordingly he was attached to the staff of General Worth and proceeded with the army all the way to its final destination. This is doubly fortunate for posterity, as Semmes's book on his Mexican interlude is at least one of the most interesting of all the literature on that war. All this was in 1847 and he is credited with eleven months of continuous "sea duty" (!) in that year.

Next, Semmes was ordered to take over command of the U.S.S. *Electra* which he did in January, 1848, serving five uneventful months in her. The war ended before this duty was completed. There was another tour in the Pensacola Navy Yard which lasted six months. His last service in a United States naval vessel was a short cruise in command of the *Flirt* which terminated in 1849. Up to this time, in the opinion of one of his sons, he had had more real sea duty than any other officer of comparable rank and length of service. Here, however, the dead hand of a reduced Navy laid him up "waiting orders." At this point, he moved his home to Mobile, Alabama. He was kept in an inactive status for seven long years. These were far from wasted years, however, as he turned back to his law and was able to give it his undivided attention for a sufficiently long period to progress well and far in the profession.

In spite of his naval inactivity in these years, Semmes was slowly crawling nearer the top of the list of lieutenants. He made commander in September, 1855, and was called back to active duty shortly afterwards. He served as Light-House Inspector until 1858. Then, after an inactive interval of three months, he became Secretary of the Light-House Board sitting in Washington.

At the age of fifty Semmes was sparely built, above average height but not a tall man. He had inherited certain physical characteristics of the Latin type. One can feel some tenseness concealed under his reserve. Often he seemed to be holding strong feelings in check. Likewise he appears to have had a certain inability to make close friendships, to obtain that pleasure in life which comes from sympathetic companionship with his brother officers and other associates. Of course this is a doubly difficult attainment for anyone to achieve while holding the position of commanding officer of a ship which is necessarily officered by younger men. A reader of his works acquires a feeling that he often tried without complete success to get close to his companions, though he was always liked and respected by all who came in contact with him.

We find Semmes still serving as Secretary of the Light-House Board as 1860 drew to a close. The first point of interest to us in our main story, upon which we are now entering, was his receipt of a letter from "a distinguished member of the Federal Congress from the South." In his reply Semmes outlined very correctly the best means that could and should be adopted by the Southern States for waging naval war against the North if hostilities were to come. The thesis was commerce destruction; and Semmes himself was to become the most famous exponent of his own theories.

Before the beginning of 1861 Semmes had already decided to resign his commission in the Navy when the proper time should arrive. Early in February he had written a letter to "a Southern member of the Federal Congress temporarily absent from his post," the gist of which was that he was "standing by." Just about this time, February 11, he was promoted to actual membership on the Light-House Board. It was an extremely brief term that he served. On February 14 he received a telegram from the Chairman of the Committee on Naval Affairs of the newly organized Southern government, requesting him to repair at once to Montgomery, Alabama, then the capital of the Confederacy. He replied in a few hours that he would come immediately. He resigned his commission in the Navy on February 15 and it was accepted the same day. Semmes left Washington on the 16th and reached Montgomery on the 19th.

As soon as he arrived he called upon Jefferson Davis who outlined his first duties. He was to be sent north for arms and munitions and for men skilled in their manufacture. His later dealings in this connection demonstrate the strange and anomalous situation that existed during the period just prior to the attack on Fort Sumter; and part of the story does not reflect a great deal of credit on the ethics and integrity of some of those in the North. Before leaving Montgomery, however, Semmes attended a joint session of the Military and Naval Affairs Committees of the Confederate Congress. He received a commission as Commander in the navy of the Confederacy then rapidly taking shape; he saw Davis again and left Montgomery for the North two days after arrival.

Semmes stopped off for a day in Richmond and inspected the state arsenal and the Tredegar Iron Works (Virginia having not yet seceded). In Washington he went through the Federal Arsenal, no less, examining machinery and interviewing mechanics! Passing through New York he visited his son at West Point who was then a cadet at the U. S. Military Academy; this son later became a major in the Confederate Army. Then followed a three weeks' tour of the shops of New York, Connecticut and Massachusetts, during which time Semmes carried out his mission of buying and contracting for munitions, machinery and mechanics. He arranged a code for future correspondence. The principal concrete result of his efforts was the purchase of a quantity of powder and percussion caps which he was able to ship south openly by express! But the contracts which Semmes made could not be carried out on account of the subsequent outbreak of hostilities. While in New York City he received a letter from the Secretary of the Confederate States Navy, Stephen R. Mallory, written March 3. This letter directed Semmes to try to get hold of "two or more" ships suitable for conversion into fast, shallow-draft, coast-defense vessels; the Secretary had heard that certain ones were available. Semmes could find none. As armed conflict drew nearer it become more and more difficult to accomplish what he had come north to do, and he felt obliged to give it up.

At the end of March Semmes sailed from New York for Savannah on a steamer flying the U. S. flag, with the Confederate flag at the fore! (The flag at the fore truck indicates the country of destination.) He reached Montgomery on April 4. He was made head of the Lighthouse Bureau of the new government, he being the sole naval officer in the organization. The Bureau was just about started when Fort Sumter was fired upon—April 12; and the war was on.

It took Semmes almost no time to see Secretary Mallory and request sea duty. During the same interview he expounded his thesis of commerce destruction and successfully urged the Secretary to adopt that course of action. At the time, there was a board of naval officers in session at New Orleans looking over all available ships with a view to their possible use as naval vessels. All had been rejected as unsuitable. The Secretary brought forth a list of such ships that he had just received that day. In it Semmes spied "a small propeller steamer, of five hundred tons burden [cargo carrying capacity], sea-going, with a low-pressure engine, sound, and capable of being so strengthened as to be enabled to carry an ordinary battery of four, or five guns. Her speed was reported to be between nine, and ten knots, but unfortunately, said the Board, she carries but five days' fuel, and has no accommodations for the crew of a ship of war." Semmes thought he could make her do, and asked that she be given to him. The Secretary agreed and the ship was purchased.

This vessel was the British steam packet *Habana* which had reached New Orleans before the blockade had been clamped down on the mouths of the Mississippi River. On April 18 Semmes was detached from his desk in the Lighthouse Bureau and ordered to take command of this first real man-of-war to fly the flag of the new Confederate States. She was renamed *Sumter* in honor of the recent capture of the fort of that name. Though since widely forgotten, this ship for a time brought far greater notoriety to the name of Sumter than did the fort itself. Semmes lost no time in reaching his new command. He left Montgomery the same day he received his orders, and steamed down the river to Mobile. After a few hours in that city he sailed for New Orleans. Commander Semmes, though not yet raised in rank, now became "Captain" Semmes, for he had command of a vessel. And at this point we shall let him take up the narrative, for, as the reader will immediately observe, he is eminently qualified to do so. As Semmes provided no chapter titles they have been supplied herein.

CHAPTER II

The Sumter *Runs the Gantlet*

I ARRIVED IN NEW ORLEANS, ON MONDAY, THE 22D of April, and at once put myself in communication with the commanding naval officer, the venerable Lawrence Rousseau, since gone to his long home, full of years, and full of honors. . . . On the same day of my arrival, in company with Lieutenant Chapman, I inspected, and took possession of my new ship. I found her only a dismantled packet-ship, full of upper cabins, and other top-hamper, furniture, and crockery, but as unlike a ship of war as possible. Still, I was pleased with her general appearance. Her lines were easy, and graceful, and she had a sort of saucy air about her, which seemed to say, that she was not averse to the service on which she was about to be employed.

A great change was apparent in New Orleans since I had last visited it. The levée in front of the city was no longer a great mart of commerce, piled with cotton bales, and supplies going back to the planter; densely packed with steamers, and thronged with a busy multitude. The long lines of shipping above the city had been greatly thinned, and a general air of desolation hung over the river front. It seemed as though a pestilence brooded over the doomed city, and that its inhabitants had fled before the fell destroyer. The *Sumter* lay on the opposite side of the river, at Algiers, and I crossed over every morning to superintend her refitment. I was sometimes detained at the ferry-house, waiting for the ferry-boat, and on these occasions, casting my eyes up and down the late busy river, it was not unfrequent to see it without so much as a skiff in motion on its bosom.

But this first simoon of the desert which had swept over the city, as a foretaste of what was to come, had by no means discouraged its patriotic inhabitants. The activity of commerce had ceased, it is true, but another description of activity had taken its place. War now occupied the thoughts of the multitude, and the sound of the drum, and the tramp of armed men were heard in the streets. The balconies were crowded with lovely women in gay attire, to witness the military processions, and the Confederate flag in miniature was pinned on almost every bosom. The enthusiasm of the Frenchman had been most easily and gracefully blended with the stern determination of the Southern man of English descent; the consequence of which was, that there was more demonstrative patriotism in New Orleans, than in any other of our Southern cities. Nor was this patriotism demonstrative only, it was deep and real, and was afterward sealed with some of the best Creole blood of the land, poured out, freely, on many a desperate battle-field. . . .

I now took my ship actively in hand, and set gangs of mechanics at work to remove her upper cabins, and other top-hamper, preparatory to making the necessary alterations. These latter were considerable, and I soon found that I had a tedious job on my hands. It was no longer the case, as it had been in former years, when I had had occasion to fit out a ship, that I could go into a navy-yard, with well-provided workshops, and skilled workmen ready with all the requisite materials at hand to execute my orders. Everything had to be improvised, from the manufacture of a water-tank, to the "kids, and cans" of the berth-deck messes, and from a gun-carriage to a friction-primer. I had not only to devise all the alterations but to make plans, and drawings of them, before they could be comprehended. The main deck was strengthened, by the addition of heavy beams to enable it to support the battery; a berth-deck was laid for the accommodation of the crew; the engine, which was partly above the water-line, was protected by a system of wood-work, and iron bars; the ship's rig was altered so as to convert her into a barkentine [sic], with square-sails on her fore and main-masts; the officers' quarters, including my own cabin, were re-arranged; new suits of sails were made, and new boats constructed; hammocks and bedding were procured for the crew, and guns, gun-carriages, and ammunition ordered. Two long, tedious months were consumed in making these various alterations, and additions. My battery was to consist of an eight-inch shell gun, to be pivoted amidships, and of four light thirty-two pounders, of thirteen cwt. each, in broadside.

The Secretary of the Navy, who was as anxious as myself that I should get to sea immediately, had given me all the assistance in his power, readily acceding to my requests, and promptly filling, or causing to be filled, all my requisitions. With the secession of Virginia we had become possessed of a valuable depot of naval supplies, in the Norfolk Navy Yard. It was filled with guns, shot, shell, cordage, and everything that was useful in the equipment of a ship, but it was far away from New Orleans, and such was the confusion along the different lines of railroad, that it was difficult to procure transportation. Commander Terry Sinclair, the active ordnance officer of the yard, had early dispatched my guns, by railroad, but weeks elapsed without my being able to hear anything of them. I was finally obliged to send a lieutenant in search of them, who picked them up, one by one, as they had been thrown out on the road-side, to make room for other freight. My gun-carriages I was obliged to have constructed myself, and I was fortunate enough to obtain the services of a very ingenious mechanic to assist me in this part of my duties—Mr. Roy, a former employee of the Custom-House, within whose ample walls he had established his work-shop. He contrived most ingeniously, and constructed out of railroad iron, one of the best carriages (or rather, slide and circle) for a pivot-gun, which I have ever seen. The large foundry of Leeds & Co. took the contract for casting my shot, and shells, and executed it to my satisfaction. . . .

A rendezvouz had been opened, and a crew had been shipped for her, which was temporarily berthed on board the receiving ship, *Star of the West*, a transport-steamer of the enemy, which had been gallantly captured by some Texans, and turned over to the Navy. New Orleans was full of seamen, discharged from ships that had been laid up, and more men were offering themselves for service, than I could receive. I had the advantage, therefore, of picking my crew, an advantage which no one but a seaman can fully appreciate. My lieutenants, surgeon, paymaster, and marine officer had all arrived, and, with the consent of the Navy Department, I had appointed my engineers—one chief, and three assistants—boatswain, carpenter, and sailmaker. My provisions had been purchased, and were ready to be put on board, and my funds had already arrived, but we were still waiting on the mechanics, who, though doing their best, had not yet been able to turn the ship over to us. From the following letter to the Secretary of the Navy, inclosing a requisition for funds, it will be seen that my demands upon the department were quite moderate, and that I expected to make the *Sumter pay her own expenses,* as soon as she should get to sea.

NEW ORLEANS, May 14, 1861.

SIR:—I have the honor to inclose, herewith, a requisition for the sum of $10,000, which I request may be remitted to the paymaster of the *Sumter,* in specie, for use during my contemplated cruise. I may find it necessary to coal several times, and to supply my crew with fresh provisions, &c., before I have the opportunity of replenishing my military chest from the enemy.

The ammunition remained to be provided, and on the 20th of May, I dispatched Lieutenant Chapman to the Baton Rouge Arsenal, which had been captured a short time before, for the purpose of procuring it, under the following letter of instructions:

NEW ORLEANS, May 20, 1861.

SIR:—You will proceed to Baton Rouge, and put yourself in communication with the commander of the C. S. Arsenal, at that point, for the purpose of receiving the ammunition, arms, shot, shell, &c., that may be required for the supply of the C. S. steamer *Sumter,* now fitting for sea at this port. It is presumed that the proper orders [which had been requested] have been, or will be dispatched from Montgomery, authorizing the issue of all such articles, as we may need. Should this not be the case, with regard to any of the articles, it is hoped that the ordnance officer in charge will not hesitate to deliver them, as it is highly important that the *Sumter* should not be detained, because of any oversight, or informality, in the orders of the War Department. Be pleased to present the accompanying requisition to Captain Booth, the superintendent, and ask that it may be filled. The gunner will be directed to report to you, to accompany you to Baton Rouge, on this service.

The reader will thus perceive that many difficulties lay in the way of equipping the *Sumter;* that I was obliged to pick up one material here, and another there, as I could best find it, and that I was not altogether free from the routine of the "Circumlocution

Office," as my requisitions had frequently to pass through many hands, before they could be complied with.

About this time, we met with a sad accident in the loss of one of our midshipmen, by drowning. He, with other young officers of the *Sumter*, had been stationed, temporarily, on board the receiving ship, in charge of the *Sumter's* crew, whilst the latter ship was still in the hands of the mechanics. The following letter of condolence to the father of the young gentleman will sufficiently explain the circumstances of the disaster

NEW ORLEANS, May 18, 1861.

SIR:—It becomes my melancholy duty to inform you, of the death, by drowning, yesterday, of your son, Midshipman John F. Holden, of the C. S. steamer *Sumter*. Your son was temporarily attached to the receiving ship (late *Star of the West*) at this place, whilst the *Sumter* was being prepared for sea, and whilst engaged in carrying out an anchor, in a boat belonging to that ship, met his melancholy fate, along with three of the crew, by the swamping of the boat, in which he was embarked. I offer you, my dear sir, my heartfelt condolence on this sad bereavement. You have lost a cherished son, and the Government a valuable and promising young officer.

W. B. HOLDEN, ESQ., *Louisburg, Tenn.*

War had begun, thus early, to demand of us our sacrifices. Tennessee had not yet seceded, and yet this ardent Southern youth had withdrawn from the Naval Academy, and cast his lot with his section.

A few extracts from my journal will now, perhaps, give the reader a better idea of the progress of my preparations for sea, and of passing events, than any other form of narrative. *May 27th.*—News received this morning of the appearance, at Pass à L'Outre, yesterday, of the U. S. steamer *Brooklyn*, and of the establishment of the blockade. Work is progressing satisfactorily, and I expect to be ready for sea, by Sunday next. . . .

Monday, May 30th. My patience is sorely tried by the mechanics. The water-tanks for the *Sumter* are not yet completed. The carriage for the 8-inch gun was finished, to-day, and we are busy laying down the circles for it, and cutting the holes for the fighting-bolts. The carriages for the 32-pounders are promised us, by Saturday next, and also the copper tanks for the magazine. Our ammunition, and small arms arrived, yesterday, from Baton Rouge. Besides the *Brooklyn,* at the Passes, we learn, to-day, that the *Niagara,* and *Minnesota,* two of the enemy's fastest, and heaviest steamships have arrived, to assist in enforcing the blockade, and to lie in wait for some ships expected to arrive, laden with arms and ammunition, for the Confederacy. [The *Niagara* at that time was possibly the fastest heavy United States ship, having made 10.9 knots (in smooth water) on her trials. Men-of-war were not speedy in those days.]

May 31st.—The tanks are at last finished, and they have all been delivered, to-day. Leeds & Co. have done an excellent job, and I shall be enabled to carry three months' water for my crew. We shall now get on, rapidly, with our preparations.

Saturday, June 1st, finds us not yet ready for sea! The tanks have all been taken on board, and stowed; the gun carriages for the 32s will be finished on Monday. The circles for the 8-inch gun have been laid down, and the fighting-bolts are ready for placing. On Monday I shall throw the crew on board, and by Thursday next, I shall, *without doubt* be ready for sea. We are losing a great deal of precious time. The enemy's flag is being flaunted in our faces, at all our ports by his ships of war, and his vessels of commerce are passing, and repassing, on the ocean, in defiance, or in contempt of our power, and, as yet, we have not struck a blow.

At length on the 3d of June, I was enabled to put the *Sumter,* formally, in commission. On that day her colors were hoisted, for the first time—the ensign having been presented to me, by some patriotic ladies of New Orleans—the crew was transferred to her, from the receiving ship, and the officers were ordered to mess on board. The ship was now hauled off and anchored in the stream, but we were delayed two long and tedious weeks yet, before we were finally ready. During these two weeks we made a trial trip up the river, some ten or twelve miles. Some of the principal citizens were invited on board, and a bright, and beautiful afternoon was pleasantly spent, in testing the qualities of the ship, the range of her guns, and the working of the gun-carriages; the whole ending by a collation, in partaking of which my guests were kind enough to wish me a career full of *"blazing* honors."

I was somewhat disappointed in the speed of my ship, as we did not succeed in getting more than nine knots out of her. There was another great disadvantage. With all the space I could allot to my coal-bunkers, she could be made to carry no more than about

THE *Sumter* RUNS THE GANTLET

eight days' fuel. We had masts, and sails, it is true, but these could be of but little use, when the coal was exhausted, as the propeller would remain a drag in the water, there being no means of hoisting it. It was with such drawbacks, that I was to take the sea, alone, against a vindictive and relentless enemy, whose Navy already swarmed on our coasts, and whose means of increasing it were inexhaustible. But the sailor has a saying, that "Luck is a Lord," and we trusted to luck.

On the 18th of June, after all the vexatious delays that have been described, I got up my anchor, and dropped down to the Barracks, below the city a short distance, to receive my powder on board, which, for safety, had been placed in the State magazine. At 10.30 P.M. of the same day, we got up steam, and by the soft and brilliant light of a moon near her full, threw ourselves into the broad, and swift current of the Father of Waters, and ran rapidly down to the anchorage, between Fort Jackson, and Fort St. Philip, where we came to at 4 A.M. In the course of the day, Captain Brand, an ex-officer of the old Navy, and now second in command of the forts, came on board to make us the ceremonial visit; and I subsequently paid my respects to Major Duncan, the officer in chief command, and ex-officer of the old Army. These gentlemen were both busy, as I found upon inspecting the forts, in perfecting their batteries, and drilling their men, for the hot work that was evidently before them. As was unfortunately the case with our people, generally, at this period, they were over-confident. They kindly supplied some few deficiencies, that still remained in our gunner's department, and I received from them a howitzer, which I mounted on my taffarel, to guard against boat attacks, by night.

I remained three days at my anchors between the forts, for the purpose of stationing, and drilling my crew, before venturing into the presence of the enemy; and I will take advantage of this lull to bring up some matters connected with the ship, which we have hitherto overlooked. On the 7th of June, the Secretary of the Navy—the Government having, in the mean time, removed to Richmond—sent me my sailing orders, and in my letter of the 14th of the same month, acknowledging their receipt, I had said to him: "I have an excellent set of men on board, though they are nearly all green, and will require some little practice, and drilling, at the guns, to enable them to handle them creditably. Should I be fortunate enough to reach the high seas, you may rely upon my implicit obedience of your instructions, 'to do the enemy's commerce the greatest injury, in the shortest time.' "

Here was a model of a letter of instruction—it meant "burn, sink, and destroy," always, of course, within the limits prescribed by the laws of nations, and with due attention to the laws of humanity, in the treatment of prisoners. The reader will see, as we progress, that I gave the "implicit obedience" which had been promised, to these instructions, and that if greater results were not accomplished, it was the fault of the *Sumter,* and not of her commander. In the same letter that brought me my sailing orders, the Secretary had suggested to me the propriety of adopting some means of communicating with him, by cipher, so that, my despatches, if captured by the enemy, would be unintelligible to him. The following letter in reply to this suggestion, will explain how this was arranged: "I have the honor to enclose herewith a copy of 'Reid's English Dictionary,' a duplicate of which I retain, for the purpose mentioned in your letter of instructions, of the 7th instant. I have not been able to find in the city of New Orleans, 'Cobb's Miniature Lexicon,' suggested by you, or any other suitable dictionary, with but a single column on a page. This need make no difference, however. In my communications to the Department, should I have occasion to refer to a word in the copy sent, I will designate the first column on the page, A, and the second column, B. Thus, if I wish to use the word 'prisoner,' my reference to it would be as follows: 323, B, 15; the first number referring to the page, the letter to the column, and the second number to the number of the word from the top of the column." By means of this simple, and cheap device, I was enabled, at all times, to keep my despatches out of the hands of the enemy, or, in other words, prevent him from interpreting them, when I had anything of importance to communicate. [A common device in many wars. As in this case, however, a book with wide circulation such as a dictionary is usually selected; the result is that the enemy quickly breaks the code by discovering the identity of the book through industrious trial of many volumes. In this case the search would be immediately limited to books having two columns per page.]

Before leaving New Orleans, I had, in obedience to a general order of the service, transmitted to the Navy Department, a Muster Roll of the officers, and men, serving on board the *Sumter.* Her crew, as reported by this roll, consisted of ninety-two persons, exclusive of officers. Twenty of these ninety-two persons were marines—a larger guard than was usual for so small a ship. The officers were as follows:

Commander.—Raphael Semmes.
Lieutenants.—John M. Kell; Robert T. Chapman; John M. Stribling; William E. Evans.
Paymaster.—Henry Myers.
Surgeon.—Francis L. Galt.
1st Lieutenant of Marines.—B. Howell.
Midshipmen.—William A. Hicks; Albert G. Hudgins; Richard F. Armstrong; Joseph D. Wilson.
Engineers.—Miles J. Freeman; William P. Brooks; Matthew O'Brien; Simeon W. Cummings.
Boatswain.—Benjamin P. Mecasky.
Gunner.—Thomas C. Cuddy.
Sailmaker.—W. P. Beaufort.
Carpenter.—William Robinson.
Captain's Clerk.—W. Breedlove Smith.

Commissions had been forwarded to all the officers entitled to receive them, and acting appointments had been given by me to the warrant officers. It will thus be seen, how formally all these details had been attended to. These commissions were to be our warrants for what we were to do, on the high seas. . . .

Whilst we were lying at our anchors between the forts, . . . Governor [Thomas O.] Moore of Louisiana, who had done good service to the Confederacy, by seizing the forts, and arsenals in his State, in advance of secession, and the Hon. John Slidell, lately returned from his seat in the Federal Senate, and other distinguished gentlemen came down, on a visit of inspection to the forts. I went on shore to call on them, and brought them on board the *Sumter* to lunch with me. My ship was, by this time, in excellent order, and my crew well accustomed to their stations, under the judicious management of my first lieutenant, and I took pleasure in showing these gentlemen how much a little discipline could accomplish, in the course of a few weeks. Discipline!—what a power it is everywhere, and under all circumstances; and how much the want of it lost us, as the war progressed. What a pity the officers of our army did not have their respective commands, encircled by wooden walls, with but a "single monarch to walk the peopled deck."

Just at nightfall, on the evening of the 21st of June, I received the following despatch from the commanding officer of the forts:

CAPTAIN:—I am desired by the commanding officer to state, that the *Ivy*—this was a small tender of the forts, and letter-of-marque—reports that the *Powhatan* has left, in pursuit of two ships, and that he has a telegram from Pass à L'Outre, to the effect, that a boat from the *Brooklyn* had put into the river and was making for the telegraph station, where she was expected to arrive within a few minutes.

The *Powhatan* was blockading the Southwest Pass, and it was barely possible that I might get to sea, through this pass, if a pilot could be at once procured; and so I immediately ordered steam to be raised, and getting up my anchor, steamed down to the Head of the Passes, where the river branches into its three principal outlets. Arriving here, at half-past ten P.M. I dispatched a boat to the light-house, for a pilot; but the keeper *knew nothing* of the pilots, and was unwilling to come on board, himself, though requested. The night wore away, and nothing could be done.

The telescope revealed to us, the next morning, that the *Powhatan* had returned to her station. From the sullen, and unsatisfactory message, which had been returned to me, by the keeper of the light-house, I began to suspect that there was something wrong, about the pilots; and it being quite necessary that I should have one constantly, on board, to enable me to take advantage of any temporary absence of the enemy's cruisers, without having to hunt up one for the emergency, I dispatched the *Ivy*, to the pilots' station, at the Southwest Pass, in search of one. This active little cruiser returned in the course of a few hours, and reported that none of the pilots were willing to come on board of me! I received, about the same time, a telegraphic despatch from the Southwest Pass, forwarded to me through Major Duncan, which read as follows: "Applied to the Captain of the Pilots' Association for a pilot for the *Sumter*. He requested me to state, that there are no pilots on duty now!" "So ho! sits the wind in that quarter," thought I— I will soon set this matter right. I, at once, sent Lieutenant Stribling on board the *Ivy*, and directed him to proceed to the Pilots' Association, and deliver, and see executed the following written order:

THE CONFEDERATE CRUISER *Sumter,* CAPTAIN SEMMES, LEAVING NEW ORLEANS JUNE 18, 1861. In six months she disorganized Yankee commerce to a degree from which it never recovered.

From a sketch made at the time.

THE U.S. STEAM SLOOP-OF-WAR *Brooklyn*. She left her blockading station and allowed the *Sumter* to get to sea.

THE U.S. SIDEWHEEL SLOOP-OF-WAR *Powhatan*. In her, David Dixon Porter gained 2,000 miles on the *Sumter* and nearly caught her.

THE *Sumter* RUNS THE GANTLET

C. S. STEAMER SUMTER, HEAD OF THE PASSES,
June 22, 1861.

SIR:—This is to command you to repair on board this ship, with three or four of the most experienced pilots of the Bar. I am surprised to learn, that an unwillingness has been expressed, by some of the pilots of your Association, to come on board the *Sumter;* and my purpose is to test the fact of such disloyalty to the Confederate States. If any man disobeys this summons I will not only have his Branch taken from him, but I will send an armed force, and arrest, him on board.

This order had the desired effect, and in the course of the afternoon, Lieutenant Stribling returned, bringing with him, the Captain of the Association, and several of the pilots. I directed them to be brought into my cabin, and when they were assembled, demanded to know the reason of their late behavior. Some stammering excuses were offered, which I cut short, by informing them that one of them must remain on board constantly, and that they might determine for themselves, who should take the first week's service; to be relieved at the end of the week, by another, and so on, as long as I should find it necessary. One of their number being designated, I dismissed the rest....

The object of the *Brooklyn's* boat, which, as we have seen, pulled into the telegraph station at Pass à L'Outre, just before we got under way from between the forts, was to cut the wires, and break up the station, to prevent intelligence being given me of the movements of the blockading fleet. I now resorted to a little retaliation. I dispatched an officer to the different light-houses, to stave the oil-casks, and bring away the lighting apparatus, to prevent the enemy's shipping from using the lights. They were of great convenience, not only to the ships employed on the blockade, but to the enemy's transports, and other ships, bound to and from the coast of Texas. They could be of no use to our own blockade-runners, as the passes of the Mississippi, by reason of their long, and tortuous, and frequently shifting channels, were absolutely closed to them.

The last letter addressed by me to the Secretary of the Navy, before escaping through the blockade, as hereinafter described, was the following:

C. S. STEAMER SUMTER, HEAD OF THE PASSES,
June 30, 1861.

SIR:—I have the honor to inform the Department that I am still at my anchors at the "Head of the Passes"—the enemy closely investing both of the practical outlets. At Pass à L'Outre there are three ships, the *Brooklyn,* and another propeller, and a large side-wheel steamer; and at the Southwest Pass, there is the *Powhatan,* lying within half a mile of the bar, and not stirring an inch from her anchors, night or day. I am only surprised that the *Brooklyn* does not come up to this anchorage, which she might easily do—as there is water enough, and no military precautions, whatever, have been taken to hold the position—and thus effectually seal all the passes of the river, by her presence alone; which would enable the enemy to withdraw the remainder of his blockading force, for use elsewhere. [It was not quite as simple as all that, considering the Confederates' rather able ram *Manassas,* their fire rafts, their guns with a range superior to the Federal ordnance, restricted waters for maneuvering; etc. In fact, upon the occasion referred to briefly and inaccurately by Semmes on page 23, the *Manassas* just barely failed to sink the U. S. S. *Richmond* one inky night at the Head of the Passes. By great good luck the latter ship happened, at the time, to be coaling from a schooner alongside of her, and that vessel took most of the heavy impact of the ram.] With the assistance of the *Jackson,* Lieutenant Gwathmey, and the *McRae,* Lieutenant Huger—neither of which has, as yet, however, dropped down—I could probably hold my position here, until an opportunity offers of my getting to sea. I shall watch, diligently, for such an opportunity, and have no doubt, that sooner or later, it will present itself. I found, upon dropping down to this point, that the lights at Pass à L'Outre, and South Pass had been strangely overlooked, and that they were still being nightly exhibited. I caused them both to be extinguished, so that if bad weather should set in—a gale from the south-east, for instance—the blockading ships, having nothing to "hold on to," will be obliged to make an offing. At present the worst feature of the blockade of Pass à L'Outre is, that the *Brooklyn* has the speed of me; so that even if I should run the bar, I could not hope to escape her, unless I surprised her, which with her close watch of the bar, at anchor near by, both night and day, it will be exceedingly difficult to do. I should be quite willing to try speed with the *Powhatan,* if I could hope to run the gantlet of her guns, without being crippled; but here again, unfortunately, with all the buoys, and other marks removed, the bar which she is watching is a perfectly blind bar, except by daylight. [Fortunately for Semmes, he did not try conclusions with the *Powhatan*. She was faster than the *Brooklyn* and had perhaps the most effective and reliable engineering plant in the Navy during her whole life of nearly forty years. It so happened later (August 16) that the *Powhatan* left Pensacola in pursuit of the *Sumter*, then more than two thousand miles distant. Under the command of the future full admiral, David Dixon Porter, the *Powhatan* got within approximately forty miles of the *Sumter* seven weeks later. Though well below her customary fine condition the *Powhatan* steamed more than ten thousand miles during the two months of the pursuit, a remarkable performance.] In the meantime, I am drilling my green crew, to a proper use of the great guns, and small arms. With the exception of a diarrhœa, which is prevailing, to some extent, brought on by too free use of the river water, in the excessive heats which prevail, the crew continues healthy.

Nothing in fact surprised me more, during the nine days I lay at the Head of the Passes, than that the enemy did not attack me with some of his light-draught, but heavily armed steamers, or by his boats, by night. Here was the *Sumter*, a small ship, with a crew, all told, of a little over a hundred men, anchored only ten, or twelve miles from the enemy, without a gun, or an obstruction between her and him; and yet no offensive movement was made against her. The enemy watched me closely, day by day, and bent all his energies toward preventing my escape, but did not seem to think of the simple expedient of endeavoring to capture me, with a superior force. In nightly expectation of an assault, I directed the engineer to keep the water in his boilers, as near the steam-point as possible, without actually generating the vapor, and sent a patrol of boats some distance down the Southwest Pass; the boats being relieved every four hours, and returning to the ship, at the first streaks of dawn. After I went to sea, the enemy did come in, and take possession of my anchorage, until he was driven away by Commodore Hollins, in a little nondescript ram; which, by the way, was the first ram experiment of the war. The reader may imagine the tedium, and discomforts of our position, if he will reflect that it is the month of June, and that at this season of the year, the sun comes down upon the broad, and frequently calm surface of the Father of Waters, with an African glow, and that clouds of that troublesome little insect the mosquito tormented us, by night and by day. There was no sleeping at all without the mosquito bar, and I had accordingly had a supply sent down for all the crew. Rather than stand the assaults of these little *picadores*, much longer, I believe my crew would have run the gantlet of the whole Federal Navy.

My diary will now perhaps give the reader, his clearest conception of the condition of things on board the *Sumter*, for the remaining few days that she is to continue at her anchors.

Tuesday, June 25th.—A sharp thunder-storm at half-past three A.M., jarring and shaking the ship with its crashes. The very flood-gates of the heavens seem open, and the rain is descending on our decks like a cataract. Clearing toward ten o'clock. Both blockading ships still at their anchors. The British steam sloop *Jason* touched at the Southwest Pass, yesterday, and communicated with the *Powhatan*. We learn by the newspapers, to-day, that the enemy has taken possession of Ship Island, and established a blockade of the Sound. The anaconda is drawing his folds around us. We are filling some shell, and cartridges to-day, and drilling the crew at the battery.

Wednesday, June 26th.—Cloudy, with occasional rain squalls, which have tempered the excessive heats. The *Ivy* returned from the city to-day, and brought me eighty barrels of coal. Sent the pilot, in the light-house keeper's boat, to sound the S. E. bar, and unused and unwatched outlet to the eastward of the South Pass—in the hope that we may find sufficient water over it, to permit the egress of the ship. The Federal ships are keeping close watch, as usual, at both the passes, neither of them having stirred from her anchor, since we have been at the "Head of the Passes."

Thursday, June 27th.—Weather sultry, and atmosphere charged with moisture. Pilot returned this afternoon, and reports ten and a half feet water on the S. E. bar. Unfortunately the *Sumter* draws twelve feet; so we must abandon this hope.

Saturday, June 29th.—A mistake induced us to expend a little coal, to-day, uselessly. The pilot having gone aloft, to take his usual morning's survey of the "situation," reported that the *Brooklyn* was nowhere to be seen! Great excitement immediately ensued, on the decks, and the officer of the watch hurried into my cabin with the information. I ordered steam to be gotten up with all dispatch, and when, in the course of a very few minutes, it was reported ready—for we always kept our fires banked—the anchor was tripped, and the ship was under way, ploughing her way through the turbid waters, toward Pass à L'Outre. When we had steamed about four miles down the pass, the *Brooklyn* was seen riding very quietly at her anchors, *in her usual berth near the bar.* Explanation: The *Sumter* had dragged her anchor during the night, and the alteration in her position had brought a clump of trees, between her, and the enemy's ship, which had prevented the pilot from seeing the latter! With disappointed hopes we had nothing to do, but to return to our anchors, and watch and wait. In half an hour more, the sailors were lounging idly about the decks, under well-spread awnings; the jest, and banter went round, as usual, and save the low hissing and singing of the steam, which was still escaping, there was nothing to remind the beholder of our recent disappointment. Such is the school of philosophy in which the seaman is reared. Our patience, however, was soon to be rewarded.

Early on the next morning, which was the 30th of June, the steamer, *Empire Parish,* came down from the city, and coming alongside of us, put on board some fresh provisions for the crew, and about one hundred barrels of coal, which my thoughful, and attentive friend, Commodore Rousseau, had sent down to me. Having done this, the steamer shoved off, and proceeded on her trip, down Pass à L'Outre, to the pilots' station, and lighthouse. It was a bright Sunday morning, and we were thinking of nothing but the usual muster, and how we should get through another idle day. In the course of two or three hours, the steamer returned, and when she had come near us, she was seen to cast off a boat, which she had been towing, containing a single boatman—one of the fishermen, or oystermen so common in these waters. The boatman pulled rapidly under our stern, and hailing the officer of the deck, told him, that the *Brooklyn* had gone off in chase of a sail, and was no longer in sight. The crew, who had been "cleaning themselves," for Sunday muster, at once stowed away their bags, the swinging-booms were gotten alongside, the boats run up, and, in ten minutes, the steam was again hissing, as if impatient of control. The men ran round the capstan, in "double-quick," in their eagerness to get up the anchor, and in a few minutes more, the ship's head swung off gracefully with the current, and, the propeller being started, she bounded off like a thing of life, on this new race, which was to decide whether we should continue to stagnate in midsummer, in the marshes of the Mississippi, or reach those "glad waters of the dark blue sea," which form as delightful a picture in the imagination of the sailor, as in that of the poet.

Whilst we were heaving up our anchor, I had noticed the pilot, standing near me, pale, and apparently nervous, and agitated, but, as yet, he had said not a word. When we were fairly under way, however, it seemed probable, at last, that we should attempt the blockade, the fellow's courage fairly broke down, and he protested to me that he knew nothing of the bar of Pass à L'Outre, and durst not attempt to run me over. "I am," said he, "a S. W. bar pilot, and know nothing of the other passes." "What," said I, "did you not know that I was lying at the Head of the Passes, for the very purpose of taking any one of the outlets through which an opportunity of escape might present itself, and yet you dare tell me, that you know but one of them, and have been deceiving me." The fellow stammered out something in excuse, but I was too impatient to listen to him, and, turning to the first lieutenant, ordered him to hoist the "Jack" at the fore, as a signal for a pilot. I had, in fact, resolved to attempt the passage of the bar, from my own slight acquaintance with it, when I had been a light-house inspector, rather than forego the opportunity of escape, and caused the Jack to be hoisted, rather as a matter of course, than because I hoped for any good result from it. The *Brooklyn* had not "chased out of sight," as reported—she had only chased to the westward, some seven or eight miles, and had been hidden from the boatman, by one of the spurs of the Delta. She had probably, all the while, had her telescopes on the *Sumter,* and as soon as she saw the black smoke issuing from her chimney, and the ship moving rapidly toward the pass, she abandoned her chase, and commenced to retrace her steps.

We had nearly equal distances to run to the bar, but I had the advantage of a four-knot current. Several of my officers now collected around me, and we were discussing the chances of escape. "What think you of our prospect," said I, turning to one of my lieutenants, who had served a short time before, on board the *Brooklyn,* and knew well her qualities. "Prospect, sir! not the least in the world—there is no possible chance of our escaping that ship. Even if we get over the bar ahead of her, she must overhaul us, in a very short time. The *Brooklyn* is good for fourteen knots an hour, sir." "That was the report," said I, "on her trial trip, but you know how all such reports are exaggerated; ten to one, she has no better speed, if so good, as the *Sumter*." "You will see, sir," replied my lieutenant; "we made a passage in her, only a few months ago, from Tampico to Pensacola, and averaged about thirteen knots the whole distance."

Here the conversation dropped, for an officer now came to report to me that a boat had just shoved off from the pilots' station, evidently with a pilot in her. Casting my eyes in the given direction, I saw a whale-boat approaching us, pulled by four stout blacks, who were bending like good fellows to their long ashen oars, and in the stern-sheets was seated, sure enough, the welcome pilot, swaying his body to, and fro, as his boat leaped under the oft-repeated strokes of the oars, as though he would hasten her already great speed. But more beautiful still was another object which presented itself. In the balcony of the pilot's house, which had been built in the very marsh, on the margin of the river, there stood a beautiful woman, the pilot's young wife, waving him on to his duty, with her handkerchief. We could have tossed a biscuit from the *Sumter* to the shore, and I uncovered my head gallantly to my fair countrywoman. A few moments more, and a tow-line had been thrown to the boat, and the gallant young fellow stood on the horse-block beside me.

As we swept past the light-house wharf, almost close enough to touch it, there were other petticoats fluttering in the breeze, the owners of which were also waving handkerchiefs of encouragement to the *Sumter*. I could see my sailors' eyes brighten at these spectacles, for the sailor's heart is capacious enough to love the whole sex, and I now felt sure of their nerves, in case it should become necessary to tax them. Half a mile or so, from the light-house, and the bar is reached. There was a Bremen ship lying aground on the bar, and there was just room, and no more, for us to pass her. She had run out a kedge, and had a warp attached to it that was lying across the passage-way. The crew considerately slackened the line, as we approached, and in another bound the *Sumter* was outside the bar, and the Confederate flag was upon the high seas! We now slackened our speed, for an instant—only an instant, for my officers and men all had their wits about them, and worked like good fellows—to haul the pilot's boat alongside, that he might return to the shore. As the gallant young fellow grasped my hand,

and shook it warmly, as he descended from the horse-block, he said, "Now, Captain, you are all clear; give her h—ll, and let her go!"

We had now nothing to do, but turn our attention to the enemy. The *Brooklyn*, as we cleared the bar, was about three and a half, or four miles distant; we were therefore just out of reach of her guns, with nothing to spare. Thick volumes of smoke could be seen pouring from the chimneys of both ships; the firemen, and engineers of each evidently doing their best. I called a lieutenant, and directed him to heave the log. He reported our speed to be nine, and a half knots. Loth to believe that we could be making so little way, through the yet turbid waters, which were rushing past us with great apparent velocity, I directed the officer to repeat the experiment; but the same result followed, though he had paid out the line with a free hand. I now sent for the engineer, and, upon inquiry, found that he was doing his very best—"though," said he, "there is little drawback, just now, in the 'foaming' of our boilers, arising from the suddenness with which we got up steam; when this subsides, we may be able to add half a knot more."

The *Brooklyn* soon loosed, and set her sails, bracing them sharp up on the starboard tack. I loosed and set mine, also. The enemy's ship was a little on my weather quarter, say a couple of points, and had thus slightly the weather-gauge of me. As I knew I could lay nearer the wind than she, being able to brace my yards sharper, and had besides, the advantage of larger fore-and-aft sails, comparatively, stay-sails, try-sails, and a very large spanker, I resolved at once to hold my wind, so closely, as to compel her to furl her sails, though this would carry me a little athwart her bows, and bring me perhaps a little nearer to her, for the next half hour, or so. A rain squall now came up, and enveloped the two ships, hiding each from the other. As the rain blew off to leeward, and the *Brooklyn* reappeared, she seemed fearfully near to us, and I began to fear I should realize the foreboding of my lieutenant. I could not but admire the majesty of her appearance, with her broad flaring bows, and clean, and beautiful run, and her masts, and yards, as taunt and square, as those of an old time sailing frigate. The stars and stripes of a large ensign flew out from time to time, from under the lee of her spanker, and we could see an apparently anxious crowd of officers on her quarter-deck, many of them with telescopes directed toward us. She had, evidently, I thought, gained upon us, and I expected every moment to hear the whiz of a shot; but still she did not fire.

I now ordered my paymaster to get his public chest, and papers ready for throwing overboard, if it should become necessary. At this crisis the engineer came up from below, bringing the welcome intelligence that the "foaming" of his boilers had ceased, and that his engine was "working beautifully," giving the propeller several additional turns per minute. The breeze, too, favored me, for it had freshened considerably; and what was still more to the purpose, I began to perceive that I was "eating" the *Brooklyn* "out of the wind"; in other words, that she was falling more and more to leeward. I knew, of course, that as soon as she fell into my wake, she would be compelled to furl her sails. This she did an half an hour or so afterward, and I at once began to breathe more freely, for I could still hold on to my own canvas. I have witnessed many beautiful sights at sea, but the most beautiful of them all was when the *Brooklyn* let fly all her sheets, and halliards, at once, and clewed up, and furled, in man-of-war style, all her sails, from courses to royals. We now began to gain quite perceptibly on our pursuer, and at half-past three, the chase was abandoned, the baffled *Brooklyn* retracing her steps to Pass à L'Outre, and the *Sumter* bounding away on her course seaward.

[Despite the "scuttlebutt" on an earlier page about the *Brooklyn's* speed, she had made but 9.2 knots on her trials in smooth water, using steam alone. And this is but a fraction less than that made by the fastest ship in her class (which included the *Richmond* and *Hartford*). Being on blockade service she could not be expected to come as close to trial speed as could the *Sumter*. However, even though the *Sumter* gained distance, the commanding officer of the *Brooklyn* was distinctly culpable in not carrying on the pursuit *at least until the* Sumter *should be irrevocably lost to sight*. The slightest engineering casualty on the *Sumter* would have caused her to fall into his hands. He should have appreciated the fact that it was *all-important* to prevent the escape of such a raider; yet he desisted from the chase when he spied a sail standing toward his regular station. Steaming all day at full speed would, at the very least, have forced the consumption of a great deal of the *Sumter's* precious coal.]

We fired no gun of triumph in the face of the enemy—my powder was too precious for that—but I sent the crew aloft, to man the rigging, and three such cheers were given for the Confederate flag, "that little bit of striped bunting," that had waved from the *Sumter's* peak during the exciting chase, as could proceed only from the throats of American seamen, in the act of defying a tyrant—those cheers were but a repetition of many such cheers that had been given, by our ancestors, to that other bit of "striped bunting" which had defied the power of England in that olden war, of which our war was but the logical sequence. The reader must not suppose that our anxiety was wholly allayed, as soon as we saw the *Brooklyn* turn away from us.

We were, as yet, only a few miles from the land, and our coast was swarming with the enemy's cruisers. Ship Island was not a great way off, and there was a constant passing to and fro, of ships-of-war between that island and the passes of the Mississippi, and we stumble upon one of these at any moment. "Sail ho!" was now shouted from the mast head. "Where away!" cried the officer of the deck. "Right ahead," said the look-out. A few minutes only elapsed, and a second sail was descried, "broad on the starboard bow." But nothing came of these spectres; we passed on, seaward, without so much as raising either of them from the deck, and finally, the friendly robes of night enveloped us. When we at length realized that we had gained an offing; when we began to feel the welcome heave of the sea; when we looked upon the changing aspect of its waters, now darkening into the deepest blue, and breathed the pure air, fresh from the Gulf, untainted of malaria, and untouched of mosquito's wing, we felt like so many prisoners who had been turned loose from a long and painful confinement; . . .

The evening of the escape of the *Sumter* was one of those Gulf evenings, which can only be *felt,* and not described. The wind died gently away, as the sun declined, leaving a calm, and sleeping sea, to reflect a myriad of stars. The sun had gone down behind a screen of purple, and gold, and to add to the beauty of the scene, as night set in, a blazing comet, whose tail spanned nearly a quarter of the heavens, mirrored itself within a hundred feet of our little bark, as she ploughed her noiseless way through the waters. [This heavenly body, the Great Comet of 1861, appeared with great suddenness in the northern hemisphere on the night of the *Sumter's* escape. That very evening (June 30) it was reported as having a head equal in angular diameter to the full moon, and a tail 90° in length and 10° in breadth; truly a stupendous spectacle.] As I leaned on the carriage of a howitzer on the poop of my ship, and cast a glance toward the quarter of the horizon whence the land had disappeared, memory was busy with the events of the last few months. How hurried, and confused they had been! It seemed as though I had dreamed a dream, and found it difficult, upon waking, to unite the discordant parts. A great government had been broken up, family ties had been severed, and war—grim, ghastly war—was arraying a household against itself. A little while back, and I had served under the very flag which I had that day defied. . . .

My first lieutenant now approached me, and touching my elbow, said, "Captain, had we not better throw this howitzer overboard? it can be of no further service to us, and is very much in the way." My waking dream was dissolved, on the instant, and I returned at once to the duties of the ship. I assented to the lieutenant's proposition, and in a few minutes more, the poop was cleared of the incumbrance. It was the howitzer—a heavy, awkward, iron field-piece with huge wheels—which we had received on board, when we lay between the forts, as a protection against the enemy's boats. The rest of the night, to a late hour, was devoted to lashing, and otherwise securing such heavy articles, as were likely to be thrown from their places, by the rolling of the ship; getting the anchors in-board and stowing them, and, generally, in making the ship snug. I turned in after a day of excitement, and slept too soundly to continue the day-dream from which I had been aroused by my first lieutenant.

The sun rose in an unclouded sky, the next morning, with a gentle breeze from the south-west, or about abeam; our course being about south-east. The look-out at the mast-head, after having carefully scanned the horizon in every direction, informed the officer of the deck, that there was nothing in sight. The awnings were soon spread, and the usual routine of a man-of-war, at sea, commenced. The crew was mustered, in clean apparel, at quarters, at nine o'clock, and a division of guns was exercised, the rest of the crew being dispersed in idle groups about the deck; the old salts overhauling their bags, and seeing that their tobacco, and soap, and needles, and thread were all right for the cruise, and the youngsters discussing their recent escape. At noon, we found ourselves in latitude 26° 18′, and longitude 87° 23′. I had provided myself with two excellent chronometers, before leaving New Orleans, and having had much experience as a master, I was always enabled, when the sun was visible, at the proper hours, to fix my position within from a quarter, to half a mile, or, what is the same thing, within from one to two seconds of time. I appointed my junior lieutenant, navigating officer, *pro forma,* but always navigated my ship, myself. I had every confidence in the ability of my young lieutenant, but I always found, that I slept better, when surrounded by danger, after I had fixed the position of my ship, by my own observations.

We held on our course, during the rest of this day, without the least incident to break in upon the monotony—not so much as a sail having been descried in any direction; not that we were in want of excitement, for we had scarcely regained our equilibrium from the excitement of the previous day. An occasional swash of the sea against the ship's sides, the monotonous beating of time by her propeller, an occasional order from the officer of the deck, and the routine "calls" of the boatswain's whistle, as dinner, or grog was piped, were the only sounds audible, beyond the usual hum of conversation among the crew.

CHAPTER III

Cienfuegos, "The Land of a Hundred Fires"

IF THE READER WILL PERMIT ME, I WILL AVAIL MYself of this interval of calm before the storm, to introduce to him some of my officers. This is indeed but a courtesy due him, as he is to be a passenger in our midst. On the afternoon of our escape from the *Brooklyn,* the officers of the ward-room were kind enough to invite me to drink a glass of wine with them, in honor of our success, and I will avail myself of this occasion, to make the presentations. I am seated at one end of the long mess-table, and my first lieutenant at the other. The first lieutenant, as the reader has already been informed, by an inspection of the *Sumter's* muster-roll, is from Georgia. John McIntosh Kell is a descendant from one of the oldest families in that State, having the blood of the McIntoshes in his veins, through one branch of his ancestors. He was bred in the old Navy, and my acquaintance with him commenced when he was in trouble. He was serving as a passed midshipman, on board the old sailing sloop *Albany,* and being ordered, on one occasion, to perform what he considered a menial duty, he resisted the order. Some of his brother passed midshipmen were in the same category. A court-martial resulted, and, at the request of the young gentlemen, I defended them. The relation of counsel, and client, as a matter of course, brought us close together, and I discovered that young Kell had in him, the making of a man. So far from being a mutineer, he had a high respect for discipline, and had only resisted obedience to the order in question, from a refined sense of gentlemanly propriety. The reader will see these qualities in him, now, as he sits opposite me. He has developed since the time I speak of, into the tall, well-proportioned gentleman, of middle age, with brown, wavy hair, and a magnificent beard, inclining to red. See how scrupulously neat he is dressed, and how suave, and affable he is, with his associates. His eye is now beaming gentleness, and kindness. You will scarcely recognize him, as the same man, when you see him again on deck, arraigning some culprit, "at the mast," for a breach of discipline. When Georgia seceded, Lieutenant Kell was well on his way to the commander's list, in the old Navy, but he would have scorned the commission of an admiral, if it had been tendered him as the price of treason to his State. To have brought a Federal ship into the waters of Georgia, and ravaged her coasts, and fired upon her people, would have been, in his eyes, little less than matricide. He forthwith resigned his commission, and joined his fortunes with those of his people. When it was decided, at Montgomery, that I was to have the *Sumter,* I at once thought of Kell, and, at my request, he was ordered to the ship—Commodore Tattnall, with whom he had been serving on the Georgia coast, giving him up very reluctantly.

[While a captain in the Old Navy, Tattnall originated the slogan "Blood is thicker than water!" This he exclaimed as he ranged his ships alongside the British in their contest with the Chinese forts at the mouth of the Pei Ho River in 1859.]

Seated next to myself, on my right hand, is Lieutenant Robert T. Chapman. This gentleman is from Alabama; he is several years younger than Kell, not so tall, but stouter, in proportion. His complexion, as you see, is dark, and he has jet-black hair, and eyes—the latter remarkable for their brilliancy, and for a twinkle of fun, and good humor. Chapman is the life of the mess-table; always in a pleasant mood, and running over with wit and anecdote. Though he has a fashion, as you see, of wearing his hair closely cropped, he is the very reverse of a round-head, being a *preux chevalier,* as ready for the fight as the dance, and having a decided preference for the music of the band, over that of "Old Hundred." He is the second lieutenant, and has, consequently, the easiest berth among the sea lieutenants, being relieved from the drudgery of the first lieutenant, and exempt from the calls for extra duty, that are sometimes made upon the junior lieutenant. When his watch is over, and his division drilled, he is a gentleman at large, for the rest of the day. You see by his build—a slight inclination to corpulency—that he is fond of his ease, and that he has fallen as naturally into the place of second lieutenant, as if it had been cut out for him on purpose. He also was bred in the old Navy, and was found to be of the pure metal, instead of the dross, when the touchstone of secession came to be applied to separate the one from the other.

At Lieutenant Kell's right hand, sits Lieutenant John M. Stribling, the third lieutenant, and a native of the glorious little State of South Carolina. He is of medium height, somewhat spare in build, with brown hair, and whiskers, and mild and expressive blue eyes; the mildness of the eye only dwelling in it, however, in moments of repose. When excited at the thought of wrong, or oppression, it has a peculiar stare of firmness, as much as to say,

> "This rock shall fly,
> From its firm base as soon as I."

Stribling was also an *élève* [midshipman] of the old Navy, and, though tied to it, by cords that were hard to sever, he put honor above place, in the hour of trial, and came South.

Next to Stribling, sits Lieutenant William E. Evans, the fourth and junior lieutenant of the ship. He is not more than twenty-four years of age, slim in person, of medium height, and rather delicate-looking, though not from ill health. His complexion is dark, and he has black hair, and eyes. He has a very agreeable, *riante* expression about his face, and is somewhat given to casuistry, being fond of an argument, when occasion presents itself. He is but recently out of the Naval Academy, at Annapolis, and like all new graduates, feels the freshness of academic honors. He is a native of South Carolina, and a brother of General Evans of that State, who so greatly distinguished himself, afterward, at the battle of Manassas, and on other bloody fields.

If the reader will now cast his eye toward the centre of the table, on my right hand, he will see two gentlemen, both with black hair and eyes, and both somewhat under middle size, conversing together. These are Dr. Francis L. Galt, the Surgeon, and Mr. Henry Myers, the Paymaster, both from the old service; the former a native of Virginia, and the latter a native of South Carolina; and opposite these, are the Chief Engineer, and Marine Officer,—Mr. Miles J. Freeman, and Lieutenant B. Howell, the latter a brother-in-law of Mr. Jefferson Davis, our honored President. I have thus gone the circuit of the ward-room. All these officers, courteous reader, will make the cruise with us, and if you will inspect the adjoining engraving, and are a judge of character, after the rules of Lavater and Spurzheim, you will perceive in advance, how much reason I shall have to be proud of them.

We may now take up our narrative, from the point at which it was interrupted, for the purpose of these introductions. Day passed into night, and with the night came the brilliant comet again, lighting us on our way over the waste of waters. The morning of the second of July, our second day out, dawned clear, and beautiful, the *Sumter* still steaming in an almost calm sea, with nothing to impede her progress. At eight A. M. we struck the northeast trade-wind, and made sail in aid of steam, giving orders to the engineer, to make the most of his fuel, by carrying only a moderate head of steam. Toward noon, a few trade squalls passed over us, with light and refreshing showers of rain; just enough to cause me to take shelter, for a few moments, under the lee of the spanker. At noon, we observed in latitude 23° 4′ showing that we had crossed the tropic—the longitude being 86° 13′. The reader has seen that we have been steering to the S. E., diminishing both latitude, and longitude, and if he will look upon the chart of the Caribbean Sea, he will perceive, that we are approaching Cape San Antonio, the south end [west end] of the island of Cuba; but he can scarcely conjecture what sort of a cruise I had marked out for myself. The Secretary of the Navy, in those curt sailing orders which we have already seen, had considerately left me *carte blanche* as to cruising-ground, but as I was "to do the greatest injury to the enemy's commerce, in the shortest time," the implication was, that I should, at once, throw myself into some one of the chief thoroughfares of his trade. I accordingly set my eye on Cape St. Roque, in Brazil, which may be said to be the great turning-point of the commerce of the world. My intention was to make a dash, of a few days, at the enemy's ships on the south side of Cuba, coal at some convenient point, stretch over to Barbadoes, coal again, and then strike for the Brazilian coast. It is with this view, that the *Sumter* is now running for the narrow outlet, that issues from the Gulf of Mexico, between Cape Antonio, and the opposite coast of Yucatan. I shaped my course for the middle of this passage, but about midnight, made the light of Cape Antonio right ahead, showing that I had been drifted, northward, by a current setting, at the rate of from three fourths of a mile, to a mile per hour. We drew off a little to the

THE *Sumter* RUNNING THE BLOCKADE OF PASS À L'OUTRE BY THE ENEMY'S SHIP *Brooklyn,* ON THE 30TH JUNE, 1861. The distances shown here are much shorter than they were during the actual event.

From a lithograph by A. Hoen and Company, Baltimore

CAPTAIN CHARLES H. POOR OF THE U.S.S. *Brooklyn*
He was the "goat" of the entire story, being responsible for Semmes's escape to sea for his career in the *Sumter* and *Alabama*.

southward, doubled the Cape, with the light still in view, and at nine o'clock, the next morning, we found ourselves off Cape Corrientes.

The weather had now become cloudy, and we had a fresh tradewind, veering from E. to E. S. E., with some sea on. At meridian, we observed in latitude 21° 29', the longitude being 84° 06'. Running along the Cuban coast, between it and the Isle of Pines, of piratical memory, at about three in the afternoon, the cry of "Sail ho!" was heard from the mast-head, for the first time since we had left the mouths of the Mississippi. The look-out, upon being questioned, said that he saw two sail, and that they were both right ahead. We came up with them, very rapidly, for they were standing in our direction, and when we had approached within signal distance, we showed them the English colors. The nearest sail, which proved to be a brig, hoisted the Spanish colors, and, upon being boarded, was found to be from Cadiz, bound for Vera Cruz. She was at once permitted to proceed. Resuming our course, we now stood for the other sail, which, by this time, there was no mistaking; she being plainly American, although she had not yet shown her colors. A gun soon brought these to the peak, when, as I had expected, the stars and stripes unfolded themselves, gracefully, to the breeze. Here was our first prize, and a most welcome sight it was.... When I had fired the gun, as a command to the stranger to heave to, and show his colors, I had hauled down the English, and hoisted my own flag.... The boarding officer soon returned from the captured ship, bringing with him the master, with his papers. There were no knotty points of fact or law to embarrass my decision. There were the American register, and clearance, and the American character impressed upon every plank and spar of the ship. Nothing could exceed the astonishment of the master, who was rather a mild, amiable-looking gentleman, not at all disposed to go either into hysterics, or the heroics. "A clap of thunder in a cloudless sky could not have surprised me more," said he to me as I overhauled his papers, "than the appearance of the Confederate flag in these seas." "My duty is a painful one," said I, "to destroy so noble a ship as yours, but I must discharge it without vain regrets; and as for yourself, you will only have to do, as so many thousands have done before you, submit to the fortunes of war—yourself and your crew will be well treated on board my ship." The prize bore the name of *The Golden Rocket*, was a fine bark, nearly new, of about seven hundred tons, and was seeking, in ballast, a cargo of sugar in some one of the Cuban ports. Boats were dispatched to bring off the crew, and such provisions, cordage, sails, and paints as the different departments of my ship stood in need of, and at about ten o'clock at night, the order was given to apply the torch to her.

The wind, by this time, had become very light, and the night was pitch-dark—the darkness being of that kind, graphically described by old sailors, when they say, you may cut it with a knife. I regret that I cannot give to the reader the picture of the burning ship, as it presented itself to the silent, and solemn watchers on board the *Sumter* as they leaned over her hammock rails to witness it. The boat, which had been sent on this errand of destruction, had pulled out of sight, and her oars ceasing to resound, we knew that she had reached the doomed ship, but so impenetrable was the darkness, that no trace of either boat, or ship could be seen, although the *Sumter* was distant only a few hundred yards. Not a sound could be heard on board the *Sumter*, although her deck was crowded with men. Every one seemed busy with his own thoughts, and gazing eagerly in the direction of the doomed ship, endeavoring, in vain, to penetrate the thick darkness. Suddenly, one of the crew exclaimed, "There is the flame! She is on fire!" The decks of this Maine-built ship were of pine, calked with old-fashioned oakum, and paid with pitch; the wood-work of the cabin was like so much tinder, having been seasoned by many voyages to the tropics, and the forecastle was stowed with paints, and oils. The consequence was, that the flame was not long in kindling, but leaped, full-grown, into the air, in a very few minutes after its first faint glimmer had been seen. The boarding officer, to do his work more effectually, had applied the torch simultaneously in three places, the cabin, the mainhold, and the forecastle; and now the devouring flames rushed up these three apertures, with a fury which nothing could resist. The burning ship, with the *Sumter's* boat in the act of shoving off from her side; the *Sumter* herself, with her grim, black sides, lying in repose like some great sea-monster, gloating upon the spectacle, and the sleeping sea, for there was scarce a ripple upon the water, were all brilliantly lighted. The indraught into the burning ship's holds, and cabins, added every moment new fury to the flames, and now they could be heard roaring like the fires of a hundred furnaces, in full blast. The prize ship had been laid to, with her main-topsail to the mast, and all her light sails, though clewed up, were flying loose about the yards. The forked tongues of the devouring element, leaping into the rigging, newly tarred, ran rapidly up the shrouds, first into the tops, then to the topmast-heads, thence to the top-gallant, and royal mast-heads, and in a moment more to the trucks; and whilst this rapid ascent of the main current of fire was going on, other currents had run out upon the yards, and ignited all the sails. A top-gallant sail, all on fire, would now fly off from the yard, and sailing leisurely in the direction of the light breeze that was fanning, rather than blowing, break into bright, and sparkling patches of flame, and settle, or rather silt into the sea. The yard would then follow, and not being wholly submerged by its descent into the sea, would retain a portion of its flame, and continue to burn, as a floating brand, for some minutes. At one time, the intricate net-work of the cordage of the burning ship was traced, as with a pencil of fire, upon the black sky beyond, the many threads of flame twisting, and writhing, like so many serpents that had received their death wounds. The mizzen-mast now went by the board, then the fore-mast, and in a few minutes afterward, the great main-mast tottered, reeled, and fell over the ship's side into the sea, making a noise like that of the sturdy oak of the forests when it falls by the stroke of the axeman.

By the light of this flambeau, upon the lonely and silent sea, lighted of the passions of bad men who should have been our brothers, the *Sumter,* having aroused herself from her dream of vengeance, and run up her boats, moved forward on her course. The captain of the *Golden Rocket* watched the destruction of his ship from the quarter-deck of the *Sumter,* apparently with the calm eye of a philosopher, though, doubtless, he felt the emotions which the true sailor always feels, when he looks upon the dying agonies of his beloved ship, whether she be broken up by the storm, or perish in any other way.

The flag! what was done with the "old flag"? It was marked with the day, and the latitude and longitude of the capture, and consigned to the keeping of the signal quartermaster, who prepared a bag for its reception; and when this bag was full, he prepared another, and another, as the cruise progressed, and occasion required. It was the especial pride of this veteran American seaman to count over his trophies, and when the weather was fine, he invariably asked permission of the officer of the deck, under pretence of damage from moths, to "air" his flags; and as he would bend on his signal-halliards, and throw them out to the breeze, one by one, his old eye would glisten, and a grim smile of satisfaction would settle upon his sun-burned, and weather-beaten features. This was our practice also on board the *Alabama,* and when that ship was sunk in the British channel, in her engagement with the enemy's ship *Kearsarge,* as the reader will learn in due time, if he has the patience to follow me in these memoirs, we committed to the keeping of the guardian spirits of that famous old battle-ground, a great many bags-full of "old flags," to be stored away in the caves of the sea, . . .

The prisoners—what did we do with them? The captain was invited to mess in the ward-room, and when he was afterward landed, the officers generously made him up a purse to supply his immediate necessities. The crew was put into a mess by themselves, with their own cook, and was put on a footing, with regard to rations, with the *Sumter's* own men. . . .

The weather still continued cloudy, with a few rain squalls passing with the trade wind, during the morning. I had turned into my cot, late on the previous night, and was still sleeping soundly, when, at daylight, an officer came below to inform me, that there were two sails in sight from the mast-head. We were steaming, as before, up the south side of Cuba, with the land plainly in sight, and soon came close enough to distinguish that the vessels ahead were both brigantines, and probably Americans. There being no occasion to resort to *ruse,* or stratagem, as the wind was light, and there was no possibility of the ships running away from us, we showed them at once the Confederate colors, and at the same time fired a blank cartridge to heave them to. They obeyed our signal, promptly, and came to the wind, with their foretopsails aback, and the United States colors at their peaks. When within a few hundred yards, we stopped our engine, and lowered, and sent a boat on board of them—the boarding officer remaining only a few minutes on board of each, and bringing back with him, their respective masters, with their ships' papers. Upon examination of these, it appeared that one of the brigantines was called the *Cuba,* and the other the *Machias;* that they were both laden with sugar and molasses, for English ports, and that they had recently come out of the port of Trinidad-de-Cuba. Indeed the recency of their sailing was tested, by the way in which their stern-boats were garlanded, with festoons of luscious bananas, and pine-apples, and by sundry nets filled with golden-hued oranges—all of which was very tempting to the eyes and olfactories of men, who had recently issued from a blockaded port, in which such luxuries were tabooed. The cargoes of these small vessels being neutral, as certified by the papers—and indeed of this there could be little doubt, as they were going from one neutral port to another—I could not burn the vessels as I had done the *Golden Rocket*, and so after transferring prize crews to them, which occupied us an hour or two, we took them both in tow, and steamed away for Cienfuegos—it being my intention to test the disposition of Spain toward us, in this matter of taking in prizes. England and France had issued proclamations, prohibiting both belligerents, alike, from bringing prizes into their ports, but Spain had not yet spoken, and I had hopes that she might be induced to pursue a different course.

Nothing worthy of note occurred during the rest of this day; we steamed leisurely along the coast, making about five knots an hour. Finding our speed too much diminished, by the towage of two heavily laden vessels, we cast off one of them—the *Cuba*—during the night and directed the prize-master to make sail, and follow us into port. The *Cuba* did not rejoin us, and we afterward learned through the medium of the enemy's papers, that she had been recaptured by her crew. I had only sent a midshipman and four men on board of her as a prize crew; and the midshipman incautiously going aloft, to look out for the land, as he was approaching his port, and a portion of his prize crew proving treacherous—they were not native Americans I am glad to say—he was fired upon by the master, and crew of the brig, who had gotten possession of the revolvers of the prize crew, and compelled to surrender, after defending himself the best he could, and being wounded in one or two places. The vessel then changed her course and made haste to get out of the Caribbean Sea.

The morning of the fifth dawned cloudy, with the usual moderate trade-wind. It cleared toward noon, and at two P. M. we crossed the shoal off the east end of the Jardinillos reef, in from seven to five fathoms of water. The sea, by this time, had become quite smooth, and the rays of a bright sun penetrated the clear waters to the very bottom of the shoal, revealing everything to us, as clearly as though the medium through which we were viewing it were atmosphere instead of water. Every rock, sea-shell, and pebble lying at the bottom of the sea were distinctly visible to us, and we could see the little fish darting into their holes, and hiding-places, as the steamer ploughed her way through their usually quiet domain. It was quite startling to look over the side, so shallow did the waters appear. The chart showed that there was no danger, and the faithful lead line, in the hands of a skilful seaman, gave us several fathoms of water to spare, and yet one could hardly divest himself of the belief, that at the next moment the steamer would run aground.

Crossing this shoal, we now hauled up N. E. by N., for the Cienfuegos lighthouse. As we approached the lights, we descried two more sail in the south-east, making an offing with all diligence, to which we immediately gave chase. They were eight or nine miles distant from the land, and to facilitate our pursuit, we cast off our remaining tow, directing the prize-master to heave to, off the lighthouse, and await our return. We had already captured three prizes, in twenty-four hours, and, as here were probably two more, I could perceive that my crew were becoming enamoured of their business, pretty much as the veteran fox-hunter does in view of the chase. They moved about with great alacrity, in obedience to orders; the seamen springing aloft to furl the sails like so many squirrels, and the firemen below sending up thick volumes of black smoke, from their furnaces. The *Sumter,* feeling the renewed impulse of her engines, sprang forward in pursuit of the doomed craft ahead, as if she too knew what was going on. We had just daylight enough left to enable us to accomplish our purpose; an hour or two later, and at least one of the vessels might have escaped. Coming up, first with one, and then the other, we hove them to, successively, by "hail," and brought the masters on board. They both proved to be brigantines, and were American, as we had supposed: —one, the *Ben. Dunning,* of Maine, and the other, the *Albert Adams,* of Massachusetts. They had come out of the port of Cienfuegos, only a few hours before, were both sugar laden, and their cargoes were documented as Spanish property. We hastily threw prize crews on board of them, and directed the prize-masters to stand in for the light, still in sight, distant about twelve miles, and hold on to it until daylight. It was now about ten P. M. Some appeal was made to me by the master of one of the brigantines, in behalf of his wife and a lady companion of hers, who were both invalids from the effects of yellow fever, which they had taken in Cienfuegos, and from which they were just convalescing. I desired him to assure the ladies, that they should be treated with every tenderness, and respect, and that if they desired it, I would send my surgeon to visit them; but I declined to release the captured vessel on this account.

We now stood in for the light ourselves, and letting our steam go down, to the lowest point consistent with locomotion, lay off, and on, until daylight. The next morning dawned beautiful, and bright, as a tropic morning only can dawn. We were close in under the land, and our prizes were lying around us, moving to and fro, gracefully, to preserve their positions. The most profuse, and luxuriant vegetation, of that peculiarly dark green known only to the tropics, ran down to the very water's edge; the beautiful little stream, on which Cienfuegos lies, disembogued itself at the foot of the lighthouse perched on a base of blackened limestone rock; and the neat, white fort, that sat a mile or two up the river, was now glistening in the rays of the sun, just lifting himself above the central range of mountains. The sea breeze had died away during the night, and been replaced by the land breeze, in obedience to certain laws which prevail in all countries swept by the trade-winds; and this land breeze, blowing so gently, as scarce to disturb a tress on the brow of beauty, came laden with the most delicious perfume of shrub and flower.

But, "what smoke is that we perceive, coming down the river?" said I, to the officer of the deck. "I will see in a moment," said this active young officer, and springing several ratlines up the rigging, to enable him to obtain a view over the intervening foliage, he said, "There is a small steam-tug coming down, with three vessels in tow, two barks and a brig." "Can you make out the nationality of the ships in tow?" I inquired. "Plainly," he replied, "they all have the American colors set." Here was a piece of unlooked-for good fortune. I had not reckoned upon carrying more than three, or four prizes into port, but here were three others. But to secure these latter, a little management would be necessary. I could not molest them, within neutral jurisdiction, and the neutral jurisdiction extended to a marine league, or three geographical miles from the land. I immediately hoisted a Spanish jack at the fore, as a signal for a pilot, and directed the officer of the deck, to disarrange his yards, a little, cock-billing this one, slightly, in one direction, and that one, in another, and to send all but about a dozen men below, to give the strangers the idea that we were a common merchant steamer, instead of a ship of war. To carry still further the illusion, we hoisted the Spanish merchant flag. But the real trouble was with the prizes—two of these must surely be recognized by their companions of only the day before! Luckily my prize masters took the hint I had given them, and hoisted their respective flags, at the fore, for a pilot also. This mystified the new-comers, and they concluded that the two brigantines, though very like, could not be the same. Besides, there was a third brigantine in company, and she evidently was a new arrival. And so they came on, quite unsuspiciously, and when the little steamer had towed them clear of the mouth of the harbor, she let them go, and they made sail. The fellows worked very industriously, and soon had their ships under clouds of canvas, pressing them out to get an offing, before the sea breeze should come in. The steam-tug, as soon as she had let go her tows, came alongside the *Sumter,* and a Spanish pilot jumped on board of me, asking me in his native tongue, if I desired to go up to town; showing that my ruse of the Spanish flag had even deceived him. I replied in the affirmative, and said to him, pleasantly, "but I am waiting a little, to take back those ships you have just towed down." "Diablo!" said he, "how can that be; they are *Americanos del Norte,* bound to Boston, and *la Nueva York!*" "That is just what I want," said I, "we are *Confederados,* and we have *la guerra* with the *Americanos del Norte!*" "*Caramba!*" said he, "that is good; give her the steam quick, Captain!" "No, no," replied I, "wait a while. I must pay due respect to your Queen, and the Captain-General; they command in these waters, within the league, and I must wait until the ships have passed beyond that." I accordingly waited until the ships had proceeded some five miles from the coast, as estimated both by the pilot, and myself, when we turned the *Sumter's* head seaward, and again removed the leash. She was not long in pouncing upon the astonished prey. A booming gun, and the simultaneous descent of the Spanish, and ascent of the Confederate flag to the *Sumter's* peak, when we had approached within about a mile of them, cleared up the mystery of the chase, and brought the fugitives to the wind. In half an hour more, their papers had been examined, prize crews had been thrown on board of them, and they were standing back in company with the *Sumter,* to rejoin the other prizes.

I had now a fleet of six sail, and when the sea breeze set in next morning, which it did between nine and ten o'clock, I led into the harbor, the fleet following. The three newly captured vessels were the bark *West Wind*, of Rhode Island; the bark *Louisa Kilham*, of Massachusetts, and the brigantine *Naiad*, of New York. They had all cargoes of sugar, which were covered by certificates of neutral property. When the *Sumter* came abreast of the small fort, which has already been noticed, we were surprised to see the sentinels on post fire a couple of loaded muskets, the balls of which whistled over our heads, and to observe them making gestures, indicating that we must come to anchor. This we immediately did; but the prizes, all of which had the United States colors flying, were permitted to pass, and they sped on their way to the town, some miles above, as they had been ordered. When we had let go our anchor, I dispatched Lieutenant Evans to the fort, to call on the Commandant, and ask for an explanation of his conduct, in bringing us to. The explanation was simple enough. He did not know what to make of the new-born Confederate flag. He had never seen it before. It did not belong to any of the nations of the earth, of which he had any knowledge, and we might be a buccaneer for aught he knew. In the afternoon, the Commandant himself came on board to visit me, and inform me, on the part of the Governor of Cienfuegos, with whom he had communicated, that I might proceed to the town, in the *Sumter*, if I desired. We drank a glass of wine together, and I satisfied him, that I had not come in to carry his fort by storm—which would have been an easy operation enough, as he had only about a corporal's guard under his command—or to sack the town of Cienfuegos, after the fashion of the Drakes, and other English sea-robbers, who have left so vivid an impression upon Spanish memory, as to make Spanish commandants of small forts, cautious of all strange craft.

It had only been a week since the *Sumter* had run the blockade of New Orleans, and already she was out of fuel! having only coal enough left for about twenty-four hours steaming. Here was food for reflection. Active operations which would require the constant use of steam, would never do; for, by-and-by, when the enemy should get on my track, it would be easy for him to trace me from port to port, if I went into port once a week. I must endeavor to reach some cruising-ground, where I could lie in wait for ships, under sail, and dispense with the use of steam, except for a few hours, at a time, for the purpose of picking up such prizes, as I could not decoy within reach of my guns. I was glad to learn from the pilot, that there was plenty of coal to be had in Cienfuegos, and I dispatched Lieutenant Chapman to town, in one of the ship's cutters, for the double purpose of arranging for a supply, and communicating with the Governor, on the subject of my prizes, and the position which Spain was likely to occupy, during the war. The following letter addressed by me to his Excellency will explain the object I had in view in coming into Cienfuegos, and the hopes I entertained of the conduct of Spain, whose important island of Cuba lay, as it were, athwart our main gateway to the sea—the Gulf of Mexico.

> CONFEDERATE STATES STEAMER SUMTER,
> ISLAND OF CUBA, July 6, 1861

SIR:—I have the honor to inform you, of my arrival at the port of Cienfuegos, with seven prizes of war. These vessels are the brigantines *Cuba*,* *Machias, Ben. Dunning, Albert Adams,* and *Naiad;* and barks *West Wind,* and *Louisa Kilham,* property of citizens of the United States, which States, as your Excellency is aware, are waging an aggressive and unjust war upon the Confederate States, which I have the honor, with this ship under my command, to represent. I have sought a port of Cuba, with these prizes, with the expectation that Spain will extend to the cruisers of the Confederate States, the same friendly reception that, in similar circumstances, she would extend to the cruisers of the enemy; in other words, that she will permit me to leave the captured vessels within her jurisdiction, until they can be adjudicated by a Court of Admiralty of the Confederate States. As a people maintaining a government *de facto,* and not only holding the enemy in check, but gaining advantages over him, we are entitled to all the rights of belligerents, and I confidently rely upon the friendly disposition of Spain, who is our near neighbor, in the most important of her colonial possessions, to receive us with equal and even-handed justice, if not with the sympathy which our identity of interests and policy, with regard to an important social and industrial institution, are so well calculated to inspire. A rule which would exclude our prizes from her ports, during the war, although it should be applied, in terms, equally to the enemy, would not, I respectfully suggest, be an equitable,

*The *Cuba* was hourly expected to arrive, but, as the reader has seen, was recaptured, and did not make her appearance.

or just rule. The basis of such a rule, as indeed, of all the conduct of a neutral during war, is equal and impartial justice to all the belligerents, without inclining to the side of either; and this should be a substantial and practical justice, and not exist in terms merely, which may be deceptive. Now, a little reflection will, I think, show your Excellency that the rule in question—the exclusion of the prizes of both belligerents from neutral ports—cannot be applied in the present war, without operating with great injustice to the Confederate States. It is well known to your Excellency, that the United States are a manufacturing and commercial people, whilst the Confederate States are an agricultural people. The consequence of this dissimilarity of pursuits was, that at the breaking out of the war, the former had within their limits, and control, almost all the naval force of the old government. This naval force they have dishonestly seized, and turned against the Confederate States, regardless of the just claims of the latter to a large proportion of it, as tax-payers, out of whose contributions to the common Treasury it was created. The United States, by this disseizin of the property of the Confederate States, are enabled, in the first months of the war, to blockade all the ports of the latter States. In this condition of things, observe the *practical* working of the rule I am discussing, whatever may be the seeming fairness of its terms. It will be admitted that we have equal belligerent rights with the enemy. One of the most important of these rights, in a war against a commercial people, is that which I have just exercised, of capturing his property, on the high seas. But how are the Confederate States to enjoy, to its full extent, the benefit of this right, if their cruisers are not permitted to enter neutral ports, with their prizes, and retain them there, in safe custody, until they can be condemned, and disposed of? They cannot send them into their own ports, for the reason already mentioned, viz.: that those ports are hermetically sealed by the agency of their own ships, forcibly wrested from them. If they cannot send them into neutral ports, where are they to send them? Nowhere. Except for the purpose of destruction, therefore, their right of capture would be entirely defeated by the adoption of the rule in question, whilst the opposite belligerent would not be inconvenienced by it, at all, as all his own ports are open to him. I take it for granted, that Spain will not think of acting upon so unjust, and unequal a rule.

But another question arises, indeed has already arisen, in the cases of some of the very captures which I have brought into port. The cargoes of several of the vessels are claimed, as appears by certificates found among the papers, as Spanish property. This fact cannot, of course, be verified, except by a judicial proceeding, in the Prize Courts of the Confederate States. But if the prizes cannot be sent either into the ports of the Confederate States, or into neutral ports, how can this verification be made? Further—supposing there to be no dispute about the title to the cargo, how is it to be unladen, and delivered to the neutral claimant, unless the captured ship can make a port? Indeed, one of the motives which influenced me in making a Spanish colonial port, was the fact that these cargoes were claimed by Spanish subjects, whom I was desirous of putting to as little inconvenience as possible, in the unlading and reception of their property, should it be restored to them, by a decree of the Confederate Courts. It will be for your Excellency to consider, and act upon these grave questions, touching alike the interests of both our governments.

I have the honor to be, &c., &c.,

RAPHAEL SEMMES.

I did not expect much to grow immediately out of the above communication. Indeed, as the reader will probably surmise, I had written it more for the eye of the Spanish Premier, than for that of the Governor of a small provincial town, who had no diplomatic power, and whom I knew to be timid, as are all the subordinate officers of absolute governments. I presumed that the Governor would telegraph it to the Captain-General, at Havana, and that the latter would hold the subject in abeyance, until he could hear from the Home Government. Nor was I disappointed in this expectation, for Lieutenant Chapman returned from Cienfuegos, the next morning, and brought me intelligence to this effect.

To dispose of the questions raised, without the necessity of again returning to them, the reader is informed, that Spain, in due time, followed the lead of England and France, in the matter of excluding prizes from her ports; and that my prizes were delivered—to whom, do you think, reader? You will naturally say, to myself, or my duly appointed agent, with instructions to take them out of the Spanish port. This was the result to be logically expected. The Captain-General had received them, in trust, as it were, to abide the decision of his Government. If that decision should be in favor of receiving the prizes of both belligerents, well; if not, I expected to be notified to take them away. But nothing was further, it seems, from the intention of the Captain-General, than this simple and just proceeding; for as soon as the Queen's proclamation was received, he deliberately handed back all my prizes to their original owners! This was so barefaced a proceeding, that it was necessary to allege some excuse for it, and the excuse given was, that I had violated the neutral waters of Cuba, and captured my three last prizes within the marine league—my sympathizing friend, the Spanish pilot, and an English sailor, on board the tug, being vouched as the respectable witnesses to the fact! Such was the power of Spanish gold, and Yankee unscrupulousness in the use of it.

[A neutral is obligated to release to their owners any prizes brought into its ports. According to Semmes's own original journal he was informed on the very day of his arrival that the *Sumter* might go wherever he wished but "that the governor would detain his prizes." Thus Spain's procedure was correct even if not for the reasons alleged in the text. All of the prizes apparently were captured outside of the three-mile limit all right; the seizure of at least the last three, however, was distinctly tainted, in that the *Sumter* issued from neutral waters to seize ships which had just left those waters. Probably, however, the Spaniards had neither the power nor the will to prevent this, even had they known the *Sumter's* identity at the time. On page 173 Semmes himself admits the illegality of identical procedure.]

Great excitement was produced, as may be supposed, by the arrival of the *Sumter*, with her six prizes, at the quiet little town of Cienfuegos. Lieutenant Chapman was met by a host of sympathizers, and carried to their club, and afterward to the house of one of the principal citizens, who would not hear of his spending the night at a hotel, and installed as his honored guest. Neighbors were called in, and the night was made merry, to a late hour, by the popping of champagne-corks and the story, and the song; and when the festivities had ceased, my tempest-tossed lieutenant was laid away in the sweetest and whitest of sheets, to dream of the eyes of the houries of the household, that had beamed upon him so kindly, that he was in danger of forgetting that he was a married man. For weeks afterward, his messmates could get nothing out of him, but something about Don this, and Doña that. There was a hurrying to and fro, too, of the stewards, and mess boys, as the cutter in which he returned, came alongside of the ship, for there were sundry boxes, marked Bordeaux, and Cette, and sundry baskets branded with anchors; and there were fruits, and flowers, and squalling chickens to be passed up.

The principal coffee-house of the place had been agog with wonders; the billiard-players had rested idly on their cues, to listen to Madam Rumor with her thousand tongues—how the fort had fired into the *Sumter*, and how the *Sumter* had fired back at the fort, and how the matter had finally been settled by the *Pirata* and the *Comandante,* over a bottle of champagne. Yankee captains, and consignees, supercargoes, and consuls passed in, and out, in consultation, like so many ants whose nest had been trodden upon, and nothing could be talked of but freights, and insurance, with, and without the war risk; bills of lading, invoices, consul's certificates to cover cargoes, and last, though not least, where the d—l all the Federal gunboats were, that this Confederate hawk should be permitted to make such a flutter in the Yankee dove-cot.

From what has been said, . . . the reader will have observed how anxious I was to conform my conduct, in all respects, to the laws of war. My hope was, that *some* of the nations of the earth, at least, would give me an asylum for my prizes, so that I might have them formally condemned by the Confederate States Prize Courts, instead of being obliged to destroy them. It was with this hope, that I had entered the port of Cienfuegos, as the reader has seen; and it was in furtherance of this object, that I now drew up the following appointment of a Prize Agent, who had come well recommended to me, as a gentleman of integrity and capacity.

C. S. Steamer Sumter, Cienfuegos,
July 6, 1861.

Sir:—You are hereby appointed Prize Agent, for, and in behalf of the Confederate States of America, of the following prizes, to wit: The *Cuba, Machias, Ben. Dunning, Albert Adams, Naiad, West Wind,* and *Louisa Kilham,* and their cargoes, until the same can be adjudicated, by the Prize Courts of the Confederate States, and disposed of by the proper authorities. You will take the necessary steps for the safe custody of these prizes, and you will not permit anything to be removed from, or disturbed on board of them. You will be pleased, also, to take the examinations of the master, and mate of each of these vessels, before a notary, touching the property of the vessels, and cargoes; and making a copy thereof, to be retained in your own possession, you will send, by some safe conveyance, the originals, addressed to "The Judge of the Confederate States District Court, New Orleans, La."

I have the honor to be, &c.,

RAPHAEL SEMMES.

Señor Don MARIANO DIAS.

During the day, the steam-tug towed down from the town, for me, a couple of lighters, containing about one hundred tons of coal, five thousands gallons of water, and some fresh provisions for the crew.* It was necessary that we should prepare for sea, with some dispatch, as there was a line of telegraph, from Cienfuegos to Havana, where there were always a number of the enemy's ships of war stationed. As a matter of course, the U. S. Consul at Cienfuegos had telegraphed to his brother Consul, in Havana, the arrival of the *Sumter*, in the first ten minutes after she had let go her anchor; and as another matter of course, there must already be several fast steamers on their way, to capture this piratical craft, which had thus so unceremoniously broken in upon the quiet of the Cuban waters, and the Yankee sugar, and rum trade. I had recourse to the chart, and having ascertained at what hour these steamers would be enabled to arrive, I fixed my own departure, a few hours ahead, so as to give them the satisfaction of finding that the bird, which they were in pursuit of, had flown. My excellent first lieutenant came up to time, and the ship was reported ready for sea before sunset, or in a little more than twenty-four hours, after our arrival.

To avoid the coal dust, which is one of the pests of a steamer, and the confusion, and noise which necessarily accompany the exceedingly poetic operation of coaling, I landed, as the sun was approaching the western horizon, in company with my junior lieutenant and sailing-master, for a stroll, and to obtain sights for testing my chronometers, as well. Having disposed of the business part of the operation first, in obedience to the old maxim; that is to say, having made our observations upon the sun, for time, we wandered about, for an hour, and more, amid the rich tropical vegetation of this queen of islands, now passing under

*[As was the case on several later occasions, it was improper for the neutral to provide the coal when it was to be used in operations against the enemy. Steam was young then but this law was already fairly well established. However, it was not nearly so conscientiously enforced as it is at present.]

the flowering acacia, and now under the deep-foliaged orange-tree, which charmed two senses at once—that of smell, by the fragrance of its young flowers, and that of sight, by the golden hue of its luscious and tempting fruit. We had landed abreast of our ship, and a few steps sufficed to put us in the midst of a dense wilderness, of floral beauty, with nothing to commune with but nature. What a contrast there was between this peaceful, and lovely scene, and the life we had led for the last week! We almost loathed to go back to the dingy walls, and close quarters of our little craft, where everything told us of war, and admonished us that a life of toil, vexation, and danger lay before us, and that we must bid a long farewell to rural scenes, and rural pleasures. As we still wandered, absorbed in such speculations as these, unconscious of the flight of time, the sound of the evening gun came booming on the ear, to recall us to our senses, and retracing our steps, we hurriedly re-embarked. That evening's stroll lingered long in my memory, and was often recalled, amid the whistling, and surging of the gale, and the tumbling, and discomforts of the ship.

I had been looking anxiously, for the last few hours, for the arrival of our prize brigantine, the *Cuba,* but she failed to make her appearance, and I was forced to abandon the hope of getting back my prize crew from her. I left with my prize agent, the following letter of instructions for the midshipman in command of the *Cuba.*

CONFEDERATE STATES STEAMER SUMTER,
CIENFUEGOS, July 7, 1861.

SIR:—Upon your arrival at this place, you will put the master, mate, and crew of the *Cuba* on *parole,* not to serve against the Confederate States, during the present war, unless exchanged, and release them. You will then deliver the brigantine to the Governor, for safe custody, until the orders of the Captain-General can be known in regard to her. I regret much that you are not able to arrive in time, to rejoin the ship, and you must exercise your judgment, as to the mode in which you shall regain your country. You will, no doubt, be able to raise sufficient funds for transporting yourself, and the four seamen who are with you, to some point in the Confederate States, upon a bill of exchange, which you are hereby authorized to draw, upon the Secretary

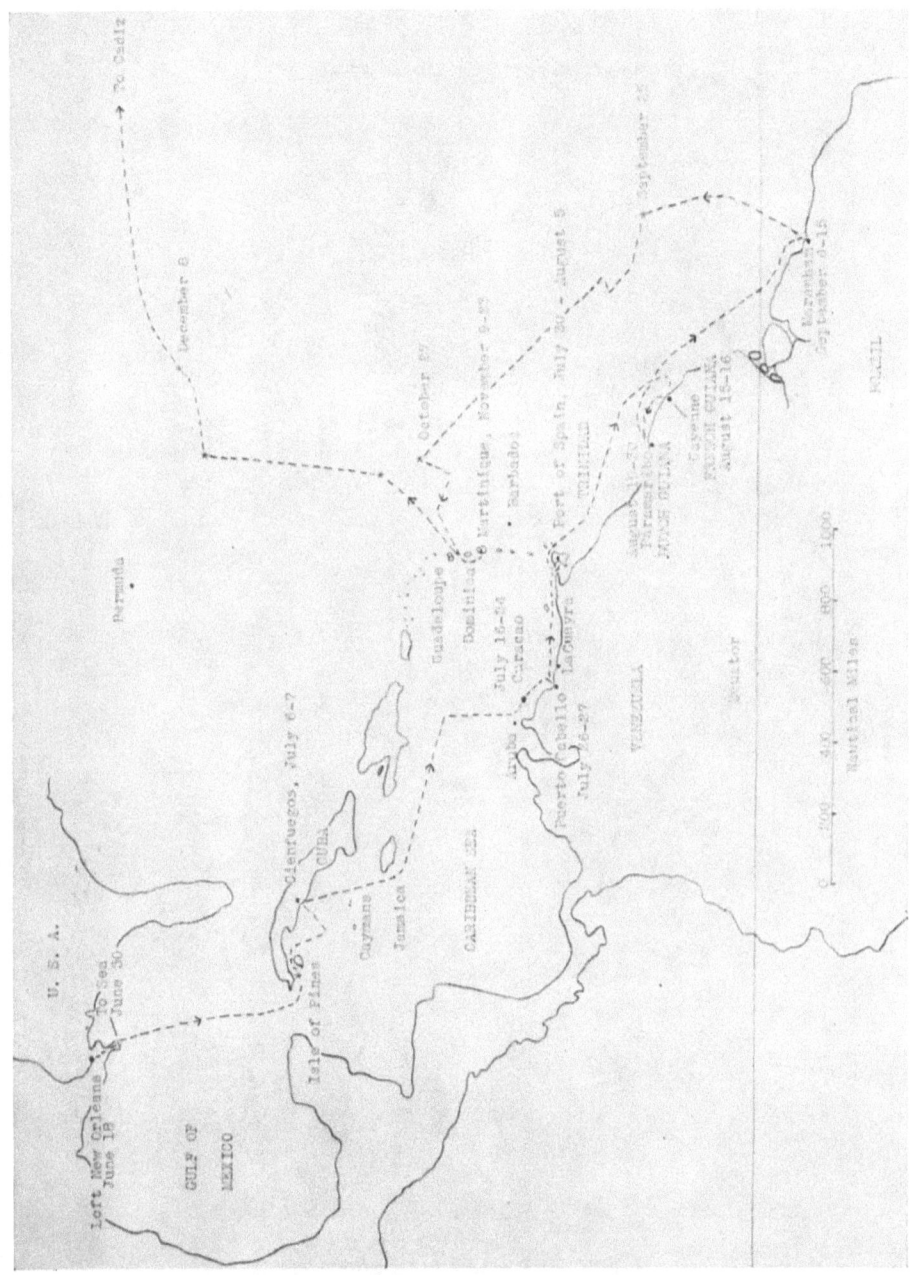

TRACK OF THE C.S.S. *Sumter* IN THE YEAR 1861
Asterisks mark positions where prizes were burned.

OFFICERS OF THE C.S.S. *Sumter*
This is the "adjoining engraving" to which Semmes refers on page 36

of the Navy. Upon your arrival within our territory, you will report yourself to that officer. Your baggage has been sent you by the pilot.
Midshipman A. G. HUDGINS.

I did not meet Mr. Hudgins, afterward, until as a rear admiral, I was ordered to the command of the James River fleet, in the winter of 1864. He was then attached to one of my ships, as a lieutenant. On the retreat from Richmond, I made him a captain of light artillery, and he was paroled with me, at Greensboro', North Carolina, in May 1865. How he has settled with my friend, the Spanish pilot, who agreed with *me* that the prizes which I captured, off Cienfuegos, were *five* miles from the land, and with the Northern claimants, and the Captain-General of Cuba, that they were less than *three* miles from it, about his baggage, I have never learned.

Everything being in readiness for sea, on board the *Sumter*, and the officers having all returned from their visits to the town, at eleven P.M., we got under way, and as the bell struck the midnight hour, we steamed out of the harbor, the lamps from the light-house throwing a bright glare upon our deck, as we passed under its shadow, close enough to "have tossed a biscuit" to the keeper; so bold is the entrance of the little river. The sea was nearly calm, and the usual land breeze was gently breathing, rather than blowing. Having given the course to the officer of the deck, I was glad to go below, and turn in, after the excitement, and confusion of the last forty-eight hours.

CHAPTER IV

On the Spanish Main

WHEN SOME SEVEN OR EIGHT MILES FROM THE land, we lost the land breeze, and were struck by the sea breeze, nearly ahead, with some force. We steamed on, all the next day, without any incident to break in upon the monotony, except a short chase which we gave to a brigantine, which proved, upon our coming up with her, to be Spanish. Between nine, and ten o'clock in the evening, we passed the small islands of the Caymans, which we found to be laid down in the charts we were using, some fifteen or sixteen miles too far to the westward. As there is a current setting in the vicinity of these islands, and as the islands themselves are so low, as to be seen with difficulty, in a dark night,—and the night on which we were passing them was dark,— I make this observation, to put navigators on their guard.

The morning of the ninth of July dawned clear, and beautifully, but as the sun gained power, the trade-wind increased, until it blew half a gale, raising considerable sea, and impeding the progress of the ship. Indeed, so little speed did we make, that the island of Jamaica, which we had descried with the first streaks of dawn, remained in sight all day; its blue mountains softened but not obliterated by the distance as the evening set in. The sea was as blue as the mountains, and the waves seemed almost as large, to our eyes, as the little steamer plunged into, and struggled with them, in her vain attempt to make headway. All the force of her engine was incapable of driving her at a greater speed than five knots. The next day, and the day after were equally unpropitious. Indeed the weather went from bad, to worse, for now the sky became densely overcast, with black, and angry-looking clouds, and the wind began to whistle through the rigging, with all the symptoms of a gale. We were approaching the hurricane season, and there was no telling at what moment, one of those terrible cyclones of the Caribbean Sea might sweep over us. To add to the gloominess of the prospect, we were comparatively out of the track of commerce, and had seen no sail, since we had overhauled the Spanish brigantine.

As explained to the reader, in one of the opening chapters, it was my intention to proceed from Cuba, to Barbadoes, there recoal, and thence make the best of my way to Cape St. Roque, in Brazil, where I expected to reap a rich harvest from the enemy's commerce. I was now obliged to abandon, or at least to modify this design. It would not be possible for me to reach Barbadoes, with my present supply of coal, in the teeth of such trade-winds, as I had been encountering for the last few days. I therefore determined to bend down toward the Spanish Main; converting the present head-wind, into a fair wind, for at least a part of the way, and hoping to find the weather more propitious, on that coast. It was now the thirteenth of July, and as we had sailed from Cienfuegos, on the seventh, we had consumed six out of our eight days' supply of fuel. Steaming was no longer to be thought of, and we must make some port under sail. The Dutch island of Curaçoa lay under our lee, and we accordingly made sail for that island. The engineer was ordered to let his fires go down, and uncouple his propeller that it might not retard the speed of the ship, and the sailors were sent aloft to loose the topsails.

This was the first time that we were to make use of our sails, unaided by steam, and the old sailors of the ship, who had not bestridden a yard for some months, leaped aloft, with a will, to obey the welcome order. . . .

Our first night under canvas, I find thus described, in my journal: "Heavy sea all night, ship rolling, and tumbling about, though doing pretty well. The propeller revolves freely, and we are making about five knots." The next day was Sunday, and the weather was somewhat ameliorated. The wind continued nearly as fresh as before, but as we were now running a point free, this was no objection, and the black, angry clouds had disappeared, leaving a bright, and cheerful sky. A sail was seen on the distant horizon, but it was too rough to chase. This was our usual muster-day, but the decks were wet, and uncomfortable, and I permitted my crew to rest, they having scarcely yet recovered from the fatigue of the last few days.

There is, perhaps, no part of the world where the weather is so uniformly fine, as on the Spanish Main. The cyclones never bend in that direction, and even the ordinary gales are unknown. We were already beginning to feel the influence of this meteorological change; for on Monday, the 15th of July, the weather was thus described in my journal: "Weather moderating, and the sea going down, though still rough. Nothing seen. In the afternoon, pleasant, with a moderate breeze, and the clouds assuming their usual soft, fleecy, trade-wind appearance." The next day was still clear, though the wind had freshened, and the ship was making good speed.

At nine A.M. we made the land, on the starboard bow, which proved to be the island of Oruba, to leeward, a few miles, of Curaçoa. For some hours past, we had been within the influence of the equatorial current, which sets westward, along this coast, with considerable velocity, and it had carried us a little out of our course, though we had made some allowance for it. We hauled up, a point, or two, and at eleven A.M. we made the island of Curaçoa, on the port bow. We doubled the northwest end of the island, at about four P.M. and hauling up on the south side of it we soon brought the wind ahead, when it became necessary to put the ship under steam again, and to furl the sails.

The afternoon proved beautifully bright, and clear; the sea was of a deep indigo-blue, and we were all charmed, even with this barren little island, as we steamed along its bold, and blackened shores, of limestone rock, alongside of which the heaviest ship might have run, and throwing out her bow and stern lines, made herself fast with impunity, so perpendicularly deep were the waters. Our average distance from the land, as we steamed along, was not greater than a quarter of a mile. There were a few stunted trees, only, to be seen, in the little ravines, and some wild shrubbery, and sickly looking grass, struggling for existence on the hills' sides. A few goats were browsing about here, and there, and the only evidence of commerce, or thrift, that we saw, were some piles of salt, that had been raked up from the lagoons, ready for shipment. And yet the Dutch live, and thrive here, and have built up quite a pretty little town—that of St. Anne's, to which we were bound. The explanation of which is, that the island lies contiguous to the Venezuelan coast, and is a free port, for the introduction of European, and American goods, in which a considerable trade is carried on, with the main land.

We arrived off the town, with its imposing battlements frowning on either side of the harbor, about dusk, and immediately hoisted a jack, and fired a gun, for a pilot. In the course of half an hour, or so, this indispensable individual appeared, but it was too late, he said, for us to attempt the entrance, that night. He would come off, the first thing in the morning, and take us in. With this assurance we rested satisfied, and lay off, and on, during the night, under easy steam. But we were not to gain entrance to this quaint little Dutch town, so easily, as had been supposed. We were to have here a foretaste of the trouble, that the Federal Consuls were to give us in the future....

Soon after the pilot had landed, from the *Sumter,* carrying with him to the shore, the intelligence that she was a Confederate States cruiser, the Federal Consul made his appearance at the Government-House, and claimed that the "pirate" should not be permitted to enter the harbor; informing his Excellency, the Governor, that Mr. Seward would be irate, if such a thing were permitted, and that he might expect to have the stone, and mortar of his two forts knocked about his ears, in double quick, by the ships of war of the Great Republic.

This bold, and defiant tone, of the doughty little Consul, seemed to stagger his Excellency; it would not be so pleasant to have St. Anne's demolished, merely because a steamer with a flag that nobody had seen before, wanted some coal; and so, the next morning, bright and early, he sent the pilot off, to say to me, that "the Governor could not permit the *Sumter* to enter, having received recent orders from Holland to that effect." Here was a pretty kettle of fish! The *Sumter* had only one day's fuel left, and it was some distance from Curaçoa, to any other place, where coal was to be had. I immediately sent for Lieutenant Chapman, and directed him to prepare himself for a visit to the shore; and calling my clerk, caused him to write, after my dictation, the following despatch to his Excellency:—

CONFEDERATE STATES STEAMER SUMTER,
OFF ST. ANNE'S, CURAÇOA, July 17, 1861.

HIS EXCELLENCY GOVERNOR CROL:—

I was surprised to receive, by the pilot, this morning, a message from your Excellency, to the effect that this ship would not be permitted to enter the harbor, unless she was in distress, as your Excellency had received orders from his Government not to admit vessels of war of the Confederate States of America, to the hospitality of the ports, under your Excellency's command. I most respectfully suggest that there must be some mistake here; and I have sent to you the bearer, Lieutenant Chapman, of the Confederate States Navy, for the purpose of an explanation. Your Excellency must be under some misapprehension as to the character of this vessel. She is a ship of war, duly commissioned by the government of the Confederate States, which States have been recognized, as belligerents, in the present war, by all the leading Powers of Europe, viz.:—Great Britain, France, Spain, &c., as your Excellency must be aware.

It is true, that these Powers have prohibited both belligerents, alike, from bringing prizes into their several jurisdictions;* but no one of them has made a distinction, either between the respective prizes, or the cruisers, themselves, of the two belligerents—the cruisers of both governments, unaccompanied by prizes, being admitted to the hospitalities of the ports of all these great Powers on terms of perfect equality. In the face of these facts, am I to understand from your Excellency, that Holland has adopted a different rule, and that she not only excludes the prizes, but the ships of war, themselves, of the Confederate States? And this, at the same time, that she admits the cruisers of the United States; thus departing from her neutrality, in this war, ignoring the Confederate States, as belligerents, and aiding and abetting their enemy? If this be the position which Holland has assumed, in this contest, I pray your Excellency to be kind enough to say as much to me in writing.

When this epistle was ready, Chapman shoved off for the shore, and a long conference ensued. The Governor called around him, as I afterward learned, all the dignitaries of the island, civil and

---

*[Semmes did not learn until later that Spain had turned him down in the case of the Cienfuegos ships. From this letter, however, he must have had little or no hope. Or possibly his inclusion of Spain in this sentence was due to carelessness only.]

military, and a grand council of State was held. These Dutchmen have a ponderous way of doing things, and I have no doubt, the gravity of this council was equal to that held in New Amsterdam in colonial days, as described by the renowned historian Diederick Knickerbocker, at which Woutter Van Twiller, the doubter, was present. Judging by the time that Chapman was waiting for his answer, during which he had nothing to do but sip the most delightful mint juleps—for these islanders seemed to have robbed old Virginia of some of her famous mint patches—in company with an admiring crowd of friends, the councillors must have "smoked and talked, and smoked again;" pondered with true Dutch gravity, all the arguments, *pro* and *con*, that were offered, and weighed my despatch, along with the "recent order from Holland," in a torsion balance, to see which was heaviest.

After the lapse of an hour, or two, becoming impatient, I told my first lieutenant, that as our men had not been practised at the guns, for some time, I thought it would be as well to let them burst a few of our eight-inch shells, at a target. Accordingly the drum beat to quarters, a great stir was made about the deck, as the guns were cast loose, and pretty soon, whiz! went a shell, across the windows of the council-chamber, which overlooked the sea; the shell bursting like a clap of rather sharp, ragged thunder, a little beyond, in close proximity, to the target. Sundry heads were seen immediately to pop out of the windows of the chamber, and then to be withdrawn very suddenly, as though the owners of them feared that another shell was coming, and that my gunners might make some mistake in their aim. By the time we had fired three or four shells, all of which bursted with beautiful precision, Chapman's boat was seen returning, and thinking that our men had had exercise enough, we ran out and secured the guns.

My lieutenant came on board, smiling, and looking pleasantly, as men will do, when they are bearers of good news, and said that the Governor had given us permission to enter. We were lying close in with the entrance, and in a few minutes more, the *Sumter* was gliding gracefully past the houses, on either side of her, as she ran up the little canal, or river, that split the town in two. The quays were crowded with a motley gathering of the townspeople, men, women, and children, to see us pass, and sailors waved their hats to us, from the shipping in the port. Running through the town into a land-locked basin, in its rear, the *Sumter* let go her anchor, hoisted out her boats, and spread her awnings,—and we were once more in port.

The *Sumter* had scarcely swung to her anchors, in the small land-locked harbor described, before she was surrounded by a fleet of bum-boats, laden with a profusion of tropical fruits, and filled with men, and women, indifferently—the women rather preponderating. These bum-boat women are an institution in Curaçoa; the profession descends from mother to daughter, and time seems to operate no change among them. It had been nearly a generation since I was last at Curaçoa. I was then a gay, rollicking young midshipman, in the "old" Navy, and it seemed as though I were looking upon the same faces, and listening to the same confusion of voices as before. The individual women had passed away, of course, but the bum-boat women remained. They wore the same parti-colored handkerchiefs wound gracefully around their heads, the same gingham or muslin dresses, and exposed similar, if not the same, bare arms, and unstockinged legs. They were admitted freely on board, with their stocks in trade, and pretty soon Jack was on capital terms with them, converting his small change into fragrant bananas, and blood-red oranges, and replenishing his tobacco-pouch for the next cruise. As Jack is a gallant fellow, a little flirtation was going on too with the purchasing, and I was occasionally highly amused at these joint efforts at trade and love-making. No one but a bum-boat woman is ever a sailor's *blanchiseuse, et par consequence* a number of well-filled clothes'-bags soon made their appearance on deck, from the different apartments of the ship, and were passed into the boats alongside.

These people all speak excellent English, though with a drawl, which is not unmusical, when the speaker is a sprightly young woman. Jack has a great fondness for pets, and no wonder, poor fellow, debarred, as he is, from all family ties, and with no place he can call his home, but his ship; and pretty soon my good-natured first lieutenant had been seduced into giving him leave to bring sundry monkeys, and parrots on board, the former of which were now gambolling about the rigging, and the latter waking the echoes of the harbor with their squalling. Such was the crowd upon our decks, and so serious was the interruption to business, that we were soon obliged to lay restrictions upon the bum-boat fleet, by prohibiting it from coming alongside, except at meal-hours, which we always designated by hoisting a red pennant, at the mizzen. It was curious to watch the movements of the fleet, as these hours approached. Some twenty or thirty boats would be lying upon their oars, a few yards from the ship, each with from two to half a dozen inmates, eagerly watching the old quartermaster, whose duty it was to hoist the pennant; the women chattering, and the parrots squalling, whilst the oarsmen were poising their oars, that they might get the first stroke over their competitors in the race. At length, away goes the flag! and then what a rushing and clattering, and bespattering until the boats are alongside.

In an hour after our anchor had been let go, the business of the ship, for the next few days, had all been arranged. The first lieutenant had visited a neighboring ship-yard, and contracted for a new foretop-mast, to supply the place of the old one which had been sprung; the paymaster had contracted for a supply of coal, and fresh provisions, daily, for the crew, and for having the ship watered; the latter no unimportant matter, in this rainless region, and I had sent an officer to call on the Governor, *with my card*, being too unwell to make the visit, in person. Upon visiting the shore the next day, I found that we were in a *quasi* enemy's territory, for besides the Federal Consul before spoken of, a Boston man had intrenched himself in the best hotel in the place, as proprietor, and was doing a thriving business, far away from "war's alarms," and a New Yorker had the monopoly of taking all the phizes of the staid old Dutchmen—"John Smith, of New York, Photographer," hanging high above the artist's windows, on a sign-board that evidently had not been painted by a Curaçoan. Mr. Smith had already taken an excellent photograph of the *Sumter*, which he naively enough told me, was intended for the New York illustrated papers. If I had had ever so much objection, to having the likeness of my ship hung up in such a "rogues' gallery," I had no means of preventing it. Besides, it could do us but little damage, in the way of identification, as we had the art of disguising the *Sumter* so that we would not know her, ourselves, at half a dozen miles distance.

I was surprised, one morning, during our stay here, whilst I was lounging, listlessly, in my cabin, making a vain attempt to read, under the infliction of the caulkers overhead, who were striking their caulking-irons with a vigor, and rapidity, that made the tympanum of my ears ring again, at the announcement that Don somebody or other, the private secretary of President [Julián] Castro, desired to see me. The caulkers were sent away, and his Excellency's private secretary brought below. President Castro was one of those unfortunate South American chiefs, who had been beaten in a battle of ragamuffins, and compelled to fly his country. He was President of Venezuela, and had been deprived of his office, before the expiration of his term, by some military aspirant, who had seated himself in the presidential chair, instead, and was now in exile in Curaçoa, with four of the members of his cabinet. The object of the visit of his secretary was to propose to me to reinstate the exiled President, in his lost position, by engaging in a military expedition, with him, to the mainland.

Here was a chance, now, for an ambitious man! I might become the Warwick of Venezuela, and put the crown on another's head, if I might not wear it myself. I might hoist my admiral's flag, on board the *Sumter,* and take charge of all the piraguas, and canoes, that composed the Venezuelan navy, whilst my colleague mustered those men in buckram, so graphically described by Sir John Falstaff, and made an onslaught upon his despoiler. But unfortunately for friend Castro, I was like one of those damsels who had already plighted her faith to another, before the new wooer appeared—I was not in the market. I listened courteously, however, to what the secretary had to say; told him, that I felt flattered by the offer of his chief, but that I was unable to accept it. "I cannot," I continued, "consistently with my obligations to my own country, engage in any of the revolutionary movements of other countries." "But," said he, "Señor Castro is the *de jure* President of Venezuela, and you would be upholding the right in assisting him;—can you not, at least, land us, with some arms and ammunition, on the main land?" I replied that, "as a Confederate States officer, I could not look into *de jure* claims. These questions were for the Venezuelans, themselves, to decide. The only government I could know in Venezuela was the *de facto* government, for the time being, and *that,* by his own showing, was in the hands of his antagonists." Here the conversation closed, and my visitor, who had the bearing and speech of a cultivated gentleman, departed. The jottings of my diary for the next few days, will perhaps now inform the reader, of our movements, better than any other form of narrative.

July 19th.—Wind unusually blustering this morning, with partial obscuration of the heavens. The engineers are busy, overhauling and repairing damages to their engine and boilers; the gunner is at work, polishing up his battery and ventilating his magazine, and the sailors are busy renewing ratlines and tarring down their rigging. An English bark entered the harbor to-day from Liverpool.

July 20th.—Painting and refitting ship; got off the new foretopmast from the shore. It is a good pine stick, evidently from our Southern States, and has been well fashioned. The monthly packet from the island of St. Thomas arrived, to-day, bringing newspapers from the enemy's country as late as the 26th of June. We get nothing new from these papers, except that the Northern bee-hive is all agog, with the marching and countermarching of troops.

July 21st.—Fresh trade-winds, with flying clouds—atmosphere highly charged with moisture, but no rain. This being Sunday, we mustered and inspected the crew. The washer-women have decidedly improved the appearance of the young officers, the glistening of white shirt-bosoms and collars having been somewhat unusual on board of the *Sumter,* of late. The crew look improved too, by their change of diet, and the use of antiscorbutics, which have been supplied to them, at the request of the surgeon; though some of them, having been on shore, "on liberty," have brought off a blackened eye. No matter—the more frequently Jack settles his accounts, on shore, the fewer he will have to settle on board ship, in breach of discipline. We read, at the muster, to-day, the finding and sentence of the first court-martial, that has sat on board the *Sumter,* since she reached the high seas.

July 22d.—Warped alongside a wharf, in the edge of the town, and commenced receiving coal on board. Refitting, and repainting ship. In the afternoon, I took a lonely stroll through the town, mainly in the suburbs. It is a quaint, picturesque old place, with some few modern houses, but the general air is that of dilapidation, and a decay of trade. The lower classes are simple, and primitive in their habits, and but little suffices to supply their wants. The St. Thomas packet sailed, to-day, and, as a consequence, the Federal cruisers, in and about that island, will have intelligence of our whereabouts, in four or five days. To mislead them, I have told the pilot, and several gentlemen from the shore, *in great confidence,* that I am going back to cruise on the coast of Cuba. The packet will of course take that intelligence to St. Thomas.

July 23d.—Still coaling, refitting and painting. Weather more cloudy, and wind not so constantly fresh, within the last few days.

Having taken sights for our chronometers, on the morning after our arrival, and again to-day, I have been enabled to verify their rates. They are running very well. The chronometer of the *Golden Rocket* proves to be a good instrument. We fix the longitude of Curaçoa to be 68° 58′ 30″, west of Greenwich.

July 24th.—Sky occasionally obscured, with a moderate trade-wind. Our men have all returned from their visits to the shore, except one, a simple lad named Orr, who, as I learn, has been seduced away, by a Yankee skipper, in port, aided by the Boston hotel-keeper, and our particular friend, the consul. As these persons have tampered with my whole crew, I am gratified to know, that there has been but one traitor found among them.

We had now been a week in Curaçoa, during which time, besides recruiting, and refreshing my crew, I had made all the necessary preparations for another cruise. The ship had been thoroughly overhauled, inside and out, and her coal-bunkers were full of good English coal. It only remained for us to put to sea. Accordingly, at twelve o'clock precisely, on the day last above mentioned, as had been previously appointed, the *Sumter,* bidding farewell to her new-made friends, moved gracefully out of the harbor—this time, amid the waving of handkerchiefs, in female hands, as well as of hats in the hands of the males; the quay being lined, as before, to see us depart. The photographer took a last shot at the ship, as she glided past his sanctum, and we looked with some little interest to the future numbers of that "Journal of Civilization," vulgarly yclept "Harper's Weekly," for the interesting portrait; which came along in due time, accompanied by a lengthy description, veracious, of course, of the "Pirate."

Curaçoa lies a short distance off the coast of Venezuela, between Laguayra, and Puerto Cabello, and as both of these places had some commerce with the United States, I resolved to look into them.* The morning after our departure found us on a smooth sea, with a light breeze off the land. The mountains, back of Laguayra, loomed up blue, mystic, and majestic, at a distance of about thirty miles, and the lookout, at the mast-head, was on the *qui vive* for strange sails. He had not to wait long. In the tropics, there is very little of that bewitching portion of the twenty-four hours, which, in other parts of the world, is called twilight. Day passes into night, and night into day, almost at a single bound. The rapidly approach-

---

*[Both well to the eastward of Curaçoa.]

ing dawn had scarcely revealed to us the bold outline of the coast, above mentioned, when sail ho! resounded from the mast-head. The sail bore on our port-bow, and was standing obliquely toward us. We at once gave chase, and at half-past six A. M., came up with, and captured the schooner *Abby Bradford,* from New York, bound for Puerto Cabello.

We knew our prize to be American, long before she showed us her colors. She was a "down-East," fore-and-aft schooner, and there are no other such vessels in the world. They are as thoroughly marked, as the Puritans who build them, and there is no more mistaking the "cut of their jib." The little schooner was provision laden, and there was no attempt to cover her cargo. The news of the escape of the *Sumter* had not reached New York, at the date of her sailing, and the few privateers that we had put afloat, at the beginning of the war, had confined their operations to our own, and the enemy's coasts. Hence the neglect of the owners of the *Bradford,* in not providing her with some good English, or Spanish certificates, protesting that her cargo was neutral. . . .

The *Bradford* being bound for Puerto Cabello, and that port being but a short distance, under my lee, I resolved to run down, with the prize, and try my hand with my friend Castro's opponent, the *de facto* President of Venezuela, to see whether I could not prevail upon him, to admit my prizes into his ports. I thought, surely, an arrangement could be made with some of these beggarly South American republics, the revenue of which did not amount to a cargo of provisions, annually, and which were too weak, besides, to be worth kicking by the stronger powers. What right had *they,* thought I, to be putting on the airs of nations, and talking about acknowledging other people, when they had lived a whole generation, themselves, without the acknowledgment of Spain.

But, as the reader will see, I reckoned without my host. I found that they had a wholesome fear of the Federal gunboats, and that even their cupidity could not tempt them to be just, or generous. If they had admitted my prizes into their ports, I could, in the course of a few months, have made those same ports more busy with the hum and thrift of commerce, than they had ever been before; I could have given a new impulse to their revolutions, and made them rich enough to indulge in the luxury of a *pronunciamiento* [insurrection], once a week. The bait was tempting, but there stood the great lion in their path—the model Republic. The fact is, I must do this model Republic the justice to say, that it not only bullied the little South American republics, but all the world besides. Even old John Bull, grown rich, and plethoric, and asthmatic and gouty, trembled when he thought of his rich argosies, and of the possibility of Yankee privateers chasing them.

Taking the *Bradford* in tow, then, we squared away for Puerto Cabello, but darkness came on before we could reach the entrance of the harbor, and we were compelled to stand off and on, during the night—the schooner being cast off, and taking care of herself, under sail. The *Sumter* lay on the still waters, all night, like a huge monster asleep, with the light from the light-house, on the battlements of the fort, glaring full upon her, and in plain hearing of the shrill cry of *"Alerta!"* from the sentinels. So quietly did she repose, with banked fires, being fanned, but not moved, by the gentle land-breeze that was blowing, that she scarcely needed to turn over her propeller during the night, to preserve her relative position with the light. There was no occasion to be in a hurry to run in, the next morning, as no business could be transacted before ten, or eleven o'clock, and so I waited until the sun, with his broad disk glaring upon us, like an angry furnace, had rolled away the mists of the morning, and the first lieutenant had holy-stoned his decks, and arranged his hammock-nettings, with his neat, white hammocks stowed in them, before we put the ship in motion.

We had, some time before, hoisted the Confederate States flag, and the Venezuelan colors were flying from the fort in response. The prize accompanied us in, and we both anchored, within a stone's throw of the town, the latter looking like some old Moorish city, that had been transported by magic to the new world, *gallinazos* [vultures], and all. Whilst my clerk was copying my despatch to the Governor, and the lieutenant was preparing himself, and his boat's crew, to take it on shore, I made a hasty *reconnoissance* of the fort, which had a few iron pieces, of small calibre mounted on it, well eaten by rust, and whose carriages had rotted from under them. The following is a copy of my letter to his Excellency.

CONFEDERATE STATES STEAMER SUMTER,
PUERTO CABELLO, July 26, 1861.

HIS EXCELLENCY, THE GOVERNOR:—

I have the honor to inform your Excellency of my arrival at this place, in this ship, under my command, with the prize schooner, *Abby*

Bradford, in company, captured by me about seventy miles to the northward and eastward. The *Abby Bradford* is the property of citizens of the United States, with which States, as your Excellency is aware, the Confederate States, which I have the honor to represent, are at war, and the cargo would appear to belong, also, to citizens of the United States, who have shipped it on consignment, to a house in Puerto Cabello. Should any claim, however, be given for the cargo, or any part of it, the question of ownership can only be decided by the Prize Courts of the Confederate States. In the meantime, I have the honor to request, that your Excellency will permit me to leave this prize vessel, with her cargo, in the port of Puerto Cabello, until the question of prize can be adjudicated by the proper tribunals of my country. This will be a convenience to all parties; as well to any citizens of Venezuela, who may have an interest in the cargo, as to the captors, who have also valuable interests to protect.

In making this request, I do not propose that the Venezuelan government shall depart from a strict neutrality between the belligerents, as the same rule it applies to us, it can give the other party the benefit of, also. In other words, with the most scrupulous regard for her neutrality, she may permit both belligerents to bring their prizes into her waters; and, of this, neither belligerent could complain, since whatever justice is extended to its enemy, is extended also to itself * * * [Here follows a repetition of the facts with regard to the seizure of the Navy by the Federal authorities, and the establishment of the blockade of the Southern ports, already stated in my letter to the Governor of Cienfuegos.] * * * Thus, your Excellency sees, that under the rule of exclusion, the enemy could enjoy his right of capture, to its full extent—all his own ports being open to him—whilst the cruisers of the Confederate States could enjoy it, *sub modo,* only; that is, for the purpose of destroying their prizes. A rule which would produce such unequal results as this, is not a just rule (although it might, in terms, be extended to both parties), and as equality and justice, are of the essence of neutrality, I take it for granted, that Venezuela will not adopt it.

On the other hand, the rule admitting both parties, alike, with their prizes into your ports, until the prize courts of the respective countries could have time to adjudicate the cases, would work equal and exact justice to both; and this is all that the Confederate States demand.

With reference to the present case, as the cargo consists chiefly of provisions, which are perishable, I would ask leave to sell them, at public auction, for the benefit of "whom it may concern," depositing the proceeds with a suitable prize agent, until the decision of the court can be known. With regard to the vessel, I request that she may remain in the custody of the same agent, until condemned and sold.

When the *Sumter* entered Puerto Cabello, with her prize, she found an empty harbor, there being only two or three coasting schooners anchored along the coast; there was a general dearth of business, and the quiet little city was panting for an excitement. A bomb-shell, thrown into the midst of the stagnant commercial community, could not have startled them more, than the rattling of the chain cable of the *Sumter* through her hawse-hole, as she let go her anchor; and when my missive was handed to the Governor, there was a racing, and chasing of bare-footed orderlies, that indicated a prospective gathering of the clans, similar to the one which had occurred at Curaçoa. A grand council was held, at which the Confederate States had not the honor to be represented.

That the reader may understand the odds against which we now had to struggle, he must recollect, that all these small South American towns are, more or less, dependent upon American trade. The New England States, and New York supply them with their domestic cottons, flour, bacon, and notions; sell them all their worthless old muskets, and damaged ammunition, and now and then, smuggle out a small craft to them, for naval purposes. The American Consul, who is also a merchant, represents not only those "grand moral ideas," that characterize our Northern people, but Sand's sarsaparilla, and Smith's wooden clocks. He is, *par excellence,* the big dog of the village. The big dog was present on the present occasion, looking portentous, and savage, and when he ope'd his mouth, all the little dogs were silent. Of course, the poor *Sumter,* anchored away off in the bay, could have no chance before so august an assemblage, and, pretty soon, an orderly came down to the boat, where my patient lieutenant was waiting, bearing a most ominous-looking letter, put up in true South American style, about a foot square, and bearing on it, *"Dios y Libertad."*

When I came to break the seal of this letter, I found it to purport, that the Governor had not the necessary *funciones,* to reply to me, diplomatically, but that he would *elevate* my despatch, to the *Supreme* Government; and that, in the mean time, I had better take the *Abby Bradford* and get out of Puerto Cabello, as

Lieutenant John McIntosh Kell, C.S.N.
First Lieutenant of both the *Sumter* and the *Alabama*. He was one of the South's ablest naval officers. From a photograph taken one day before departure from New Orleans.

THE U.S. STEAM SLOOP-OF-WAR *Iroquois*. She was unable to prevent the *Sumter* from slipping out from St. Pierre.

THE BURNING OF THE CLIPPER SHIP *Harvey Birch* IN THE ENGLISH CHANNEL BY THE C.S.S. *Nashville*, NOVEMBER 19, 1861.
Courtesy of the Peabody Museum

soon as possible! This was all said, very politely, for your petty South American chieftain is

"As mild a mannered man, as ever cut a throat,"

but it was none the less strong for all that. The missive of the Governor reached me early, in the afternoon, but I paid not the least attention to it. I sent the paymaster on shore, to purchase some fresh provisions, and fruits, for the crew, and gave such of the officers "liberty," as desired it. The next morning I sent a prize crew on board the *Bradford*, and determined to send her to New Orleans. Being loth to part with any more of my officers, after the experience I had had, with the prize brig *Cuba*, I selected an intelligent quartermaster, who had been mate of a merchantman, as prize-master. My men I could replace—my officers I could not. The following letter of instructions was prepared for the guidance of the prize-master:

CONFEDERATE STATES STEAMER SUMTER,
OFF PUERTO CABELLO, July 26, 1861.

QUARTERMASTER AND PRIZE-MASTER, EUGENE RUHL:

You will take charge of the prize schooner, *Abby Bradford*, and proceed with her, to New Orleans—making the land to the westward of the passes of the Mississippi, and endeavoring to run into Barrataria Bay, Berwick's Bay, or some of the other small inlets. Upon your arrival, you will proceed to the city of New Orleans, in person, and report yourself to Commodore Rousseau, for orders. You will take especial care of the accompanying package of papers, as they are the papers of the captured schooner, and you will deliver them, with the seals unbroken, to the judge of the Prize Court, Judge Moise. You will batten down your hatches, and see that no part of the cargo is touched, during the voyage, and you will deliver both vessel, and cargo, to the proper law officers, in the condition in which you find them, as nearly as possible.

I availed myself of this opportunity, to address the following letter to Mr. Mallory, the Secretary of the Navy; having nothing very important to communicate, I did not resort to the use of the cipher, that had been established between us.

CONFEDERATE STATES STEAMER SUMTER,
PUERTO CABELLO, July 26, 1861.

SIR:—Having captured a schooner of light draught, which, with her cargo, I estimate to be worth some twenty-five thousand dollars, and being denied the privilege of leaving her at this port, until she could be adjudicated, I have resolved to dispatch her for New Orleans, in charge of a prize crew, with the hope that she may be able to elude the vigilance of the blockading squadron, of the enemy, and run into some one of the shoal passes, to the westward of the mouth of the Mississippi, as Barrataria, or Berwick's Bay. In great haste, I avail myself of this opportunity to send you my first despatch, since leaving New Orleans. I can do no more, for want of time, than barely enumerate, without describing events.

We ran the blockade of Pass à L'Outre, by the *Brooklyn*, on the 30th of June, that ship giving us chase. On the morning of the 3d of July, I doubled Cape Antonio, the western extremity of Cuba, and, on the same day, captured, off the Isle of Pines, the American ship, *Golden Rocket*, belonging to parties in Bangor, in Maine. She was a fine ship of 600 tons, and worth between thirty and forty thousand dollars. I burned her. On the next day, the 4th, I captured the brigantines *Cuba* and *Machias*, both of Maine, also. They were laden with sugars. I sent them to Cienfuegos, Cuba. On the 5th of July, I captured the brigs *Ben. Dunning*, and *Albert Adams*, owned in New York, and Massachusetts. They were laden, also, with sugars. I sent them to Cienfuegos. On the next day, the 6th, I captured the barks *West Wind*, and *Louisa Kilham*, and the brig *Naiad*, all owned in New York, Rhode Island, and Massachusetts. I sent them, also, to Cienfuegos.

On the same day, I ran into that port, myself, reported my captures to the authorities, and asked leave for them to remain, until they could be adjudicated. The Government took them in charge, until the Home Government should give directions concerning them. I coaled ship, and sailed, again, on the 7th. On the 17th I arrived at the Island of Curaçoa, without having fallen in with any of the enemy's ships. I coaled again, here—having had some little difficulty with the Governor, about entering—and sailed on the 24th. On the morning of the 25th, I captured, off Laguayra, the schooner *Abby Bradford*, which is the vessel, by which I send this despatch. I do not deem it prudent to speak, here, of my future movements, lest my despatch should fall into the hands of the enemy. We are all well, and "doing a pretty fair business," in mercantile parlance, having made nine captures in twenty-six days.

The *Bradford* reached the coast of Louisiana, in due time, but approaching too near to the principal passes of the Mississippi, against which I had warned her, she was re-captured, by one of the enemy's steamers, and my prize crew were made prisoners, but soon afterward released, though they did not rejoin me.* I am thus particular, in giving the reader an account of these, my first transactions, for the purpose of showing him, that I made every effort to avoid the necessity of destroying my prizes, at sea; and that I only resorted to this practice, when it became evident that there was nothing else to be done. Not that I had not the right to burn them, under the laws of war, when there was no dispute about the property—as was the case with the *Golden Rocket,* she having had no cargo on board—but because I desired to avoid all possible complication with neutrals.

Having dispatched the *Bradford,* we got under way, in the *Sumter,* to continue our cruise. We had scarcely gotten clear of the harbor, before a sail was discovered, in plain sight, from the deck. The breeze was light, and she was running down the coast, with all her studding sails set. Her taunt and graceful spars, and her whitest of cotton sails, glistening in the morning's sun, revealed at once the secret of her nationality. We chased, and, at the distance of full seven miles from the land, came up with, and captured her. She proved to be the bark *Joseph Maxwell,* of Philadelphia, last from Laguayra, where she had touched, to land a part of her cargo. The remainder she was bringing to Puerto Cabello. Upon inspection of her papers, I ascertained that one-half of the cargo, remaining on board of her, belonged to a neutral owner, doing business in Puerto Cabello.

Heaving the bark to, in charge of a prize crew, beyond the marine league, I took her master on board the *Sumter,* and steaming back into the harbor, sent Paymaster Myers on shore with him, to see if some arrangement could not be made, by which the interests of the neutral half-owner of the cargo could be protected;

*[The *Powhatan* recaptured the *Abby Bradford.* It was this capture combined with information obtained from a member of the *Bradford*'s crew that led to the *Powhatan*'s pursuit of the *Sumter* described on page 23.]

to see, in other words, whether *this* prize, in which a Venezuelan citizen was interested, would not be permitted to enter, and remain until she could be adjudicated. Much to my surprise, upon the return of my boat, the paymaster handed me a written *command* from the Governor, to bring the *Maxwell* in, and deliver her to him, until the *Venezuelan courts* could determine whether she had been captured within the marine league, or not! This insolence was refreshing. I scarcely knew whether to laugh, or be angry at it. I believe I indulged in both emotions. The *Sumter* had not let go her anchor, but had been waiting for the return of her boat, under steam. She was lying close under the guns of the fort, and we could see that the tompions had been taken out of the guns, and that they were manned by some half-naked soldiers. Not knowing but the foolish Governor might order his commandant to fire upon me, in case I should attempt to proceed to sea, in my ship, before I had sent a boat out to bring in the *Maxwell*, I beat to quarters, and with my crew standing by my guns, steamed out to rejoin my prize. When I had a little leisure to converse with my paymaster, he told me, that the Federal consul had been consulted, on the occasion, and that the nice little *ruse* of the Governor's order had been resorted to in the hope of intimidating me. I would have burned the *Maxwell*, on the spot, but, unfortunately, as the reader has seen, she had some neutral cargo on board, and this I had no right to destroy. I resolved, therefore, to send her in; not to the Confederate States, for she drew too much water to enter any, except the principal ports, and these being all blockaded, by steamers, it was useless for her to make the attempt. The following letter of instructions to her prize-master, will show what disposition was made of her.

CONFEDERATE STATES STEAMER SUMTER,
AT SEA, July 27, 1861.

MIDSHIPMAN AND PRIZE-MASTER WM. A. HICKS:—

You will take charge of the prize bark, *Joseph Maxwell*, and proceed, with her, to some port on the south side of the island of Cuba, say St. Jago [Santiago], Trinidad, or Cienfuegos. I think it would be safest for you to go into Cienfuegos, as the enemy, from the very fact of our having been there, recently, will scarcely be on the look for us a second time. The steamers which were probably sent thither from Havana in pursuit of the *Sumter* must, long since, have departed, to hunt her in some other quarter.

Upon your arrival, you will inform the Governor, or Commandant of the Port, of the fact, state to him that your vessel is the prize of a ship of war, and not of a privateer, and ask leave for her to remain in port, in charge of a prize agent, until she can be adjudicated by a prize court of the Confederate States. Should he grant you this request, you will, if you go into Cienfuegos, put the vessel in charge of Don Mariano Dias, our agent for the other prizes; but should you go into either of the other ports, you will appoint some reliable person to take charge of the prize, but without power to sell, until further orders—taking from him a bond, with sufficient sureties for the faithful performance of his duties.

Should the Governor decline to permit the prize to remain, you will store the cargo, with some responsible person, if permitted to land it, taking his receipt therefor, and then take the ship outside the port, beyond the marine league, and burn her. Should you need funds for the unlading and storage of the cargo, you are authorized to sell so much of it as may be necessary for this purpose. You will then make the best of your way to the Confederate States, and report yourself to the Secretary of the Navy. You will keep in close custody the accompanying sealed package of papers, being the papers of the captured vessel, and deliver it, in person, to the Judge of the Admiralty Court, in New Orleans. The paymaster will hand you the sum of one hundred dollars, and you are authorized to draw on the Secretary of the Navy for such further sum as you may need, to defray the expenses of yourself, and crew, to the Confederate States.

I had not yet seen the proclamation of neutrality by Spain, and the reader will perceive, from the above letter, that I still clung to the hope that that Power would dare to be just, even in the face of the truckling of England and France. The master of the *Maxwell* had his wife on board, and the sea being smooth, I made him a present of one of the best of his boats, and sent him and his wife on shore in her. He repaid my kindness by stealing the ship's chronometer, which he falsely told the midshipman in charge of the prize I had given him leave to take with him. At three P. M., taking a final leave of Puerto Cabello, there being neither waving of hats or handkerchiefs, or regrets on either side, we shaped our course to the eastward, and put our ship under a full head of steam.

[The *Maxwell* was returned to her owners by the Cuban (Spanish) authorities, as was done with the earlier prizes.]

There was a fresh trade-wind blowing, and some sea on, as the *Sumter* brought her head around to the eastward, and commenced buffeting her way, again, to windward. She had, in addition, a current to contend with, which sets along this coast in the direction of the trade-wind, at the rate of about a knot an hour. We were steaming at a distance of seven or eight miles from the land, and, as the shades of evening closed in, we descried a Federal brigantine, running down the coast—probably for the port we had just left—hugging the bold shore very affectionately, to keep within the charmed marine league, within which she knew she was safe from capture. We did not, of course, molest her, as I made it a point always to respect the jurisdiction of neutrals, though never so weak. I might have offended against the sovereignty of Venezuela, by capturing this vessel, with impunity, so far as Venezuela was herself concerned, but then I should have committed an offence against the laws of nations, and it was these laws that I was, myself, looking to, for protection. Besides, the Secretary of the Navy, in preparing my instructions, had been particular to enjoin upon me, not only to respect the rights of neutrals, but to conciliate their good will.

As we were running along the land, sufficiently near for its influence to be felt upon the trade-winds, it became nearly calm during the night, the land and sea breezes, each struggling for the mastery, and thus neutralizing each other's forces. The steamer sprang forward with renewed speed, and when the day dawned the next morning, we were far to windward of Laguayra. The sun rose in a sky, without a cloud, and the wind did not freshen, as the day advanced, so much as it had done the day before. The mountains of Venezuela lay sleeping in the distance, robed in a mantle of heavenly blue, numerous sea-birds were on the wing, and the sail of a fishing-boat, here and there, added picturesqueness to the scene. At half-past nine, we gave chase to a fore-and-aft schooner, which proved to be a Venezuala coaster.

In the afternoon, we passed sufficiently near the island of Tortuga, to run over some of its coral banks. The sun was declining behind the yet visible mountains, and the sea breeze had died away to nearly a calm, leaving the bright, and sparkling waters, with a mirrored surface. We now entered upon a scene of transcendent beauty, but the beauty was that of the deep, and not of the surface landscape. . . .

We are in five or six fathoms of water, but this water is so clear, that we are enabled to see the most minute object, quite distinctly. We have "slowed" the engine the better to enjoy the beautiful submarine landscape; and look! we are passing over a miniature forest, instinct with life. There are beautifully branching trees of madrepores, whose prongs are from one to two feet in length, and sometimes curiously interlaced. Each one of the branches, as well as the trunk, has a number of little notches in it. These are the cells in which the little stone-mason is at work. Adhering to the branches of these miniature trees, like mosses, and lichens, you see sundry formations that you might mistake for leaves. These are also cellular, and are the workshops of the little masons. Scattered around, among the trees, are waving the most gorgeous of fans, and, what we might call sea-ferns, and palms. These are of a variety of brilliant colors, purple predominating.

Lying on the smooth, white sand, are boulders of coral in a variety of shapes—some, like the domes of miniature cathedrals; some, perfectly spherical; some, cylindrical. These and the trees, are mostly of a creamy white, though occasionally, pink, violet, and green are discovered. As the passage of the steamer gives motion to the otherwise smooth sea, the fans, ferns, and palms wave, gracefully, changing their tints as the light flashes upon them, through the pellucid waters. The beholder looks entranced, as though he were gazing upon a fairy scene, by moonlight; and to add to the illusion, there is a movement of life, all new to the eye, in every direction. The beautiful star-fish, with its five points, as equally, and regularly arranged, as though it had been done by the rule of the mathematician, with great worm-like molluscs, lie torpid on the white sand. Jelly-fish, polypi, and other nondescript shapes, float about in the miniature forest; and darting hither and thither, among the many-tinted ferns, some apparently in sport, and some in pursuit of their prey, are hundreds of little fishes, sparkling, and gleaming in silver, and gold, and green, and scarlet.

The most curious of these is the parrot-fish, whose head is shaped like the beak of the parrot, and whose color is light green. How wonderfully full is the sea of animal life! All this picture is animal life; for what appears to be the vegetable portion of this sub-marine landscape, is scarcely vegetable at all. The waving ferns, fans, and palms are all instinct with animal life. The patient little toiler of the sea, the coralline insect, is busy with them, as he is with his limestone trees. He is helping on their formation by his secretions, and it is difficult to say what portion of them is vegetable, what, mineral, and what, animal.

I had been an hour, and more, entranced by the fairy submarine forest, and its denizens, which I have so imperfectly described, when the sun sank behind the Andes, and night threw her mantle upon the waters, changing all the sparkling colors of forest, and fish, to sombre gray, and admonishing me, that it was time to return to every-day life, and the duties of the ship. "Let her have the steam," said I to the officer of the deck, as I arose from my bent posture over the ship's rail; and, in a moment more, the propeller was thundering us along at our usual speed.

At eleven P. M., we were up with the island of Margarita and as I designed to run the passage between it, and the main land, I preferred daylight for the operation; and so, sounding in thirty-two fathoms of water, I hove the ship to, under her trysails for the night, permitting her steam to go down. The next day, the weather still continued clear and pleasant, the trade-wind being sufficiently light not to impede our headway, for we were steaming, as the reader will recollect, nearly head to wind. We had experienced but little adverse current during the last twenty-four hours, and were making very satisfactory progress. I was now making a passage, rather than cruising, as a sail is a rare sight, in the part of the ocean I was traversing.

At meridian we passed that singular group of islands called the Frayles—*Anglice,* friars—jutting up from the sea in cones of different shapes, and looking, at a distance, not unlike so many hooded monks. With the exception of a transient fisherman, who now and then hauls up his boat out of the reach of the surf, on these harborless islands, and pitches his tent, made of his boat's sail, for a few days of rest and refreshment, they have no inhabitants.

July 30th.—"Thick, cloudy weather, with incessant, and heavy rains; hauling in for the coast of Venezuela, near the entrance to the Gulf of Paria. So thick is the weather, that to 'hold on to the land,' I am obliged to run the coast within a mile, and this is close running on a coast not minutely surveyed." So said my journal. Indeed the day in question was a memorable one, from its scenery, and surroundings. Few landscapes present so bold, and imposing a picture as this part of the South American coast. The Andes here rise abruptly out of the sea, to a great height. Our little craft running along their base, in the bluest and deepest of water, looked like a mere cockle-shell, or nautilus. Besides the torrents of rain, that were coming down upon our decks, and through which, at times, we could barely catch a glimpse of the majestic, and sombre-looking mountains, we were blinded by the most vivid flashes of lightning, simultaneously with which, the rolling and crashing of the thunder deafened our ears. I had stood on the banks of the Lake of Geneva, and witnessed a storm in the Alps, during which Byron's celebrated lines occurred to me. They occurred to me more forcibly here, for literally—

>   "Far along
> From peak to peak, the rattling crags among,
>   Leaps the live thunder! Not from one cloud,
> But every mountain now had found a tongue,
>   And Jura answers, through her misty shroud,
> Back to the joyous Alps, who call to her aloud!"

That word "joyous" was well chosen by the poet, for the mountains did indeed seem to rejoice in this grand display of nature. Of wind there was scarcely any—what little there was, was frequently off the land, and even blew in the direction opposite to that of the trade-wind. We were in the rainy season, along this coast, and all the vegetable kingdom was in full luxuriance. The cocoanut, and other palms, giving an Eastern aspect to the scenery, waved the greenest of feathery branches, and every shrub, and almost every tree rejoiced in its flower. It was delightful to inhale the fragrance, as the whirling aërial current brought us an occasional puff from the land.

On board the ship, we looked like so many half-drowned rats. The officer of the deck, trumpet in hand, was ensconced, to his ears, in his india-rubber pea-jacket, his long beard looking like a wet mop, and little rills of rain trickling down his neck, and shoulders, from his slouched "Sou'wester." The midshipman of the watch had taken off his shoes, and rolled up his trousers, and was paddling about in the pools on deck, as well pleased as a young duck. And as for the old salt, he was in his element. There was plenty of fresh water to wash his clothes in, and accordingly the decks were filled with industrious washers, or rather scrubbers, each with his scrubbing-brush, and bit of soap, and a little pile of soiled duck frocks and trousers by his side.

CHAPTER V

The English, the French, and the Dutch

THE READER HAS BEEN INFORMED, THAT WE were running along the coast, within a mile of it, to enable us to keep sight of the land. The object of this was to make the proper landfall for running into the Gulf of Paria, on which is situated the Port of Spain, in the island of Trinidad, to which we were bound. We opened the gulf as early as nine A. M., and soon afterward identified the three islands that form the Bocas del Drago, or dragon's mouth. The scenery is remarkably bold and striking at the entrance of this gulf or bay. The islands rise to the height of mountains, in abrupt and sheer precipices, out of the now muddy waters—for the great Orinoco, traversing its thousands of miles of alluvial soil, disembogues near by. Indeed, we may be said to have been already within the delta of that great stream.

Memory was busy with me, as the *Sumter* passed through the Dragon's Mouth. I had made my first cruise to this identical island of Trinidad, when a green midshipman in the Federal Navy. A few years before, the elder Commodore Perry—he of Lake Erie memory —had died of yellow fever, when on a visit, in one of the small schooners of his squadron, up the Orinoco. The old sloop-of-war *Lexington,* under the command of Commander, now Rear-Admiral Shubrick, was sent to the Port of Spain to bring home his remains. I was one of the midshipmen of that ship. A generation had since elapsed. An infant people had, in that short space of time, grown old and decrepid, and its government had broken in twain. But there stood the everlasting mountains, as I remembered them, unchanged! . . .

We entered through the Huevo passage—named from its egg-shaped island—and striking soundings, pretty soon afterward, ran up by our chart and lead-line, there being no pilot-boat in sight. We anchored off the Port of Spain a little after mid-day—an English merchant brig paying us the compliment of a salute.

I dispatched a lieutenant to call on the Governor. The orders of neutrality of the English government had already been received, and his Excellency informed me that, in accordance therewith, he would extend to me the same hospitality that he would show, in similar circumstances, to the enemy; which was nothing more, of course, than I had a right to expect. The Paymaster was dispatched to the shore, to see about getting a supply of coal, and send off some fresh provisions and fruit for the crew; and such of the officers as desired went on liberty.

The first thing to be thought of was the discharge of our prisoners, for, with the exception of the Captain, whom I had permitted to land in Puerto Cabello, with his wife, I had the crew of the *Joseph Maxwell*, prize-ship, still on board. . . .

Our decks were crowded with visitors, on the afternoon of our arrival; some of these coming off to shake us warmly by the hand, out of genuine sympathy, whilst others had no higher motive than that of mere curiosity. The officers of the garrison were very civil to us, but we were amused at their diplomatic precaution, in coming to visit us in *citizens' dress*. There are no people in the world, perhaps, who attach so much importance to matters of mere form and ceremony, bluff and hearty as John Bull is, as the English people. Lord Russell had dubbed us a "so-called" government, and this expression had become a law to all his subordinates; no official visits could be exchanged, no salutes reciprocated, and none other of the thousand and one courtesies of red-tapedom observed toward us; and, strange to say, whilst all this nonsense of form was being practised, the substance of nationality, that is to say, the acknowledgment that we possessed belligerent rights, had been frankly and freely accorded to us. It was like saying to a man, "I should like, above all things, to have you come and dine with me, but as you hav n't got the right sort of a dining-dress, you can't come, you know!" Some ridiculous consequences resulted from this etiquette of nations. Important matters of business frequently remained unattended to, because the parties could not address each other officially. An *informal* note would take the place of an official despatch.

The advent of the *Sumter* invariably caused more, or less commotion, in official circles; the small colonial officials fearing lest she might complicate them with their governments. There was now another important council to be held. The opinion of the "law-officers of the crown" was to be taken by his Excellency, upon the question, whether the *Sumter* was entitled to be coaled in her Majesty's dominions. The paymaster had found a lot of indifferent coal, on shore, which could be purchased at about double its value, but nothing could be done until the "council" moved; and it is proverbial that large bodies like provincial councils, move slowly. The Attorney-General of the Colony, and other big wigs got together, however, after due ceremony, and, thanks to the fact, that the steamer is an infernal machine of modern invention, they were not very long in coming to a decision. If there had been anything about a steamer, in Coke upon Littleton, Bacon, or Bracton, or any other of those old fellows who deal in black letter, I am afraid the *Sumter* would have been blockaded by the enemy, before she could have gotten to sea. The *pros* and *cons* being discussed—I had too much respect for the calibre of certain guns on shore, to throw any shells across the windows of the council-chamber—it was decided that coal was not contraband of war, and that the *Sumter* might purchase the necessary article in the market.

But though she might purchase it, it was not so easy to get it on board. It was hard to move the good people on shore. The climate was relaxing, the rainy season had set in, and there was only negro labor to be had, about the wharves and quays. We were four tedious days in filling our coal-bunkers. It had rained, off and on, the whole time. I did not visit the shore, but I amused myself frequently by inspecting the magnificent scenery by which I was surrounded, through an excellent telescope. The vegetation of Trinidad is varied, and luxuriant beyond description. As the clouds would break away, and the sun light up the wilderness of waving palms, and other tropical trees and plants of strange and rich foliage, amid which the little town lay embowered, the imagination was enchanted with the picture.

The emancipation of the slave ruined this, as it did the other West India islands. As a predial laborer, the freedman was nearly worthless, and the sugar crop, which is the staple, went down to zero. In despair, the planters resorted to the introduction of the coolie; large numbers of them have been imported, and under their skilful and industrious cultivation, the island is regaining a share of its lost prosperity.

A day or two after my arrival, I had a visit from the master of a Baltimore brig, lying in the port. He was ready for sea, he said, and had come on board, to learn whether I would capture him. I told him to make himself easy, that I should not molest him, and referred him to the act of the Confederate Congress, declaring that a state of war existed, to show him that, as yet, we regarded Maryland as a friend. [The act of the Southern Congress excluded Maryland from enemy status, the Confederates still hoping at that time that she too might yet secede.] He went away rejoicing, and sailed the next day.

We had, as usual, some little refitting of the ship to do. Off Puerto Cabello, we had carried away our main yard, by coming in contact with the *Abby Bradford,* and the first lieutenant having ordered another on our arrival, it was now towed off, and gotten on board, fitted, and sent aloft.

Sunday, August 4th.—Morning calm and clear. The chimes of the church-bells fall pleasantly and suggestively on the ear. An American schooner came in from some point, up the bay, and anchored well in shore, some distance from us, as though distrustful of our good faith, and of our respect for British neutrality. Being all ready for sea, at half-past ten A. M., I gave the order to get up steam; but the paymaster reporting to me that his vouchers were not all complete, the order was countermanded, and we remained another day.

Her Majesty's steam-frigate *Cadmus* having come in, from one of the neighboring islands, I sent a lieutenant on board to call on her captain. This was the first foreign ship of war to which I had extended the courtesy of a visit, and, in a few hours afterward, my visit was returned. I had, from this time onward, much agreeable intercourse with the naval officers of the several nations, with whom I came in contact. I found them much more independent, than the civil, and military officers. They did not seem to care a straw, about *de factos,* or *de jures,* and had a sailor's contempt for red tape and unmeaning forms. They invariably received my officers, and myself, when we visited their ships, with the honors of the side, appropriate to our rank, without stopping to ask, in the jargon of Lord Russell, whether we were "So-Called," or Simon

Pure. After the usual courtesies had passed between the lieutenant of the *Cadmus* and myself, I invited him into my cabin, when, upon being seated, he said his captain had desired him to say to me, that, as the *Sumter* was the first ship of the Confederate States he had fallen in with, he would take it, as a favor, if I would show him my commission. I replied, "Certainly, but there is a little ceremony to be complied with, on your part, first." "What is that?" said he. "How do I know," I rejoined, "that you have any *authority* to demand a sight of my commission—the flag at your peak may be a cheat, and you may be no better than you take me for, a ship of war of some hitherto unknown government—you must show me *your* commission first." This was said, pleasantly, on my part, for the idea was quite ludicrous, that a large, and stately steam-frigate, bearing the proud cross of St. George, could be such as I had hypothetically described her. But I was right as to the point I had made, to wit, that one ship of war has no right to demand a sight of the commission of another, without first showing her own. Indeed, this principle is so well known among naval men, that the lieutenant had come prepared for my demand, having brought his commission with him. Smiling, himself, now, in return, he said: "Certainly, your request is but reasonable; here is her Majesty's commission," unrolling, at the same time, a large square parchment, beautifully engraved with nautical devices, and with sundry seals, pendent therefrom. In return, I handed him a small piece of coarse, and rather dingy Confederate paper, at the bottom of which was inscribed the name of Jefferson Davis. He read the commission carefully, and when he had done, remarked, as he handed it back to me, "Mr. Davis's is a smooth, bold signature." I replied "You are an observer of signatures, and you have hit it exactly, in the present instance. I could not describe his character to you more correctly, if I were to try—our President has all the smoothness, and polish of the ripe scholar and refined gentleman, with the boldness of a man, who dares strike for the right, against odds."

Monday, August 5th.—Weather clear, and fine. Flocks of parrots are flying overhead, and all nature is rejoicing in the sunshine, after the long, drenching rains. Far as the eye can reach, there is but one sea of verdure, giving evidence, at once, of the fruitfulness of the soil, and the ardor of the sun. At eleven A. M., Captain Hillyar, of the *Cadmus,* came on board, to visit me, and we had a long and pleasant conversation on American affairs. He considerately brought me a New York newspaper, of as late a date, as the 12th of July. . . .

The Captain now rose to depart. I accompanied him on deck, and when he had shoved off, I ordered the ship to be gotten under way—the fires having been started some time before, the steam was already up. The *Sumter,* as she moved out of the harbor of the Port of Spain, looked more like a comfortable passenger steamer, bound on a voyage, than a ship of war, her stern nettings, and stern and quarter boats being filled with oranges, and bananas, and all the other luscious fruits that are produced so abundantly in this rich tropical island. Other luxuries were added, for Jack had brought, on board, one or two more sad-looking old monkeys, and a score more of squalling parrots.

We passed out of the Gulf of Paria, through the eastern, or Mona passage, a deep strait, not more than a third of a mile in width, with the land rising, on both sides, to a great height, almost perpendicularly. The water of the Orinoco here begins to mix with the sea-water, and the two waters, as they come into unwilling contact, carry on a perpetual struggle, whirling about in small circles, and writhing and twisting like a serpent in pain.

We met the first heave of the sea at about two o'clock in the afternoon, and turning our head again to the eastward, we continued to run along the mountainous and picturesque coast of Trinidad, until an hour or two after nightfall. The coast is quite precipitous, but, steep as it is, a number of negro cabins had climbed the hill-sides, and now revealed their presence to us by the twinkle of their lights, as the shades of evening fell over the scene. These cabins were quite invisible, by daylight, so dense was the foliage of the trees amid which they nestled. . . .

The night was quite light, and taking a fresh departure, at about ten P. M., from the east end of Trinidad, we passed through the strait between it and the island of Tobago, and soon afterward emerged from the Caribbean Sea, upon the broad bosom of the . . . Atlantic. Judging by the tide rips, that were quite visible in the moonlight, there must have been considerable current setting through this strait, to the westward. The next day the weather was still fine, and the wind light from about E. N. E., and the *Sumter* made good speed through the smooth sea. At about ten A. M. a sail was descried, some twelve or fourteen miles distant. She was away off on our port beam, running before the trade-wind, and I forbode to chase. As before remarked, I was not now cruising, but anxious to make a passage, and could not afford the fuel to chase, away from the track I was pursuing, the few straggling sail I might discover in this lonely sea. Once in the track of commerce, where the sails would come fast and thick, I could make up for lost time. At noon, we observed in latitude 9° 14'; the longitude, by chronometer, being 59° 10'.

Wednesday, August 7th.—Weather clear, and delightful, and the sea smooth. Nothing but the broad expanse of the ocean visible, except, indeed, numerous flocks of flying-fish, which we are flushing, now and then like so many flocks of partridges, as we disturb the still waters. These little creatures have about the flight of the partridge, and it is a pretty sight to see them skim away over the billows with their transparent finny wings glistening in the sun, until they drop again into their "cover," as suddenly as they rose. Our crew having been somewhat broken in upon, by the sending away of so many prize crews, the first lieutenant is re-arranging his watch and quarter-bills, and the men are being exercised at the guns, to accustom them to the changes which have become necessary, in their stations. Officers and men are enjoying, alike, the fine weather. With the fore-castle, and quarter-deck awnings spread, we do not feel the heat, though the sun is nearly perpendicular at noon. Jack is "overhauling" his clothes'-bag, and busy with his needle and thread, stopping, now and then, to have a "lark" with his monkey, or to listen to the prattle of his parrot. The boys of the ship are taking lessons, in knotting, and splicing, and listening to the "yarn" of some old salt, as he indoctrinates them in these mysteries. The midshipmen have their books of navigation spread out before them, and slate in hand, are discussing sine and tangent, base, and hypothenuse. The only place in which a lounger is not seen is the quarter-deck. This precinct is always sacred to duty, and etiquette. No one ever presumes to seat himself upon it, not even the Commander. Here the officer of the deck is pacing to and fro, swinging his trumpet idly about, for the want of something to do. But hold a moment! he has at last found a job. It is seven bells (half-past eleven) and the ship's cook has come to the mast, to report dinner. The cook is a darkey, and see how he grins, as the officer of the deck, having tasted of the fat pork, in his tin pan, and mashed some of his beans, with a spoon, to see if they are done, tells him, "that will do." The Commander now comes on deck, with his sextant, having been informed that it is time to "look out for the sun." See, he gathers the midshipmen around him, each also with his instrument, and, from time to time, asks them what "altitude they have on," and compares the altitude which they give him with his own, to see if they are making satisfactory progress as observers. The latitude being obtained, and reported to the officer of the deck, that officer now comes up to the Commander, and touching his hat, reports twelve o'clock, as though the Commander didn't know it already. The Commander says to him, sententiously, "make it so," as though the sun could not make it so, without the Commander's leave. See, now what a stir there is about the hitherto silent decks. Since we last cast a glance at them, Jack has put up his clothes'-bag, and the sweepers have "swept down," fore and aft, and the boatswain having piped to dinner, the cooks of the different messes are spreading their "mess-cloths" on the deck, and arranging their viands. The drum has rolled, "to grog," and the master's mate of the spirit-room, muster-book in hand, is calling over the names of the crew, each man as his name is called, waddling up to the tub, and taking the "tot" that is handed to him, by the "Jack-of-the-dust," who is the master's mate's assistant. Dinner now proceeds with somewhat noisy jest and joke, and the hands are not "turned to," that is, set to work again, until one o'clock.

We have averaged, in the last twenty-four hours, eight knots and a half, and have not, as yet, experienced any adverse current, though we are daily on the lookout for this enemy; latitude 8° 31'; longitude 56° 12'. In the course of the afternoon, a brigantine passing near us, we hove her to, with a blank cartridge, when she showed us the Dutch colors. She was from Dutch Surinam, bound for Europe. Toward nightfall, it became quite calm, and naught was heard but the thumping of the ship's propeller, as she urged her ceaseless way through the vast expanse of waters.

August 8th.—Weather still beautifully clear, with an occasional rain squall enclosing us as in a gauze veil, and shutting out from view for a few minutes, at a time, the distant horizon. The wind is light, and variable, but always from the Eastern board; following the sun as the chariot follows the steed. We are making good speed through the water, but we have at length encountered our dreaded enemy, the great equatorial current, which sets, with such regularity, along this coast. Its set is about W. N. W., and its drift about one knot per hour. Nothing has been seen to-day. The water has changed its deep blue color, to green, indicating that we are on soundings. We are about ninety miles from the coast of Guiana. The sun went down behind banks, or rather cumuli of pink and lilac clouds. We are fast sinking the north polar star, and new constellations arise, nightly, above the southern horizon. Amid other starry wonders, we had a fine view this evening, of the southern cross; latitude 7° 19'; longitude 53° 04'.

The next day was cloudy, and the direction of the current was somewhat changed, for its set was now N. W., half N. This current is proving a serious drawback, and I begin to fear, that I shall not be able to make the run to Maranham, as I had hoped. Not only are the elements adverse, but my engineer tells me, that we were badly cheated, in our coal measure, at Trinidad, the sharp coal-dealer having failed to put on board of us as many tons as he had been paid for; for which the said engineer got a rowing. We observed, to-day, in latitude 6° 01' and longitude 50° 48'.

August 10th.—Weather clear, with a deep blue sea, and a fresh breeze, from the south-east. The south-east trade-winds have thus crossed the equator, and reached us in latitude 5° north, which is our latitude to-day. I was apprehensive of this, for we are in the middle of August, and in this month these winds frequently drive back the north-east trades, and usurp their place, to a considerable extent, until the sun crosses back into the southern hemisphere. We thus have both wind, and current ahead; the current alone has retarded us fifty miles, or a fraction over two knots an hour; which is about equal to the drift of the Gulf Stream off Cape Hatteras.

Things were beginning now to look decidedly serious. I had but three days of fuel on board, and, upon consulting my chart, I found that I was still 550 miles from my port, current taken into account. It was not possible for the dull little *Sumter* to make this distance, in the given time, if the wind, and current should continue of the same strength. I resolved to try her, however, another night, hoping that some change for the better might take place. My journal tells the tale of that night as follows:—

August 11th.—"The morning has dawned with a fresh breeze, and rather rough sea, into which we have been plunging all night, making but little headway. The genius of the east wind refuses to permit even steam to invade his domain, and drives us back, with disdain. His ally, the current, has retarded us sixty miles in the last twenty-four hours!" I now no longer hesitated, but directing the engineer to let his fires go down, turned my ship's head, to the westward, and made sail; it being my intention to run down the coast to Cayenne in French Guiana, with the hope of obtaining a fresh supply of fuel at that place. We soon had the studding sails on the ship, and were rolling along to the northward and westward, with more grace than speed, our rate of sailing being only four knots. The afternoon proved to be remarkably fine, and we should have enjoyed this *far niente* change, but for our disappointment. Our chief regret was that we were losing so much valuable time, in the midst of the stirring events of the war.

Hauling in for the coast, in the vicinity of Cape Orange, we struck soundings about nightfall. The sea now became quite smooth, and the wind fell very light during the night—the current, however, is hurrying us on, though its set is not exactly in the right direction. Its tendency is to drive us too far from the coast. The next day, it became perfectly calm, and so continued all day. We were in twenty-three fathoms of water, and could see by the lead line that we were drifting over the bottom at the rate of about two knots an hour. We got out our fishing-lines, and caught some deep sea-fish, of the grouper species. The sea was alive with the nautilus, and the curious sea-nettle, with its warps and hawsers thrown out, and its semi-transparent, gelatinous disc contracting and expanding, as the little animal extracted its food from the water. Schools of fish, large and small, were playing about in every direction, and flocks of sea-gulls, and other marine birds of prey, were hovering over them, and making occasional forays in their midst. During the day, a sail was descried, far in shore, but we were unable to make it out; indeed sails were of the least importance to us now, as we were unable to chase. Just before sunset, we had a fine view of the Silver Mountains, some forty or fifty miles distant, in the southwest.

August 15th.—During the past night, we made the "Great Constable," a small island, off the coast, and one of the landmarks for Cayenne. The night was fine, and moonlit, and we ran in, and anchored about midnight, in fourteen fathoms of water. At daylight, the next morning, after waiting for the passage of a rain-squall, we got under way, and proceeding along the coast, came up with the Remize Islands, in the course of the afternoon, where we found a French pilot-lugger lying to, waiting for us. We were off Cayenne, and the lugger had come out to show us the way into the anchorage. A pilot jumping on board, we ran in, and anchored to the north-west of the "Child"—a small island—in three and a quarter fathoms of water. I could scarcely realize, that this was the famous penal settlement of Cayenne, painted in French history, as the very abode of death, and fraught with all other human horrors, so beautiful, and picturesque did it appear. The outlying islands are high, rising, generally, in a conical form, and are densely wooded, to their very summits. Sweet little nooks and coves, overhung by the waving foliage of strange-looking tropical trees, indent their shores, and invite the fisherman, or pleasure-seeker to explore their recesses. The main land is equally rich in vegetation, and though the sea-coast is low, distant ranges of mountains, inland, break in, agreeably, upon the monotony. A perennial summer prevails, and storms, and hurricanes are unknown. It was here that some of the most desperate and bloodthirsty of the French revolutionists of 1790, were banished. Many of them died of yellow fever; others escaped, and wandered off to find inhospitable graves, in other countries; few of them ever returned to France. Shortly after we came to anchor, the batteries of the town, and some small French steamers of war, that lay in the harbor, fired salutes in honor of the birthday of Louis Napoleon—this being the 15th of August.

The next morning, at daylight, I dispatched Lieutenant Evans, and Paymaster Myers, to the town—the former to call on the Governor, and the latter to see if any coal could be had. Their errand was fruitless. Not only was there no coal to be purchased, but my officers thought that they had been received rather ungraciously. The fact is, we found here, as in Curaçoa, that the enemy was in possession of the neutral territory. There was a Federal Consul resident in the place, who was the principal contractor, for supplying the French garrison with fresh beef! and there were three, or four Yankee schooners in the harbor, whose skippers had a monopoly of the trade in flour and notions. What could the *Sumter* effect against such odds?

In the course of an hour after my boat returned, we were again under way, running down the coast, in the direction of Surinam, to see if the Dutchmen would prove more propitious, than the Frenchmen had done. About six P. M., we passed the "Salut"

Islands, three in number, on the summit of one of which shone the white walls of a French military hospital, contrasting prettily with the deep-green foliage of the shade-trees around it. It was surrounded by low walls, on which were mounted some small guns *en barbette.* Hither are sent all the sick sailors, and soldiers from Cayenne.

August 17th.—Morning clear, and beautiful, as usual, in this delightful climate, with a fresh breeze from the south-east. We are now in latitude 6° north, and still the south-east tradewind is following us—the calm belt having been pushed farther and farther to the northward. We are running along in ten fathoms of water, at an average distance of seven, or eight miles, from the land, with the soundings surprisingly regular. Passed the mouth of the small river Maroni, at noon. At four P. M., ran across a bank, in very muddy water, some fifteen miles to the northward and eastward, of the entrance of this river, with only three fathoms of water on it; rather close shaving on a strange coast, having but six feet of water under our keel. Becoming a little nervous, we "hauled out," and soon deepened into five fathoms. There is little danger of shipwreck, on this coast, however, owing to the regularity of the soundings, and the almost perpetual smoothness of the sea. The bars off the mouths of the rivers, too, are, for the most part, of mud, where a ship *sticks,* rather than *thumps.* Hence, the temerity with which we ran into shallow waters.

Sunday, August 18th.—The south-east wind came to us, as softly, and almost as sweetly, this morning, as if it were "breathing o'er a bed of violets;" but it freshened as the day advanced, in obedience to the mandate of its master, the sun, and we had a fresh breeze, toward nightfall. After passing Port Orange, we ran over another three-fathom bank, the water deepening beyond, and enabling us to haul in toward the coast, as we approached Bram's Point, at the mouth of the Surinam River, off which we anchored, (near the buoy on the bar,) at twenty minutes past five P. M., in four fathoms of water. This being Sunday, as we were running along the coast, we had mustered and inspected the crew, and caused the clerk to read the articles "for the better government of the Navy" to them —the same old articles, though not read under the same old flag, as formerly. This was my invariable practice on the Sabbath. It broke in, pleasantly, and agreeably, upon the routine duties of the week, pretty much as church-going does, on shore, and had a capital eftect, besides, upon discipline, reminding the sailor of his responsibility to the laws, and that there were such merciless tribunals, as Courts-Martial, for their enforcement. The very shaving, and washing, and dressing, of a Sunday morning, contributed to the sailor's self-respect. The "muster" gratified, too, one of his passions, as it gave him the opportunity of displaying all those anchors, and stars, which he had so industriously embroidered, in floss silk, on his ample shirt-collar, and on the sleeve of his jacket. We had some dandies on board the *Sumter,* and it was amusing to witness the self-complacent air, with which these gentlemen would move around the capstan, with the blackest, and most carefully polished of pumps, and the whitest, and finest of sinnott hats, from which would be streaming yards enough of ribbon, to make the ship a pennant.

I had had considerable difficulty in identifying the mouth of the Surinam River, so low and uniform in appearance was the coast, as seen from the distance at which we had been compelled to run along it, by the shallowness of the water. There is great similarity between these shelving banks, running off to a great distance, at sea, and the banks on the coast of West Florida. The rule of soundings, on some parts of the latter coast, is a foot to the mile, so that, when the navigator is in ten feet of water, he is ten miles from the land. This is not quite the case, on the coast of Guiana, but on some parts of it, a large ship can scarcely come within sight of the land. A small craft, drawing but a few feet of water, has no need of making a harbor, on either coast, for the whole coast is a harbor—the sea, in bad weather, breaking in from three to five fathoms of water, miles outside of her, leaving all smooth and calm within. There is a difference, however, between the two coasts—the Florida coast is scourged by the hurricane, whilst the Guiana coast is entirely free from storms.

Soon after we came to anchor, as related, we descried a steamer in the west, steering for the mouth of the river. Nothing was more likely than that, by this time, the enemy should have sent some of his fast gun-boats in pursuit of us, and the smoke of a steamer on the horizon, therefore, caused me some uneasiness....

The steamer, now approaching, having been descried, at a great distance, by the curling of her black smoke high into the still air, night set in before she was near enough to be made out. We could see her form indistinctly, in the darkness, but no certain conclusion could be arrived at as to her size or nationality. I, at once, caused my fires to be lighted, and, beating to quarters, prepared my ship for action. We stood at our guns for some time, but seeing, about ten P.M., that the strange steamer came to anchor, some three or four miles out-side of us, I permitted the men to leave their quarters, cautioning the officer of the watch, however, to keep a bright lookout, during the night, for the approach of boats, and to call me if there should be any cause for alarm. As I turned in, I thought things looked a little squally. If the strange vessel were a mail-steamer, she would, of course, be familiar with the waters in which she plied, and, instead of anchoring outside, would have run boldly into the river without waiting for daylight. Besides, she had no lights about her as she approached, and packet steamers always go well lighted up. That she was a steamer of war, therefore, appeared quite certain; but, of course, it was of no use to speculate upon the chances of her being an enemy; daylight only could reveal that. In the meantime, the best thing we could do would be to get a good night's rest, so as to rise refreshed for the morning's work, if work there should be.

At daylight, all hands were again summoned to their quarters; and pretty soon the strange steamer was observed to be under way, and standing toward us. We got up our own anchor in a trice—the men running around the capstan in "double-quick,"— and putting the ship under steam, started to meet her. Neither of us had, as yet, any colors hoisted. We soon perceived that the stranger was no heavier than ourselves. This greatly encouraged me, and I could see a corresponding lighting up of the faces of my crew, all standing silently at their guns. Desiring to make the stranger reveal her nationality to me first, I now hoisted the French colors—a fine new flag, that I had had made in New Orleans. To my astonishment, and no little perplexity, up went the same colors, on board the stranger! I was alongside of a French ship of war, pretending to be a Frenchman myself! Of course, there was but one thing to be done, and that was, to haul down the French flag and hoist my own, which was done in an instant, when we mutually hailed. A colloquy ensued, when the names of the two ships were interchanged, and we ascertained that the stranger was bound into the Surinam, like ourselves. We now both ran in for the light-ship, and the Frenchman receiving a pilot on board from her, I permitted him to take the lead, and we followed him up the long and narrow channel, having sometimes scarcely a foot of water to spare under our keel.

After we had passed inside of Bram's Point, the tide being out, both ships anchored to wait for the returning flood. I took advantage of the opportunity, and sent a lieutenant to visit the French ship. The *Vulture,* for such was her name, was one of the old-fashioned, side-wheel steamers, mounting only carronades, and was last from Martinique, with convicts on board, for Cayenne. Running short of coal, she was putting into Paramaribo, for a supply. Getting under way again, soon after mid-day, we continued our course up the river. We were much reminded, by the scenery of the Surinam, of that of some of our Southern rivers—the Mississippi, for instance, after the voyager from the Gulf has left the marshes behind him, and is approaching New Orleans. The bottom lands, near the river, are cleared, and occupied by sugar, and other plantations, the back-ground of the picture presenting a dense, and unbroken forest. As we passed the well-known sugar-house, with its tall chimney, emitting volumes of black smoke, and saw gangs of slaves, cutting, and hauling in the cane, the illusion was quite perfect. Nothing can exceed the fertility of these alluvial lands. They are absolutely inexhaustible, yielding crop after crop, in continual succession, without rest or interval; there being no frosts to interfere with vegetation, in this genial climate. Some of the planters' dwellings were tasteful, and even elegant, surrounded by galleries whose green Venetian blinds gave promise of coolness within, and sheltered besides by the umbrageous arms of giant forest-trees. Cattle wandered over the pasture lands, the negroes were well clothed, and there was a general air of abundance, and contentment. Slavery is held by a very precarious tenure, here, and will doubtless soon disappear, there being a strong party, in Holland, in favor of its abolition. Our consort, the *Vulture,* and ourselves anchored almost at the same moment, off the town of Paramaribo, in the middle of the afternoon. There were two, or three American brigantines in the harbor, and a couple of Dutch ships of war. I sent a lieutenant to call on the Governor, and to request permission to coal, and refit; both of which requests were granted, with the usual conditions, viz.: that I should not increase my crew or armament, or receive ammunition on board. The Captain of the *Vulture* now came on board, to return the visit I had made him, through my lieutenant, and the commanding Dutch naval officer also called. But, what was more important, several coal merchants came off to negotiate with my paymaster, about supplying the ship with the very necessary article in which they dealt. The successful bidder for our contract was a *"gentleman of color,"* that is to say, a quadroon, who talked freely about whites, and blacks, always putting himself, of course, in the former category, by the use of the pronoun "we," and seemed to have no sort of objection to our flag, or the cause it was supposed to represent. I wined this "gentleman," along with my other visitors, and though I paid him a remunerative price for his coal, I am under many obligations to him, for his kindness, and assistance to us, during our stay....

August 23d.—Weather clear, during the day, but we had some heavy showers of rain, with thunder, and lightning during the night. We are receiving coal rather slowly—a small lighter-load at a time. We are making some changes in the internal arrangements of the ship. Finding, by experience, that we have more tank-room, for water, than is requisite, we are landing a couple of our larger tanks, and extending the bulkheads of the coal-bunkers. By this means, we shall be enabled to increase our coal-carrying capacity by at least a third, carrying twelve days of fuel, instead of eight. Still the *Sumter* remains fundamentally defective, as a cruiser, in her inability to lift her screw.

August 24th.—Weather clear, and pleasant, with some passing clouds, and light showers of rain. The Dutch mail-steamer, from Demerara, arrived, to-day. We are looking anxiously for news from home, as, at last accounts—July 20th from New York—a battle near Manassas Junction, seemed imminent. Demerara papers of the 19th of August contained nothing, except that some skirmishing had taken place, between the two armies. The French steamer-of-war *Abeille* arrived, and anchored near us.

Sunday, August 25th.—Morning cloudy. At half-past eight I went on shore to church. The good old Mother has her churches, and clergymen, even in this remote Dutch colony. The music of her choirs is like the "drum-beat" of England; it encircles the earth, with its never-ending melody. As the sun, "keeping company with the hours," lights up, with his newly risen beams, one degree of longitude after another, he awakens the priest to the performance of the never-ending mass. The church was a neat, well-arranged wooden building, of large dimensions, and filled to overflowing with devout worshippers. All the shades of color, from "snowy white to sooty" were there, and there did not seem to be any order in the seating of the congregation, the shades being promiscuously mixed. The preacher was fluent, and earnest in action, but his sermon, which seemed to impress the congregation, being in that beautiful and harmonious language, which we call "low Dutch," was entirely unintelligible to me. The Latin mass, and ceremonies—which are the same all over the world—were, of course, quite familiar, and awoke many tender reminiscences. I had heard, and seen them, in my own country, under the domes of grand cathedrals, and in the quiet retreat of the country house, where the good wife herself had improvised the altar. A detachment of the Government troops was present.

Some Dutch naval lieutenants visited the ship to-day. We learned, by late papers from Barbadoes, politely brought us by these gentlemen, that the enemy's steamer, *Keystone State*, was in that island, in search of us, on the 21st of July. She probably heard, there, of my intention to go back to cruise off the island of Cuba, which, as the reader has seen, I *confidently* communicated to my friends at Curaçoa, and has turned back herself. If she were on the right track she should be here before this. There was great commotion, too, as we learn by these papers, at Key West, on the 8th of July, when the news reached there of our being at Cienfuegos. Consul Shufeldt, at Havana, had been prompt, as I had foreseen. We entered Cienfuegos on the 6th, and on the 8th, he had two heavy and fast steamers, the *Niagara* and the *Crusader*, in pursuit of us. They, too, seem to have lost the trail.

August 28th.—Bright, elastic morning, with a gentle breeze from the south-east. There was a grand fandango, on shore, last night, at which some of my officers were present. The fun grew "fast and furious," as the night waned, and what with the popping of champagne-corks, and the flashing of the bright eyes of the waltzers, as they were whirled in the giddy dance, my young fellows have come off looking a little red about the eyes, and inclined to be poetical....

August 29th.—We have, at length, finished coaling, after a tedious delay of ten days. A rumor prevailed in the town, yesterday, that there were two enemy's ships of war off the bar—keeping themselves cunningly out of sight, to waylay the *Sumter*. The rumor comes with circumstance, for it is said that the fisherman, who brought the news, supplied one of the ships with fish, and said that the other ship was getting water on board from one of the coast plantations. To-day, the rumor dwindles; but one ship, it seems, has been seen, and she a merchant ship. The story is probably like that of the three white crows.

August 30th.—The pilot having come on board, we got under way, at two P.M., and steamed down to the mouth of the river, where we came to anchor. A ship, going to sea, is like a woman going on a journey—many last things remaining to be attended to, at the moment of departure. I have always found it best, to shove off shore-boats, expel all visitors, "drop down" out of the influences of the port, and send an officer or two back, to arrange these last things. A boat was now accordingly dispatched back to the town, for this purpose, and as she would not return until late in the night, inviting the surgeon and paymaster, and my clerk to accompany me, I pulled on shore, in my gig, to make a visit to an adjoining sugar plantation, that lay close by, tempting us to a stroll under its fine avenues of cocoanut and acacia trees. We were received very hospitably at the planter's mansion, where we found some agreeable ladies, and with whom we stayed late enough, to take tea, at their pressing solicitation. It was a Hollandese household, but all the inmates spoke excellent English. Whilst tea was being prepared, we wandered over the premises, the sugar-house included, where we witnessed all the processes of sugar making, from the expression of the juice from the cane, to the crystallization of the syrup. There were crowds of negroes on the place, old and young, male and female—some at work, and some at play; the players being rather the more numerous of the two classes. The grounds around the dwelling were tastefully laid out, in serpentine walks, winding through a wilderness of rare tropical shrubbery, redolent of the most exquisite of perfumes. True to the Dutch instinct for the water, the river, or rather the bay, for the river has now disembogued into an arm of the sea, washed the very walls of the flower-garden, and the plash, or rather the monotonous fretting of the tiny waves, at their base, formed no unmusical accompaniment to the hum of conversation, as the evening wore away. Among other plants, we noticed the giant maguey, and a great variety of the cactus, that favorite child of the sun. Our visit being over, we took a warm leave of our hospitable entertainers, and pulled on board the *Sumter*, by moonlight, deeply impressed, and softened as well by the harmonies of nature, and feeling as little like "pirates," as possible.

The next morning, having run up our boats, and taken a final leave of the waters of the Surinam, we steamed out to sea, crossing the bar about meridian; the weather being fine, and the wind fresh from the north-east. Having given it out that we were bound to Barbadoes, to look for the *Keystone State,* we stood north, until we had run the land out of sight, to give color to this idea, when we changed our course to E., half S. We ran along, for the next two or three days, on soundings, with a view to break the force of the current, doubling Cape Orange, on the 2d of September, and hauling more to the southward, with the trending of the coast. On the next day, we had regained the position from which we had been compelled to bear up, and my journal remarks:—"We have thus lost three days and a half of steaming, or about fifty tons of coal, but what is worse, we have lost twenty-three days of valuable time,—but this time can scarcely be said to have been wholly lost, either, since the display of the flag of our young republic, in Cayenne and Paramaribo, has had a most excellent effect."

Sept. 4th.—Weather fine, with a fresh breeze, from about E. by S. During most of the day, we have carried fore and aft sails, and have made an excellent run, for a dull ship—175 miles. We have experienced no current. We passed the mouths of the great Amazon, to-day, bearing on its bosom the waters of a continent. We were running along in the deepest and bluest of sea-water, whilst at no great distance from us, we could plainly perceive, through our telescopes, the turbid waters of the great stream, mixing and mingling, by slow degrees, with the ocean. Numerous tide rips marked the uncongenial meeting of the waters, and the sea-gull and penguin were busy diving in them, as though this neutral ground, or rather I should say, battle-ground, was a favorite resort for the small fish, on which they prey. A drift log with sedate water-fowl seated upon it, would now and then come along, and schools of porpoises were disporting themselves, now in the blue, now in the muddy waters. Unlike the mouths of the Mississippi, there were no white sails of commerce dotting the waters, in the offing, and no giant tow-boats throwing their volumes of black smoke into the air, and, with their huge side-wheels, beating time to the pulsations of the steam-engine. All was nature. The giant stream ran through a wilderness, scarcely yet opened to civilization. It disembogues a little south of the equator, and runs from west to east, nearly entirely across the continent.

We crossed the equator in the *Sumter*, on the meridian of 46° 40′, and sounded in twenty fathoms of water, bringing up from the bottom of the sea, for the first time, some of the sand, and shells of the Southern Hemisphere. We hoisted the Confederate flag, though there were no eyes to look upon it outside of our ship, to vindicate, symbolically, our right to enter this new domain of Neptune, in spite of Abraham Lincoln, and the Federal gun-boats.

September 5th.—Wind fresh from E. S. E. Doubled Cape Garupi, during the early morning, and sounded, at meridian, in eight fathoms of water, *without any land in sight*, though the day was clear. Hauled out from the coast a little. At half-past three, P.M., made the island of San Joao, for which we had been running, a little on the starboard bow. We now hauled in close with this island, and running along its white sand beach, which reminded us much of the Florida coast, about Pensacola, we doubled its north-eastern end, in six, and seven fathoms of water. Night now set in, and, shaping our course S. E. by S., we ran into some very broken ground—the soundings frequently changing, in a single cast of the lead, from seven to four fathoms. Four fathoms being rather uncomfortably shoal, on an open coast, we again hauled out, until we deepened our water to eight fathoms, in which we ran along, still in very equal soundings, until we made the light on Mount *Itacolomi,* nearly ahead. In half an hour afterward, we anchored in six and a half fathoms of water, to wait for daylight.

When I afterward told some Brazilian officers, who came on board, to visit me, in Maranham, of this eventful night's run, they held up their hands in astonishment, telling me that the chances were a hundred to one, that I had been wrecked, for, many parts of the broken ground over which I had run, were *almost dry,* at low water. Their steamers never attempt it, they said, with the best pilots on board. It is a pity this coast is not better surveyed, for the charts by which I was running, represented it free from danger. The Brazilian is a coral coast, and, as before remarked, all coral coasts are dangerous. The inequality of soundings was due to the greater industry of the little stone-mason, of which we read some pages back, in some spots than in others. This little worker of the sea will sometimes pierce a ship's bottom, with a cone, which it has brought near the surface, from surrounding deep waters. As it is constantly at work, the bottom of the sea is constantly changing, and hence, on coral coasts, surveying steamers should be almost always at work. Having anchored in the open sea, and the sea being a little rough, we found, when we came to heave up our anchor, the next morning, that we brought up only the ring, and a small piece of the shank. It had probably been caught in the rocky bottom, and broken by the force of the windlass, aided by the pitching of the ship.

There was, much to my regret, no pilot-boat in sight. The entrance to Maranham is quite difficult, but difficult as it was, I was forced to attempt it. We rounded safely, the shoals of Mount Itacolomi, and passed the middle ground of the Meio, and I was already congratulating myself that the danger was past, when the ship ran plump upon a sand-bank, and stopped! She went on, at full speed, and the shock, to those standing on deck, was almost sufficient to throw them off their feet. We had a skilful leadsman in the chains, and at his last cast, he had found no bottom, with eight fathoms of line—all that the speed of the ship would allow him to sink. Here was a catastrophe! Were the bones of the *Sumter* to be laid to rest, on the coast of Brazil, and her Commander, and crew to return to the Confederate States, and report to the Government, that they had lost its only ship of war! This idea flashed through my mind for an instant, but only for an instant, for the work of the moment pressed. The engineer on duty had stopped his engine, without waiting for orders, as soon as he felt the ship strike, and I now ordered it reversed. In a moment more the screw was revolving in the opposite direction, and the strong tide, which was running out, catching the ship, on the port bow, at the same time, she swung round to starboard, and slid off the almost perpendicular edge of the bank into the deep water, pretty much as a turtle will drop off a log. The first thing I did was to draw a long breath, and the second was to put on an air of indifference, as if nothing had happened, and tell the officer of the deck, in the coolest manner possible, to "let her go ahead." We now proceeded more cautiously, under low steam, giving the leadsman plenty of time to get his soundings, accurately. These soon proving very irregular, and there being some fishermen on the coast, half a mile distant, throwing up their arms, and gesticulating to us, as though to warn us of danger, we anchored, and sending a boat on shore, brought one of them off, who volunteered to pilot us up to the town. Upon sounding the pumps, we found that the ship had suffered no damage from the concussion. We anchored in the port of Maranham, in three or four hours afterward, and the Confederate States flag waved in the Empire of Brazil.

CHAPTER VI

The Birds Have Flown

THE PORT ADMIRAL SENT A LIEUTENANT TO call on us, soon after anchoring, and I dispatched one of my own lieutenants, to call on the Governor; returning the Admiral's visit, myself, in the course of the afternoon, at his place of business on shore.

The day after our arrival in Maranham, was a day of feasting and rejoicing by the townspeople—all business being suspended. It was the 7th of September, the anniversary of the day [1822], on which Brazil had severed her political connection with Portugal—in other words, it was her Independence-day. The forts and ships of war fired salutes, and the latter were gayly draped in flags and signals, presenting a very pretty appearance. It is customary, on such occasions, for the ships of war of other nations, in the port, to participate in the ceremonies and merry-making. We abstained from all participation, on board the *Sumter,* our flag being, as yet, unrecognized, for the purposes of form and ceremony. In the evening, a grand ball was given, at the Government House, by the President of the Province, to which all the world, except the *Sumter,* was invited—the etiquette of nations, before referred to, requiring that she should be ruled out. The only feeling excited in us, by this official slight, was one of contempt for the silliness of the proceeding— . . . The Government House being situated on the river bank, near our anchorage, the lights of the brilliantly illuminated halls and chambers, shone full upon our decks, and the music of the bands, and even the confused hum of the voices of the merry-makers, and the muffled shuffling of the dancers' feet, came to us, very distinctly, to a late hour. The *Sumter* lay dark, and motionless, and silent, amid this scene of merriment; the only answer which she sent back to the revellers, being the sonorous and startling cry, every half hour, of her marine sentinels on post, of "All's well!"

Having suffered, somewhat, in health, from the fatigue and excitement of the last few weeks, I removed on shore the next day, and took up my quarters at the hotel Porto, kept by one of those nondescripts one sometimes meets with in the larger South American cities, whose nationality it is impossible to guess at, except that he belongs to the Latin race. My landlord had followed the sea, among his thousand and one occupations, spoke half a dozen languages, and was "running"—to use a slang Americanism—a theatre and one or two fashionable restaurants, in beautifully laid out pleasure-grounds in the suburbs, in addition to his hotel. He drove a pair of fast horses, was on capital terms with all the pretty women in the town, smashed champagne-bottles, right and left, and smoked the best of Havana cigars. The reader will thus see, that being an invalid, and requiring a little nursing, I had fallen into capital hands. Whether it was that Senhor Porto—for he had given his own name to his hotel—had chased and captured merchant-ships, in former days, himself, or from some other motive, I could never tell, but he took quite a fancy to me at once, and I rode with him daily, during my stay, behind his fast ponies, and visited all the places of amusement, of which he was the *padron*. The consequence was, that I visibly improved in health, and at the end of the week which I spent with him, returned on board the *Sumter*, quite set up again; in requital whereof, I have permitted the gallant Captain to sit for his portrait in these pages.

My first duty, after being installed in my new apartments on shore, was, of course, to call on the President of the Department— the town of Maranham being the seat of government of the province of the same name. The President declined to see me then, but appointed noon, the next day, to receive me. Soon after I had returned to my hotel, Senhor Porto entered my room, to inform me that Captain Pinto, of the Brazilian Navy, the commanding naval officer on the station, accompanied by the Chief of Police, had called to see me. "What does this mean?" said I, "the Chief of Police, in our cities, is a very questionable sort of gentleman, and is usually supposed to be on the scent of malefactors." "Oh! he is a very respectable gentleman, I assure you," replied Porto, "and, as you see, he has called with the Port Admiral, so that he is in good company, at least. Indeed he is reputed to be the confidential friend of the President." Thus reassured, and making a virtue of necessity, I desired Porto, very complacently, to admit the visitors. The Port Admiral had done me the honor to visit me, immediately upon my arrival, and I had returned his visit, so that we were not strangers. He introduced the Chief of Police to me, who proved to be, as *Porto* had represented him, an agreeable gentleman, holding military rank, and, after the two had been seated, they opened their business to me. They had come, they said, on behalf of the President, to present me with a copy of a paper, which had been handed him, by the United States Consul, protesting against my being permitted to coal, or receive any other supplies in the port of Maranham. Oh ho! thought I, here is another of Mr. Seward's small fry turned up. I read the paper, and found it full of ignorance and falsehoods—ignorance of the most common principles of international law, and barefaced misrepresentations with regard to my ship; the whole composed in such execrable English, as to be highly creditable to Mr. Seward's Department. I characterized the paper, as it deserved, and said to the gentlemen, that as I had made an appointment to call on the President, on the morrow, I would take that opportunity of replying to the slanderous document. The conversation then turned on general topics, and my visitors soon after withdrew.

As I rode out, that afternoon, with Porto, he said, "Never mind! I know all that is going on, at the palace, and you will get all the coal, and everything else you want." . . .

At the appointed hour, the next day, I called to see his Excellency, the President, and being ushered, by an orderly in waiting, into a suite of spacious, and elegantly furnished apartments, I found Captain Pinto, and his Excellency, both prepared to receive me. We proceeded, at once, to business. I exhibited to his Excellency the same little piece of brownish paper, with Mr. Jefferson Davis's signature at the bottom of it, that I had shown to Captain Hillyer of the *Cadmus*—unasked, however, as no doubts had been raised as to the verity of the character of my ship. I then read to his Excellency an extract or two from the letter of instructions, which had been sent me by the Secretary of the Navy, directing me to pay all proper respect to the territory, and property of neutrals. I next read the proclamations of England and France, acknowledging us to be in the possession of belligerent rights, and said to his Excellency, that although I had not seen the proclamation of Brazil, I presumed she had followed the lead of the European powers—to which he assented. I then "rested my case," as the lawyers say, seeing, by the expression of his Excellency's countenance, that every lick had told, and that I had nothing now to fear. "But, what about coal being contraband of war," said his Excellency, at this stage of the proceeding. "The United States Consul, in the protest addressed to me, a copy of which I sent you, yesterday, by Captain Pinto, and the Chief of Police, states that you had not been permitted to coal, in any of the ports, which you have hitherto visited." The reader will recollect, that, at the British Island of Trinidad, the question of my being permitted to coal had been submitted to the "law officers of the Crown." The newspaper, at that place, had published a copy of the opinion of these officers, and also a copy of the decision of the Governor, thereupon. Having brought a copy of this paper, in my pocket, for the occasion, I now rejoined to his Excellency: "The United States Consul has made you a false statement. I have coaled, already, in the colonies of no less than three Powers—Spain, Holland, and England"—and drawing from my pocket the newspaper, and handing it to him, I continued, "and your Excellency will find, in this paper, the decision of the English authorities, upon the point in question—that is to say, that coal is not contraband of war, and may be supplied by neutrals to belligerents." Captain Pinto, to whom his Excellency handed the paper, read aloud the decision, putting it into very good Portuguese, as he went along, and when he had finished the reading, his Excellency turned again to me, and said: "I have no longer any doubts on the question. You can have free access to the markets, and purchase whatsoever you may desire—munitions of war alone excepted." . . . The official portion of my interview with the President being ended, I ventured upon some general remarks with regard to the unnatural, and wicked war which was being waged upon us, and soon afterward took my leave.

In an hour after I had left the President's quarters, my paymaster had contracted for a supply of coal, and lighters were being prepared to take it on board. The sailors were now permitted to visit the shore, in detachments, "on liberty," and the officers wandered about, in twos and threes, wherever inclination prompted. We soon found that wherever we moved, we were objects of much curiosity, the people frequently turning to stare at us; but we were always treated with respect. Nothing was thought, or talked of, during our stay, but the American war. The Provincial Congress was in session, and several of its members boarded at the hotel Porto. I found them intelligent, well-informed men. There were political parties here, as elsewhere, of course; among others as might be expected, in a slave-holding country, there was an abolition party, and this party sympathized with the North. It was very small, however, for it was quite evident, from the popular demonstrations, that the great mass of the people were with us. This state of the public feeling not only rendered our stay, very pleasant, but facilitated us in getting off our supplies. Invitations to the houses of the citizens were frequent, and we had free access to all the clubs, and other places of public resort.

I must not omit to mention here, a very agreeable fellow-countryman, whom we met in Maranham—Mr. J. Wetson, from Texas. He had been several years in Brazil. His profession was that of a steam-engineer, and mill-wright. This worthy young mechanic, full of love, and enthusiasm for his section, loaned the paymaster two thousand dollars, on a bill against the Secretary of the Navy; and during the whole of our stay, his rooms were the head-quarters of my younger officers, where he dispensed to them true Southern hospitality. We were gratified to find him a great favorite with the townspeople, and we took leave of him with regret.

Maranham lies in latitude 2° S. and we visited it, during the dry season; the sun having carried the equatorial cloud-ring, which gives it rain, farther north. We had perpetual sunshine, during our stay, but the heat was tempered by the trade-wind, which blew sometimes half a gale, so that we did not feel it oppressive. Toward night the sea-breeze would moderate, and the most heavenly of bright skies, and most balmy of atmospheres would envelop the landscape. At this witching hour, the beauties of Maranham made their appearance, at the street-doors, and at open windows, and the tinkle of the guitar and the gentle hum of conversation would be heard. Later in the night, there would arise from different parts of the town—somewhat removed from the haunts of the upper-tendom—the rumbling, and jingling of the tambourine, and the merry notes of the violin, as the national fandango was danced, with a vigor, and at the same time with a poetry of motion unknown to colder climes. The wine flowed freely on these occasions, and not unfrequently the red knife of the assassin found the heart's blood of a rival in love; for there are other climes besides those of which the poet sang, where

> "The rage of the vulture, the love of the turtle
> Now melt into sorrow, now madden to crime."

The trade of Maranham is mostly monopolized by Portugal, France, and Spain, though there is some little carried on with the United States—an occasional ship from New York, or Boston, bringing a cargo of flour, cheap but gaudy furniture, clocks, and domestic cottons, and other Yankee staples, and notions. The shopkeepers are mostly French and Germans. An excellent staple of cotton is produced in the province of Maranham.

On the 15th of September, the *Sumter* was ready for sea, having been refitted, and repainted, besides being coaled, and provisioned; and there being, as usual, according to rumor, a couple of enemy's ships waiting for her outside, we received a pilot on board, and getting up steam, took leave of Maranham, carrying with us many kindly recollections of the hospitality of the people. We swept the sea horizon, with our glasses, as we approached the bar, but the enemy's cruisers were nowhere to be seen, and at three P. M., we were again in blue water; our little craft rising, and falling gently, to the undulations of the sea, as she ploughed her way through it.

The question now was, in what direction should we steer? I was within striking distance of the cruising-ground, for which I had set out—Cape St. Roque; but we had been so long delayed, that we should reach it, if we proceeded thither at all, at a most unpropitious season—the sailing, and steaming qualities of the *Sumter* considered. The trade-winds were sweeping round the Cape, blowing half a gale, on the wings of which the dullest ship would be able to run away from us, if we trusted to sail, alone; and steam, in the present state of my exchequer, was out of the question. I had paid $17.50 per ton for the coal I had taken in, at Maranham, and but for the timely loan of Mr. Wetson, should have exhausted my treasury entirely. The trade-winds would continue to blow, with equal force, until some time in December; they would then moderate, and from that time, onward, until March, we might expect more gentle weather. This, then, was the only season, in which the *Sumter* could operate off the Cape, to advantage.

On the other hand, the calm belt of the equator lay before me—

its southern edge, at this season of the year, being in latitude of about 5° N. All the homeward-bound trade of the enemy passed through this calm belt, or used to pass through it before the war, at a well-known crossing. At that crossing, there would be a calm sea, light, and variable winds, and rain. In such weather, I could lie in wait for my prey, under sail, and, if surprise, and stratagem did not effect my purpose, I could, when a sail appeared, get up steam and chase and capture, without the expenditure of much fuel. In this way, with the coal I had on board, I could prolong my cruise, probably, for a couple of months. I did not hesitate long, therefore, between the two schemes. I turned my ship's head to the northward, and eastward, for the calm belt, and before sunset, we had run the coast of Brazil out of sight.

We recrossed the equator, the next day. In five days more, the sun would have reached the equator, when we should have had the grand spectacle, at noon, of being able to sweep him, with our instruments, entirely around the horizon, with his lower limb just touching it, at all points. We could nearly do this, as it was, and so rapidly did he dip, at noon, that we were obliged to watch him, with constant vigilance, to ascertain the precise moment of twelve o'clock.

September 17th.—The sea is of a deep, indigo blue, and we have a bright, and exceedingly transparent atmosphere, with a fresh breeze from the south-east. At half-past eleven A. M., we let the steam go down, uncoupled the propeller, and put the ship under sail. Observed at noon, in latitude 2° 19′ N.; longitude, 41° 29′.

For the next few days, we encountered a remarkable easterly current—the current, in this part of the ocean, being almost constantly to the westward. This current—which we were now stemming, for we were sailing toward the north-west—retarded us, as much as fifty miles, in a single day! So remarkable did the phenomenon appear, that if I had noticed it, for but a single day, I should have been inclined to think that I had made some mistake in my observations, or that there was some error in my instrument, but we noticed it, day after day, for four or five days.

Contemporaneously with this phenomenon, another, and even more wonderful one appeared. This was a succession of tide-rips, so remarkable, that they deserve special description.

The *Sumter* lay nearly stationary, during the whole of these phenomena—the easterly current setting her back, nearly as much as she gained under sail. She was in the average latitude of 5° N., and average longitude of 42° W. For the first three days, the rips appeared with wonderful regularity—there being an interval of just twelve hours between them. They approached us from the south, and travelled toward the north. At first, only a line of foam would be seen, on the distant horizon, approaching the ship very rapidly. As it came nearer, an almost perpendicular wall of water, extending east and west, as far as the eye could reach, would be seen, the top of the wall boiling and foaming, like a breaker rolling over a rocky bottom. As the ridge approached nearer and nearer, it assumed the form of a series of rough billows, jostling against, and struggling with each other, producing a scene of the utmost confusion, the noise resembling that of a distant cataract. Reaching the ship, these billows would strike her with such force, as to send their spray to the deck, and cause her to roll and pitch, as though she were amid breakers. The phenomenon was, indeed, that of breakers, only the cause was not apparent—there being no shoal water to account for it. The *Sumter* sometimes rolled so violently in these breakers, when broadside to, that we were obliged to keep her off her course, several points, to bring the sea on her quarter, and thus mitigate the effect. The belt of rips would not be broad, and as it travelled very rapidly—fifteen or twenty miles the hour—the ship would not be long within its influence. In the course of three quarters of an hour, it would disappear, entirely, on the distant northern horizon. So curious was the whole phenomenon, that the sailors, as well as the officers, assembled, as if by common consent, to witness it. "There come the tide rips!" some would exclaim, and, in a moment there would be a demand for the telescopes, and a rush to the ship's side, to witness the curious spectacle. These rips have frequently been noticed by navigators, and discussed by philosophers, but hitherto, no satisfactory explanation has been given of them. They are like the bores, at the mouths of great rivers; as at the mouth of the Amazon, in the western hemisphere, and of the Ganges, in the eastern; great breathings, or convulsions of the sea, the causes of which elude our research. These bores sometimes come in, in great perpendicular walls, sweeping everything before them, and causing immense destruction of life, and property. I was, at first, inclined to attribute these tide rips to the lunar influence, as they appeared twice in twenty-four hours, like the tides, and each time near the passing of the meridian, by the moon; but, in a few days, they varied their times of appearance, and came on quite irregularly, sometimes with an interval of five or six hours, only. And then the tidal wave, for it is evidently this, and not a current, should be from east to west, if it were due to lunar influence; and we have seen that it travelled from south to north. Nor could I connect it with the easterly current that was prevailing—for it travelled at right angles to the current, and not with, or against it. It was, evidently, due to some pretty uniform law, as it always travelled in the same direction.

We reached the calm belt, on the 24th of September, for, on this day, having lost the south-east trade, we had light and baffling winds from the south-west, and rain-clouds began to muster overhead. On the next day, the weather being in its normal condition of cloud, the welcome cry of "sail ho!" came resounding from the mast-head, with a more prolonged, and musical cadence than usual —the look-out, with the rest of the crew, having become tired of the inactivity of the last few days. All was bustle, immediately, about the decks; and in half an hour, with the sails snugly furled, and the ship under steam, we were in hot pursuit. The stranger was a brigantine, and was standing to the north-west, pursuing the usual crossing of the calm belt, as best he might, in the light winds, that were blowing, sometimes this way, sometimes that. We came up with him quite rapidly, there being scarcely a ripple on the surface of the smooth sea, to impede our progress, and when we had come sufficiently near to enable him to make it out, distinctly, we showed him the enemy's flag. He was evidently prepared with his own flag, for, in less than a minute, the lazy breeze was toying and playing with it, and presently blew it out sufficiently, to enable us to make out the well-known and welcome stars and stripes. We hove him to, by "hail," and hauling down the false colors, and hoisting our own, we sent a boat on board of him, and captured him. He proved to be the *Joseph Parke,* of Boston, last from Pernambuco, and six days out, *in ballast.* The *Parke* had been unable to procure a return cargo; the merchants of Pernambuco having heard of the arrival of the *Sumter,* at Maranham, in rather uncomfortable proximity.

We transferred the crew of the captured vessel to the *Sumter,* replacing it with a prize crew, and got on board from her such articles of provisions, cordage, and sails as we required; but instead of burning her, we transformed her, for the present, into a scout vessel, to assist us in discovering other prizes. I sent Lieutenant Evans on board to command her, and gave him a couple of midshipmen, as watch officers. The following was his commission:—

"Sir:—You will take charge of the prize-brig *Joseph Parke,* and cruise in company with this vessel, until further orders. During the day, you will keep from seven to eight miles, to the westward, and to windward, and keep a bright look-out, from your top-gallant yard, for sails— signalling to us, such as you may descry. Toward evening, every day, you will draw in toward this vessel, so as to be within three, or four miles of her, at dark; and, during the night you will keep close company with her, to guard against the possibility of separation. Should you, however, be separated from her, by any accident, you will make the best of your way to latitude 8° N., and longitude 45° W., where you will await her a reasonable time. Should you not join her again, you will make the best of your way to some port in the Confederate States."

In obedience to these instructions, the *Parke* drew off to her station, and letting our fires go down on board the *Sumter,* we put her under sail, again. Long before night, the excitement of the chase and capture had died away, and things had resumed their wonted course. The two ships hovered about the "crossing," for several days, keeping a bright look-out, but nothing more appeared; and on the 29th of September, the *Parke* having been called alongside, by signal, her prize crew was taken out, and the ship burned, after having been made a target, for a few hours, for the practice of the crew. It was evidently no longer of any use to bother ourselves about the crossing of the calm-belt, for, instead of falling in with a constant stream of the enemy's ships, returning home, from different parts of the world, we had been cruising in it, some ten days, and had sighted but a single sail! We had kept ourselves between the parallels of 2° 30′ N., and 9° 30′ N., and between the meridians of 41° 30′ W., and 47° 30′ W.; and if the reader have any curiosity on the subject, by referring to the map, he will perceive, that the north-western diagonal of the quadrilateral figure, formed by these parallels, and meridians, is the direct course between Cape St. Roque, and New York. But the wary seabirds had, evidently, all taken the alarm, and winged their way, home, by other routes. I was the more convinced of this, by an intercepted letter which I captured in the letter-bag of the *Parke*, which was written by the master of the ship, *Asteroid*, to his owner, and which ran as follows:—

"The *Asteroid* arrived off this port [Pernambuco], last evening, seventy-five days from Baker's Island, and came to anchor in the outer roads, this morning. I found yours of August 9th, and noted the contents, which, I must say, have made me rather *blue*. I think you had better *insure*, even at the extra premium, as the *Asteroid* is not a *clipper*, and will be a *bon* prize for the Southerners. I shall sail this evening [September 16th, three days before the *Joseph Parke*] and take a *new* route, for Hampton Roads."*

The *Asteroid* escaped us, as no doubt many more had done, by avoiding the "beaten track," and taking a new road home; thus verifying, in a very pointed manner, the old adage, that "the longest way round is the shortest way home."

We now made sail for the West India Islands, designing, after a short cruise among them, to run into the French island of Martinique, and coal. We still kept along on the beaten track of homeward-bound ships, but with little expectation of making any prizes, and for some days overhauled none but neutral ships. Many of these had cargoes for the United States, but not having the same motive to avoid me, that the enemy's ships had, they were content to travel the usual highway. Although many of them had enemy's property on board they were perfectly safe from molestation—the Confederate States' Government having adopted, as the reader has seen, in its Act declaring, that, by the conduct of the enemy, a state of war existed, the liberal principle, that "Free ships make free goods."

Among the neutrals overhauled by us, was an English brig called the *Spartan*, from Rio Janeiro, for St. Thomas, in the West Indies. We had an exciting chase after this fellow. We pursued him, under United States colors, and as the wind was blowing fresh, and the chase was a "stern-chase," it proved, as usual, to be a long one, although the *Sumter* was doing her best, under both steam and sail.

*[*Asteroid* should read *Asterion* throughout. She was lost on Baker's (Baker) Island two years later. Incidentally, private postal correspondence is inviolable under international law.]

John Bull evidently mistook us for the Yankee we pretended to be, and seemed determined to prevent us from overhauling him, if possible. His brig, as we soon discovered, had light heels, and he made the best possible use of them, by giving her every inch of canvas he could spread. Still, we gained on him, and as we came sufficiently near, we gave him a blank cartridge, to make him show his colors, and heave to. He showed his colors—the English red—but refused to heave to. The unprofessional reader may be informed, that when a merchant-ship is under full sail, and especially when she is running before a fresh breeze, as the *Spartan* was, it puts her to no little inconvenience, to come to the wind. She has to take in her sails, one by one, owing to her being short-handed, and "the clewing up," and "hauling down" occupy some minutes. The captain of the *Spartan* was loth to subject himself to this inconvenience, especially at the command of the hated Yankee. Coming up a little nearer, we now fired a shotted gun at him, taking care not to strike him, but throwing the shot so near as to give him the benefit of its rather ominous music, as it whistled past. As soon as the smoke from the gun, which obscured him for a moment, rolled away before the breeze, we could see him starting his "sheets," and "halliards," and pretty soon the saucy little *Spartan* rounded to, with her main top-sail to the mast. The reader may be curious to know, why I had been so persistent in heaving to a neutral. The answer is, that I was not sure she was neutral. The jaunty little brig looked rather more American, than English, in all but the flag that was flying at her peak. She had not only the grace and beauty of hull that characterize our American-built ships, but the long, tapering spars on which American ship-masters especially pride themselves. She did, indeed, prove to be American, in a certain sense, as we found her to hail from Halifax, in Nova Scotia. The master of the *Spartan* was in an ill-humor when my boarding-officer jumped on board of him. It was difficult to extract a civil answer from him. "What is the news?" said the boarding-officer. "Capital news!" replied the master; "you Yankees are getting whipped like h—ll; you beat the Derby boys at the Manassas races." "But what's the news from Rio?" now inquired the supposed Yankee boarding-officer. "Well, there's good news from that quarter too—all the Yankee ships are laid up, for want of freights." "You are rather hard upon us, my friend," now rejoined the boarding-officer; "why should you take such an interest in the

Confederate cause?" "Simply, because there is a little man fighting against an overgrown bully, and I like pluck."

The *Spartan* being bound to St. Thomas, and we ourselves intending to go, soon, into the West Indies, it was highly important that we should preserve our *incognito,* to which end, I had charged the boarding-officer, to represent his ship as a Federal cruiser, in search of the *Sumter.* The boarding-officer having done this, found the master of the *Spartan* complimentary to the last; for as he was stepping over the brig's side, into his boat, the master said, "I hope you will find the *Sumter,* but I rather think you will hunt for her, as the man did for the tax-collector, hoping all the time he might n't find him."

The weather now, again, became calm, and we had "cat's-paws" from all the points of the compass. The breeze, with which we had chased the *Spartan,* was a mere spasmodic effort of Nature, for we were still in the calm-belt, or, as the sailors expressively call it, the "doldrums." For the next few days, it rained almost incessantly, the heavily charged clouds sometimes settling so low, as scarcely to sweep clear of our mastheads. It did not simply rain; the water fell in torrents, and the lightning flashed, and the thunder rolled, with a magnificence and grandeur that were truly wonderful to witness. In the intervals of these drenching rains, the clouds, like so many half-wrung sponges, would lift themselves, and move about with great rapidity, in every direction—now toward, and now from, each other—convolving, in the most curious disorder, as though they were so many huge, black serpents, writhing and twisting in the powerful grasp of some invisible hand. Anon, a water-spout would appear upon the scene, with its inverted cone, sometimes travelling rapidly, but more frequently at rest. At times, so ominous, and threatening would be the aspect of the heavens, with its armies of black clouds in battle-array, its forked lightning, and crashing thunder, the perfect stillness of the atmosphere, and the rapid flight of scared water-fowl, that a hurricane would seem imminent, until we would cast our eyes upon the barometer, standing unmoved, at near the marking of thirty inches, amid all the signs, and portents around it. In half an hour, sometimes, all this paraphernalia of clouds would break in twain, and retreat, in opposite directions, to the horizon, and the sun would throw down a flood of golden light, and scalding heat upon our decks; on which would be paddling about the half-drowned sailors. The first lieutenant took advantage of these rains, to fill, anew, his water-tanks, "tenting" his awnings, during the heaviest of the showers, and catching more water than he needed; and the sailors had another such jubilee of washing, as they had had, when we were running along the Venezuelan coast.

Sunday, September 29th.—Beautiful, clear morning, with a gentle breeze from the south-east, and a smooth sea. At eleven A. M., mustered the crew, and inspected the ship. Latitude, 6° 55′ N.; longitude, 45° 08′ W. Evening set in, squally, and rainy. Running along to the north-west, under topsails.

October 2d.—This morning, when I took my seat, at the breakfast-table, I was surprised to find a very tempting-looking dish of fried fish set out before me, and upon inquiring of my faithful steward, John, (a Malayan, who had taken the place of Ned, [who had jumped ship at Paramaribo]) to what good fortune he was indebted, for the prize, his little black eyes twinkled, as he said, "Him jump aboard, last night!" Upon further inquiry, I found that it was a small sword-fish, that had honored us with a visit; the active little creature having leaped no less than fifteen feet, to reach the deck of the *Sumter*. It was lucky that its keen spear did not come in contact with any of the crew during the leap—a loss of life might have been the consequence. The full-grown sword-fish had been known to pierce a ship's bottom, floor-timber and all, with its most formidable weapon.

October 4th.—Weather clear, and beautiful, with trade-clouds, white and fleecy, and a light breeze from the eastward. The bosom of the gently heaving sea is scarcely ruffled. Schools of fish are playing around us, and the sailors have just hauled, on board, a large shark, which they have caught with hook and line. The sailor has a great antipathy to the shark, regarding him as his hereditary enemy. Accordingly, the monster receives no mercy when he falls into Jack's hands. See how Jack is tormenting him now! and how fiercely the monster is snapping, and grinding his teeth together, and beating the deck with his powerful tail, as though he would crush in the planks. He is tenacious of life, and will be a long time in dying, and, during all this time, Jack will be cutting, and slashing him, without mercy, with his long sheath-knife. The comparatively calm sea is covered, in every direction, for miles, with a golden or straw-colored dust. Whence comes it? We are four hundred miles from any land! It has, doubtless, been dropped by the trade-winds, as they have been neutralized over our heads, in this calm belt of the equator, and, in a future page, we shall have further occasion to refer to it. We have observed, to-day, in latitude 8°; the longitude being 46° 58'.

October 11th.—Morning clear and calm, after a couple of days of tempestuous weather, during which the barometer settled a little. Toward noon it clouded up again, and there were squally appearances in the south-east. The phenomenon of the tide-rips had reappeared. Malay John was in luck, again, this morning, a covey of flying-fish having fallen on the deck, last night, during the storm. He has served me a plate full of them for breakfast. The largest of them are about the size of a half-grown Potomac herring, and they are somewhat similar in taste—being a delicate, but not highly flavored fish.

October 14th.—At noon, to-day, we plotted precisely upon the diagonal between St. Roque and New York; our latitude being 8° 31', and longitude 45° 56'. We now made more sail, and on the 17th of October we had reached the latitude of 11° 37'. From this time, until the 22d, we had a constant series of bad weather, the barometer settling to 29.80, and the wind blowing half a gale, most of the time. Sometimes the wind would go all around the compass, and the weather would change half a dozen times, in twenty-four hours. On the last-mentioned day, the weather became again settled, and being now in latitude 14°, we had passed out of the calm belt, and began to receive the first breathings of the northeast trade-wind.

On the 24th, we chased and hove to a French brig, called *La Mouche Noire,* from Nantes, bound for Martinique. She had been out forty-two days, had no newspapers on board, and had no news to communicate. We boarded her under the United States flag, and when the boarding-officer apologized to the master for the trouble we had given him, in heaving him to, in the exercise of our belligerent right of search, he said, with an admirable *naiveté,* he had *heard* the United States were at war, but he did not recollect with whom! Admirable Frenchman! wonderful simplicity, to care nothing about newspapers, and to know nothing about wars!

On the 25th, we overhauled that *rara avis in mare,* a Prussian ship. The 27th was Sunday; we had a gentle breeze from the northeast, with a smooth sea, and were enjoying the fine morning, with our awnings spread, scarcely expecting to be disturbed, when the cry of "Sail ho!" again rang from the mast-head. We had been making preparations for Sunday muster; Jack having already taken down from its hiding-place his Sunday hat, and adjusted its ribbons, and now being in the act of "overhauling" his bag, for the "mustering-shirt and trousers." All these preparations were at once suspended, the firemen were ordered below, there was a passing to and fro of engineers, and in a few minutes more the welcome black smoke came pouring out of the *Sumter's* chimney. Bounding away over the sea, we soon began to raise the strange sail from the deck. She was a fore-and-aft schooner of that peculiar model and rig already described as belonging to the New Englander, and nobody else, and we felt certain, at once, that we had flushed the enemy. The little craft was "close-hauled," or, may be, she had the wind a point free, which was her best point of sailing, had the whitest kind of cotton canvas, and carried very taunt gaff-topsails. We found her exceedingly fast, and came up with her very slowly. The chase commenced at nine A. M., and it was three P. M. before we were near enough to heave her to with the accustomed blank cartridge. At the report of our gun—the Confederate States flag being at our peak—the little craft, which had probably been in an agony of apprehension, for some hours past, saw that her fate was sealed, and without further ado, put her helm down, lowered her foresail, hauled down her flying-jib, drew her jib-sheet over to windward—and was hove to; the stars and stripes streaming out from her main-topmast head. Upon being boarded, she proved to be the *Daniel Trowbridge,* of New Haven, Connecticut, last from New York, and bound to Demerara, in British Guiana.

This was a most opportune capture for us, for the little craft was laden with an assorted cargo of provisions, and our own provisions had been nearly exhausted. With true Yankee thrift, she had economized even the available space on her deck, and had a number of sheep, geese, and pigs, on board, for the Demerara market. Another sail being discovered, almost at the moment of this capture, we hastily threw a prize crew on board the *Trowbridge,* and directing her to follow us, sped off in pursuit of the newly discovered sail. It was dark before we came up with this second chase. She proved to be an English brigantine, from Nova Scotia, for Demerara. We now stood back to rejoin our prize, and banking our fires, and hoisting a light at the peak, the better to enable the prize to keep sight of us, during the night, we lay to, until daylight. The next day, and the day after, were busy days, on board the *Sumter,* for we devoted both of them, to getting on board provisions, from the prize. The weather proved propitious, the breeze being gentle, and the sea smooth. We hoisted out the *Tallapoosa*—our launch— and employed her, and the quarterboats—the gig included, for war admits of little ceremony—in transporting barrels, bales, boxes, and every other conceivable kind of package, to the *Sumter.* The paymaster was in ecstasy, for, upon examination, he found the *Trowbridge's* cargo to be all that he could desire—the beef, pork, canvased hams, ship-bread, fancy crackers, cheese, flour, everything being of the very best quality. We were, indeed, under many obligations to our Connecticut friends. To get at the cargo, we were obliged to throw overboard many articles, that we had no use for, and treated old Ocean to a gayly painted fleet of Connecticut woodenware, buckets, foot-tubs, bath-tubs, wash-tubs, churns. We found the sheep, pigs, and poultry in excellent condition; and sending the butcher on board each evening, we caused those innocents to be slaughtered, in sufficient numbers to supply all hands. Jack was in his glory. He had passed suddenly, from mouldy and worm-eaten bread, and the toughest and leanest of "old horse," to the enjoyment of all these luxuries. My Malayan steward's eyes fairly danced, as he stowed away in the cabin lockers, sundry cans of preserved meats, lobster, milk, and fruits. John was a real artist, in his line, and knew the value of such things; and as he busied himself, arranging his luxuries, on the different shelves, I could hear him muttering to himself, "Dem Connecticut mans, bery good mans—me wish we find him often." We laid in, from the *Trowbridge,* full five months' provisions, and getting on board, from her, besides, as much of the live stock, as we could manage to take care of, we delivered her to the flames, on the morning of the 30th of October. On the same day, we chased, and boarded the Danish brig, *Una,* from Copenhagen, bound to Santa Cruz. Being sixty-six days out, she had no news to communicate. We showed her the United States colors, and when she arrived, at Santa Cruz, she reported that she had fallen in with a Federal cruiser. The brig *Spartan,* which we boarded, a few pages back, made the same report, at St. Thomas; so that the enemy's cruisers, that were in pursuit of us, had not, as yet, the least idea that we had returned to the West Indies.

For the next few days, we chased and overhauled a number of

ships, but they were all neutral. The enemy's West India trade seemed to have disappeared almost entirely. Many of his ships had been laid up, in alarm, in his own ports, and a number of others had found it more to their advantage, to enter the public service, as transports. . . .

November 2d.—Morning, heavy clouds, with rain, breaking away partially, toward noon, and giving us some fitful sunshine. Sail ho! at early dawn. Got up steam, and chased, and at 7 A. M. came up with, and sent a boat on board of the English brigantine, *Falcon,* from Halifax, for Barbadoes. Banked fires. Latitude 16° 32′; longitude 56° 55′. Wore ship to the northward, at meridian. Received some newspapers, by the *Falcon,* from which we learn, that the enemy's cruiser *Keystone State,* which, when last heard from, was at Barbadoes, had gone to Trinidad, in pursuit of us. At Trinidad, she lost the trail, and, instead of pursuing us to Paramaribo, and Maranham, turned back to the westward. We learn from the same papers, that the enemy's steam-frigate, *Powhatan,* Lieutenant Porter, with more sagacity, pursued us to Maranham, arriving just one week [only five days] after our departure. At a subsequent date, Lieutenant—now Admiral—Porter's official report fell into my hands, and, plotting his track, I found that, on one occasion, we had been within forty miles of each other; almost near enough, on a still day, to see each other's smoke.

November 3d.—Weather fine, with a smooth sea, and a light breeze from the north-east. A sail being reported from the masthead, we got up steam, and chased, and upon coming near enough to make out the chase, found her to be a large steamer. We approached her, very warily, of course, until it was discovered that she was English, when we altered our course, and banked fires. Our live-stock still gives us fresh provisions, and the abundant supply of Irish potatoes, that we received on board, at the same time, is beginning to have a very beneficial effect, upon the health of the crew—some scorbutic symptoms having previously appeared.

Nov. 5th.—Weather fine, with the wind light from the eastward, and a smooth sea. At daylight, a sail was descried in the north-east, to which we immediately gave chase. Coming up with her, about nine A. M., we sent a boat on board of her. She proved to be the English brigantine, *Rothsay,* from Berbice, on the coast of Guiana, bound for Liverpool. Whilst we had been pursuing the *Rothsay,* a second sail had been reported. We now pursued this second sail, and, coming up with her, found her to be a French brigantine, called *Le Pauvre Orphelin,* from St. Pierre (in France) bound for Martinique. We had scarcely turned away from the *Orphelin,* before a third sail was announced. This latter sail was a large ship, standing, close-hauled, to the N. N. W., and we chased her rather reluctantly, as she led us away from our intended course. She, too, proved to be neutral, being the *Plover,* from Barbadoes, for London. The *Sumter* being, by this time out of breath, and no more sails being reported, we let the steam go down, and gave her a little rest. We observed, to-day, in latitude 17° 10′ N.; the longitude being 59° 06′ W. We had shown the United States colors to all these ships to preserve our *incognito,* as long as possible. We found them all impatient, at being "hove to," and no doubt many curses escaped, *sotto voce,* against the d—d Yankee, as our boats shoved off, from their sides. We observed that none of them saluted the venerable "old flag," which was flying at our peak, whereas, whenever we had shown the Confederate flag to neutrals, down went, at once, the neutral flag, in compliment—showing the estimate, which generous seamen, the world over, put upon this ruthless war, which the strong were waging against the weak.

The 6th of November passed without incident. On the 7th, we overhauled three more neutral ships—the English schooner *Weymouth,* from Weymouth, in Nova Scotia, for Martinique; an English barque, which we refrained from boarding, as there was no mistaking her bluff English bows, and stump top-gallant masts; and a French brig, called the *Fleur de Bois,* last from Martinique, and bound for Bordeaux. In the afternoon of the same day, we made the islands, first of Marie Galante, and then of Guadeloupe, and the Saints. At ten P. M., we doubled the north end of the island of Dominica, and, banking our fires, ran off some thirty or forty miles to the south-west, to throw ourselves in the track of the enemy's vessels, homeward bound from the Windward Islands. The next day, after overhauling an English brigantine, from Demerara, for Yarmouth, we got up steam, and ran for the island of Martinique approaching the town of St. Pierre near enough, by eight P. M., to hear the evening gun-fire. A number of small schooners and sail-boats were plying along the coast, and as night threw her mantle over the scene, the twinkling lights of the town appeared, one by one, until there was quite an illumination, relieved by the sombre back-ground of the mountain. The *Sumter,* as was usual with her, when she had no work in hand, lay off, and on, under sail, all night. The next morning at daylight, we again got up steam, and drawing in with the coast, ran along down it, near enough to enjoy its beautiful scenery, with its waving palms, fields of sugar-cane, and picturesque country houses, until we reached the quiet little town of Fort de France, where we anchored.

The *Sumter* having sailed from Maranham, on the 15th of September, and arrived at Martinique, on the 9th of November, had been nearly two months at sea, during all of which time, she had been actively cruising in the track of the enemy's commerce. She had overhauled a great many vessels, but, for reasons already explained, most of these were neutral. But the damage which she did the enemy's commerce, must not be estimated by the amount of property actually destroyed. She had caused consternation, and alarm among the enemy's ship-masters, and they were making, as we have seen, long and circuitous voyages, to avoid her. Insurance had risen to a high rate, and, for want of freights, the enemy's ships—such of them, at least, as could not purchase those lucrative contracts from the Government, of which I have spoken in a former page—were beginning to be tied up, at his wharves, where they must rot, unless they could be sold, at a sacrifice, to neutrals.

CHAPTER VII

In the Shadow of Mont Pelée

IMMEDIATELY AFTER ANCHORING, IN FORT DE France, I sent a lieutenant on shore, to call on the Governor, report our arrival, and ask for the usual hospitalities of the port,—these hospitalities being, as the reader is aware, such as Goldsmith described as welcoming him at his inn, the more cheerfully rendered, for being paid for. I directed my lieutenant to use rather the language of demand—courteously, of course—than of petition, for I had seen the French proclamation of neutrality, and knew that I was entitled, under the orders of the Emperor, to the same treatment, that a Federal cruiser might receive. I called, the next day, on the Governor myself. I found him a very affable, and agreeable gentleman. He was a rear admiral, in the French Navy, and bore the aristocratic name of Condé. Having observed a large supply of excellent coal in the government dock-yard, as I pulled in to the landing, I proposed to his Excellency that he should supply me from that source, upon my paying cost, and expenses. He declined doing this, but said that I might have free access to the market, for this and other supplies. Mentioning that I had a number of prisoners on board, he at once gave me permission to land them, provided the United States Consul, who lived at St. Pierre, the commercial metropolis of the island, would consent to become responsible for their maintenance during their stay in the island. There being no difference of opinion between the Governor and myself, as to our respective rights and duties, our business-matters were soon arranged, and an agreeable chat of half an hour ensued, on general topics, when I withdrew, much pleased with my visit.

Returning on board the *Sumter,* I dispatched the paymaster to St. Pierre—there was a small passenger-steamer plying between the two ports—to contract for coal and some articles of clothing for the crew. Of provisions we had plenty, as the reader has seen. Lieutenant Chapman accompanied him, and I sent up, also, the masters of the two captured ships, that were on board, that they might see their Consul and arrange for their release.

The next day was Sunday, and I went on shore, with Mr. Guerin, a French gentleman, who had been educated in the United States, and who had called on board to see me, to the Governor's mass. In this burning climate the church-hours are early, and we found ourselves comfortably seated in our pews as early as eight o'clock. The building was spacious and well ventilated. The Governor and his staff entered punctually at the hour, as did, also, a detachment of troops—the latter taking their stations, in double lines, in the main aisle. A military band gave us excellent sacred music from the choir. The whole service was concluded in three-quarters of an hour. The whites and blacks occupied pews promiscuously, as at Paramaribo, though there was no social admixture of races visible. I mean to say that the pews were mixed, though the people were not—each pew was all white or all black; the mulattoes, and others of mixed blood, being counted as blacks. I returned on board for "muster," which took place at the usual hour of eleven o'clock. Already the ship was full of visitors, and I was struck with the absorbed attention with which they witnessed the calling of the names of the crew, and the reading of the articles of war by the clerk. They were evidently not prepared for so interesting a spectacle. The officers were all dressed in bright and new uniforms of navy blue—we had not yet been put in gray along with the army—the gorgeous epaulettes of the lieutenants flashing in the sun, and the midshipmen rejoicing in their gold-embroidered anchors and stars. The men attracted no less attention than the officers, with their lithe and active forms and bronzed countenances, heavy, well-kept beards, and whitest of duck frocks and trousers. One of my visitors, turning to me, after the muster was over, said, pleasantly, in allusion to the denunciations of us by the Yankee newspapers, which he had been reading, *"Ces hommes sont des pirates bien polis, Monsieur Capitaine."*

In the afternoon, one watch of the crew was permitted to visit the shore, on liberty. To each seaman was given a sovereign, for pocket-money. They waked up the echoes of the quaint old town, drank dry all the grog-shops, fagged out the fiddlers, with the constant music that was demanded of them, and "turned up Jack" generally; coming off, the next morning, looking rather solemn and seedy, and not quite so *polis* as when the Frenchman had seen them the day before. The United States Consul having come down from St. Pierre to receive his imprisoned countrymen, himself, I caused them all—except three of them, who had signed articles for service on board the *Sumter*—to be parolled and sent on shore to him. Before landing them, I caused them to be mustered on the quarter-deck, and questioned them, in person, as to the treatment they had received on board—addressing myself, especially, to the two masters. They replied, without exception, that they had been well treated, and thanked me for my kindness. . . .

My paymaster, and lieutenant returned, in good time, from St. Pierre, and reported that they had found an abundance of excellent coal, at reasonable rates, in the market, but that the Collector of the Customs had interposed, to prevent it from being sold to them. Knowing that this officer had acted without authority, I addressed a note to the Governor, reminding him of the conversation we had had the day before, and asking him for the necessary order to overrule the action of his subordinate. My messenger brought back with him the following reply:—

FORT DE FRANCE, November 12, 1861.

TO THE CAPTAIN:—

I have the honor to send you the enclosed letter, which I ask you to hand to the Collector of Customs, at St. Pierre, in which I request him to permit you to embark freely, as much coal as you wish to purchase, in the market. * * *

With the expression of my highest regard for the Captain,

MAUSSION DE CONDÉ.

I remained a few days longer, at Fort de France, for the convenience of watering ship, from the public reservoir, and to enable the rest of my crew to have their run on shore. Unless Jack has his periodical frolic, he is very apt to become moody, and discontented; and my sailors had now been cooped up, in their ship, a couple of months. This giving of "liberty" to them is a little troublesome, to be sure, as some of them will come off drunk, and noisy, and others, overstaying their time, have to be hunted up, in the grog-shops, and other sailor haunts, and brought off by force. My men behaved tolerably well, on the present occasion. No complaint came to me from the shore, though a good many "bills," for "nights' lodgings," and "drinks," followed them on board. Poor Jack! how strong upon him is the thirst for drink! We had an illustration of this, whilst we were lying at Fort de France. It was about nine P. M., and I was below in my cabin, making preparations to retire. Presently, I heard a plunge into the water, a hail, and almost simultaneously, a shot fired from one of the sentinels' rifles. The boatswain's-mate's whistle now sounded, as a boat "was called away," and a rapid shuffling of feet was heard overhead, as the boat was being lowered. Upon reaching the deck, I found that one of the firemen, who had come off from "liberty," a little tight, had jumped overboard, and, in defiance of the hail, and shot of the sentinel, struck out, lustily, for the shore. The moon was shining brightly, and an amusing scene now occurred. The boat was in hot pursuit, and soon came upon the swimmer; but the latter, who dived like a duck, had no notion of being taken. As the boat would come up with him, and "back all," for the purpose of picking him up, he would dive under her bottom, and presently would be seen, either abeam, or astern, "striking out," like a good fellow, again. By the time the boat could turn, and get headway once more, the swimmer would have some yards the start of her, and when she again came up with him, the same tactics would follow. The crew, hearing what was going on, had all turned out of their hammocks, and come on deck to witness the fun; and fun it really was for some minutes, as the doubling, and diving, and twisting, and turning went on—the boat now being sure she had him and now sure she had n't. The fellow finally escaped, and probably a more chop-fallen boat's crew never returned alongside of a ship, than was the *Sumter's* that night. An officer was now sent on shore in pursuit of the fugitive. He had no difficulty in finding him. In half an hour after the performance of his clever feat, the fireman was lying—dead drunk—in one of the *cabarets*, in the sailor quarter of the town. He had had no intention of deserting, but had braved the sentinel's bullet, the shark—which abounds in these waters—and discipline—all for the sake of a glass of grog!

Our time was made remarkably pleasant, during our stay; the inhabitants showing us every mark of respect and politeness, and the officers of the garrison, and of a couple of small French vessels of war, in the port, extending to us the courtesies of their clubs, and mess-rooms. I declined all invitations, myself, but my officers frequently dined on shore; and on the evening before our departure, they returned the hospitalities of their friends, by an elegant supper in the ward-room, at which the festivities were kept up to a late hour. Riding, and breakfast-parties, in the country, were frequent, and bright eyes, peeping out of pretty French bonnets, shone benignantly upon my young "pirates." The war was frequently the topic of conversation, when such expressions as *"les barbares du Nord!"* would escape, not unmusically, from the prettiest of pouting lips. I passed several agreeable evenings, at the hospitable mansion of my friend, Mr. Guerin, the ladies of whose family were accomplished musicians. The sailor is, above all others of his sex, susceptible of female influences. The difference arises, naturally, out of his mode of life, which removes him so often, and so long, from the affections, and refinements of home. After roughing it, for months, upon the deep, in contact only with coarse male creatures, how delightful I found it to sink into a luxurious seat, by the side of a pretty woman, and listen to the sweet notes of her guitar, accompanied by the sweeter notes, still, of her voice, as she warbled, rather than sang some lay of the sea.

In these delightful tropical climates, night is turned into day. The sun, beating down his fierce rays upon heated walls and streets, drives all but the busy merchant and the laborer in-doors during the day. Windows are raised, blinds closed and all the members of the household, not compelled to exertion, betake themselves to their *fauteuils,* and luxurious hammocks. Dinner is partaken of at five or six o'clock, in the afternoon. When the sun goes down, and the shades of evening begin to fall, and the first gentle stirring of the trees and shrubbery, by the land breeze begins to awaken the katydid, and the myriads of other insects, which have been dozing in the heat, the human world is also awakened. The lazy beauty now arises from her couch, and seeking her bath-room, and tire-woman, begins to prepare for the *duties of the day.* She is coiffed, and arranged for conquest, and sallies forth to the *Place d'Armes,* to listen to the music of the military bands, if there be no other special entertainment on hand. The *Place d'Armes* of Fort de France is charmingly situated, on the very margin of the bay, where, in the intervals of the music, or of the hum of conversation, the ripple of the tide beats time, as it breaks upon the smooth, pebbly beach. Ships are anchored in front, and far away to the left, rises a range of blue, and misty hills, which are pointed out to the stranger, as the birth-place of the Empress Josephine. The statue of the Empress also adorns the grounds, and the inhabitants are fond of referring to her history. I was quite surprised at the throng that the quiet little town of Fort de France was capable of turning out, upon the *Place d'Armes;* and even more at the quality, than the quantity of the throng. What with military and naval officers, in their gay uniforms, the multitudes of well-dressed men and women, the ecclesiastics in the habits of their several orders, the flower-girls, the venders of fruits, sherbets, and ice-creams—for the universal Yankee has invaded the colony with his ice-ships—and the delightful music of the bands, it would be difficult to find a more delightful place, in which to while away an hour....

On the 13th of November, my water-tanks being full, and my crew having all returned from "liberty"—none of them having shown any disposition to desert—we got up steam, and proceeded to the town of St. Pierre,* for the purpose of coaling; arriving at the early hour of 8 A. M., and anchoring at the man-of-war anchorage, south of the town. I immediately dispatched a lieutenant to call on the military commandant, accompanied by the paymaster, to make the necessary arrangements for coaling. St. Pierre was quite a different place, from the quiet old town we had left. A number of merchant-ships were anchored in the harbor, and there was quite an air of stir, and thrift, about the quays. Busy commerce was carrying on her exchanges, and with commerce there is always life. There were not so many idle people here, to be awakened from their noon-tide slumbers, by the katydid, as in Fort de France. A number of visitors came off, at once, to see us; rumor having preceded us, and blown the trumpet of our fame, much more than we deserved. Among the rest, there were several customhouse officers, but if these had any office of espionage to perform, they performed it, so delicately, as not to give offence. Indeed they took pains to explain to us, that they had only come on board out of civility, and as a mere matter of curiosity. I never permit myself to be out-done in politeness, and treated them with all consideration.

*[This is the place that was to suffer the loss of 30,000 lives during the frightful eruption of Mont Pelée in 1902.]

IN THE SHADOW OF MONT PELÉE

The Collector of the Customs gave prompt obedience to the Governor's despatch—commanding him not to throw any obstacle in the way of our coaling—by withdrawing the interdict of sale which he had put upon the coal-merchants; and the paymaster returning, after a short absence, with news that he had made satisfactory arrangements with the said merchants, the ship was warped up to the coal-depot, and some thirty tons of coal received, on board, the same afternoon. This was very satisfactory progress. We sent down the fore-yard, for repairs, and the engineer finding some good machinists on shore, with more facilities in the way of shop, and tools, than he had expected, took some of his own jobs, of which there are always more or less, in a steamer, on shore.

As the sun dipped his broad red disk into the sea, I landed with my clerk, and we took a delightful evening stroll, along one of the country roads, leading to the northern end of the island, and winding, occasionally, within a stone's throw of the beach. The air was soft, and filled with perfume, and we were much interested in inspecting the low-roofed and red-tiled country houses, and their half-naked inmates, of all colors, that presented themselves, from time to time, as we strolled on. We were here, as we had been in Maranham, objects of much curiosity, and the curiosity was evinced in the same way, respectfully. Wherever we stopped for water—for walking in this sultry climate produces constant thirst—the coolest "monkeys"—a sort of porous jug, or jar—and calabashes, were handed us, often accompanied by fruits and an invitation to be seated. Fields of sugar-cane stretched away on either hand, and an elaborate cultivation seemed everywhere to prevail. The island of Martinique is mountainous, and all mountainous countries are beautiful, where vegetation abounds. Within the tropics, when the soil is good, vegetation runs riot in very wantonness; and so it did here. The eye was constantly charmed with a great variety of shade and forest trees, of new and beautiful foliage, and with shrubs, and flowers, without number, ever forming new combinations, and new groups, as the road meandered now through a plane, and now through a rocky ravine, up whose precipitous sides a goat could scarcely clamber.

> "As the shades of eve came slowly down,
> The hills were clothed with deeper brown,"

and the twinkle of the lantern at the *Sumter's* peak denoting that her Captain was out of the ship, caught my eye, at one of the turnings of the road, and reminded me, that we had wandered far enough. We retraced our steps just in time to escape a shower, and sat down, upon our arrival on board, to the evening's repast, which John had prepared for us, with appetites much invigorated by the exercise. We found the market-place, situated near the ship, both upon landing and returning, filled with a curious throng, gazing eagerly upon the *Sumter*. This throng seemed never to abate during our stay—it was the first thing seen in the morning, and the last thing at night. The next morning, John brought me off a French newspaper; for St. Pierre is sufficiently large, and prosperous, to indulge in a tri-weekly. With true island marvel, a column was devoted to the *Sumter*, predicating of her, many curious exploits, and cunning devices by means of which she had escaped from the enemy, of which the little craft had never heard, and affirming, as a fact beyond dispute, that her Commander was a Frenchman, he having served, in former years, as a lieutenant on board of the French brig-of-war *Mercure!* I felt duly grateful for the compliment, for a compliment indeed it was, to be claimed as a Frenchman, *by* a Frenchman—the little foible of Gallic vanity considered.

Many rumors were now afloat as to the prospective presence, at Martinique, of the enemy's ships of war. It was known that the enemy's steam-sloop, *Iroquois*, Captain James S. Palmer, had been at the island of Trinidad, on the second of the then current month of November, whence she had returned to St. Thomas—this neutral island being unscrupulously used by the enemy, as a regular naval station, at which there was always at anchor one or more of his ships of war, and where he had a coal-depot. St. Thomas was a free port, and an important centre of trade, both for the West India Islands and the Spanish Main, and had the advantage, besides, of being a general rendezvous of the mail-steamers that plied in those seas. One of these steamers, bound to St. Thomas, had touched at Martinique, soon after the *Sumter's* arrival there, and, as a matter of course, we might expect the presence of the enemy very soon. I used every possible diligence to avoid being blockaded by the enemy, and twenty-four hours more would have enabled me to accomplish my purpose, but the Fates would have it otherwise; for at about two P. M., on the very next day after the delightful evening's stroll described in the last chapter, the *Iroquois* appeared off the north end of the island. She had purposely approached the

IN THE SHADOW OF MONT PELÉE 129

island on the side opposite to that on which the town of St. Pierre lies, the better to keep herself out of sight, until the last moment; and when she did come in sight, it was ludicrous to witness her appearance. Her commander's idea seemingly was, that the moment the *Sumter* caught sight of him, she would, if he were recognized, immediately attempt to escape. Hence it was necessary to surprise her; and to this end, he had made some most ludicrous attempts to disguise his ship. The Danish colors were flying from his peak, his yards were hanging, some this way, some that, and his guns had all been run in, and his ports closed. But the finely proportioned, taunt, saucy-looking *Iroquois*, looked no more like a merchant-ship, for this disguise, than a gay Lothario would look like a saint, by donning a cassock. The very disguise only made the cheat more apparent. We caught sight of the enemy first. He was crawling slowly from behind the land, which had hidden him from view, and we could see a number of curious human forms, above his rail, bending eagerly in our direction. The quarter-deck, in particular, was filled with officers, and we were near enough to see that some of these had telescopes in their hands, with which they were scanning the shipping in the harbor. We had a small Confederate States flag flying, and it was amusing to witness the movements on board the *Iroquois,* the moment this was discovered. A rapid passing to and fro of officers was observable, as if orders were being carried, in a great hurry, and the steamer, which had been hitherto cautiously creeping along, as a stealthy tiger might be supposed to skirt a jungle, in which he had scented, but not yet seen a human victim, sprang forward under a full head of steam. At the same moment, down came the Danish and up went the United States flag. "There she comes, with a bone in her mouth!" said the old quartermaster on the look-out; and, no doubt, Captain Palmer thought to see, every moment, the little *Sumter* flying from her anchors. But the *Sumter* went on coaling, and receiving on board some rum and sugar, as though no enemy were in sight, and at nine P. M. was ready for sea. The men were given their hammocks, as usual, and I turned in, myself, at my usual hour, not dreaming that the *Iroquois* would cut up such antics during the night as she did.

During the afternoon, she had run into the harbor,—without anchoring, however,—and sent a boat on shore to communicate, probably, with her consul, and receive any intelligence he might have to communicate. She then steamed off, seaward, a mile, or two, and moved to and fro, in front of the port until dark. At half-past one o'clock, the officer of the deck came down in great haste, to say, that the *Iroquois* had again entered the harbor, and was steaming directly for us. I ordered him to get the men immediately to their quarters, and followed him on deck, as soon as I could throw on a necessary garment or two. In a very few minutes, the battery had been cast loose, the decks lighted, and the other preparations usual for battle made. It was moonlight, and the movements of the enemy could be distinctly seen. He came along, under low steam, but, so steadily, and aiming so directly for us, that I could not doubt it was his intention to board us. The men were called to "repel boarders"; and for a moment or two, a pin might have been heard to drop, on the *Sumter's* deck, so silent was the harbor, and so still was the scene on board both ships. Presently, however, a couple of strokes on the enemy's steam gong were heard ["back engines slow"], and, in a moment more, he sheered a little, and lay off our quarter, motionless. It was as though a great sea-monster had crawled in under cover of the night, and was eying its prey, and licking its chops, in anticipation of a delicious repast. After a few minutes of apparent hesitation, and doubt, the gong was again struck ["ahead slow"], and the leviathan —for such the *Iroquois* appeared alongside the little *Sumter*—moving in a slow, and graceful curve, turned, and went back whence it came. This operation, much to my astonishment, was repeated several times during the night. . . .

The next morning, the Governor having heard of what had been done; how the neutral waters of France had been violated by manœuvre and by menace, though the actual attack had been withheld, sent up from Fort de France the steamer-of-war *Acheron*, Captain Duchatel, with orders to Captain Palmer, either to anchor, if he desired to enter the harbor, or to withdraw beyond the marine league, if it was his object to blockade the *Sumter;* annexing to his anchoring, if he should choose this alternative, the condition imposed by the laws of nations, of giving the *Sumter* twenty-four hours the start, in case she should desire to proceed to sea. Soon after the *Acheron* came to anchor, the *Iroquois* herself ran in and anchored. The French boat then communicated with her, when she immediately hove up her anchor again! She had committed herself to the twenty-four hours' rule the moment she dropped her

IN THE SHADOW OF MONT PELÉE

anchor; but being ignorant of the rule, she had not hesitated to get her anchor again, the moment that she was informed of it, and to claim that she was not bound by her mistake. I did not insist upon the point. The *Iroquois* now withdrew beyond the marine league, by day, but, by night, invariably crept in, a mile or two nearer, fearing that she might lose sight of me, and that I might thus be enabled to escape. She kept up a constant communication, too, with the shore, both by means of her own boats, and those from the shore, in violation of the restraints imposed upon her by the laws of nations—these laws requiring, that if she would communicate, she must anchor; when, of course, the twenty-four hours' rule would attach. I had written a letter to the Governor, informing him of the conduct of Captain Palmer, on the first night after his arrival, and claiming the neutral protection to which I was entitled. His Excellency having replied to this letter, through Captain Duchatel, in a manner but little satisfactory to me, I addressed him, through that officer, the following, in rejoinder:—

> CONFEDERATE STATES STEAMER SUMTER,
> ST. PIERRE, November 22, 1861.

SIR:—I have had the honor to receive your letter of yesterday, in which you communicate to me the views of the Governor of Martinique, relative to the protection of my right of asylum, in the waters of this island; and I regret to say, that those views do not appear to me to come up to the requirements of the international code. The Governor says, that "it does not enter into his intentions, to exercise toward the *Iroquois*, either by night, or by day, so active a *surveillance* as you [I] desire"; and you tell me, that I ought to have "confidence in the strict execution of a promise, made by a commander in the military marine of the American Union, so long as he has not shown to me the evidence that this engagement has not been scrupulously fulfilled." It would appear from these expressions, that the only protection I am to receive against the blockade of the enemy, is a simple promise exacted by you, from that enemy, that he will keep himself without the marine league, the Governor, in the meantime, exercising no watch, by night or by day, to see whether this promise is complied with. In addition to the violations of neutrality reported by me, yesterday, I have, this morning, to report, that one of my officers being on shore, in the northern environs of the town, last night, between eight and nine o'clock, saw two boats, each pulling eight oars, the men dressed in dark blue clothing, with the caps usually worn by the sailors of the Federal Navy, pulling quietly in toward the beach; and that he distinctly heard a conversation, in English, between them—one of them saying to the other, "Look Harry! there she is, I see her,"—in allusion, doubtless, to this ship. These boats are neither more nor less than scout, or sentinel boats, sent to watch the movements, within neutral waters, of their enemy. Now, with all due deference to his Excellency, I cannot see the difference between the violation of the neutrality of these waters, by the enemy's boats, and by his ship; and if no surveillance is to be exercised, either by night or by day, I am receiving very much such protection as the wolf would accord to the lamb.

It is an act of war for the enemy to approach me, with his boats, for the purpose of reconnoissance, or watch, and especially during the night, and I have the same right to demand that he keep his boats beyond the marine league, as that he keep his ship, at that distance. Nor am I willing to rely upon his promise, that he will not infringe my rights, in this particular. If France owes me protection, it is her duty to accord it to me, herself, and not remit me to the good faith, or bad faith, of my enemy; in other words, I respectfully suggest, that it is her *duty*, to exercise *surveillance* over her own waters, both "by night, and by day," when one belligerent is blockading another, in those waters. I have, therefore, respectfully to request, that you will keep a watch, by means of guard boats, at both points of the harbor, to prevent a repetition of the hostile act, which was committed against me last night; or if you will not do this, that you will permit me to arm boats, and capture the enemy, when so approaching me. It would seem quite plain, either that I should be protected, or be permitted to protect myself. Further: it is in plain violation of neutrality for the enemy to be in daily communication with the shore, whether by means of his own boats, or boats from the shore. If he needs supplies, it is his duty to come in for them; and if he comes in, he must anchor; and if he anchors, he must accept the condition of remaining twenty-four hours after my departure. It is a mere subterfuge for him to remain in the offing, and supply himself with all he needs, besides reconnoitring me, closely, by means of his boats, and I protest against this act also. I trust you will excuse me, for having occupied so much of your time, by so lengthy a communication, but I deem it my duty to place myself right, upon the record, in this matter. I shall seize an early opportunity to sail from these waters, and if I shall be brought to a bloody conflict, with an enemy, of twice my force, by means of signals given to him, in the

The *Sumter* RUNNING THE BLOCKADE OF ST. PIERRE, MARTINIQUE, BY THE ENEMY'S SHIP, *Iroquois,* ON NOVEMBER 23, 1861. The directions here are reversed from the real ones; and, of course, in order to have any picture at all, the visibility is represented as many times higher than it actually was.

From a lithograph by A. Hoen and Company, Baltimore

CAPTAIN J. S. PALMER, OF THE U.S.S. *Iroquois*
Born in 1810; died of yellow fever at St. Thomas, 1867

waters of France, either by his own boats, or others, I wish my Government to know, that I protested against the unfriendly ground assumed by the Governor of Martinique, that 'it does not enter into his intentions, to exercise toward the *Iroquois*, either by night, or by day, so active a surveillance as you [I] desire.'

MR. DUCHATEL, *commanding H. I. F. M's steamer Acheron.*"

As the lawyers say, "I took nothing by my motion," with Governor Condé. The United States were strong at sea, and the Confederate States weak, and this difference was sufficient to insure the ruling against me of all but the plainest points, about which there could be no dispute, either of principle, or of fact. Whilst the Governor would probably have protected me, by force, if necessary, against an actual assault, by the *Iroquois*, he had not the moral courage to risk the ire of his master, by offending the Great Republic, on a point about which there could be any question.

The *Iroquois* was very much in earnest in endeavoring to capture me, and Captain Palmer spent many sleepless nights, and labored very zealously to accomplish his object; notwithstanding which, when my escape became known to his countrymen, he had all Yankeeland down on him. It was charged, among other things, by one indignant Yankee captain, that Palmer and myself had been school-mates, and that treachery had done the work. I must do my late opponent the justice to say, that he did all that vigilance and skill could do, and a great deal more, than the laws of war authorized him to do. He made a free use of the neutral territory, and of his own merchant-ships that were within its waters. He had left St. Thomas in a great hurry, upon getting news of the *Sumter*, without waiting to coal. In a day or two after his arrival at St. Pierre, he chartered a Yankee schooner, and sent her to St. Thomas, for a supply of coal; and taking virtual possession of another—a small lumber schooner, from Maine, that lay discharging her cargo, a short distance from the *Sumter*—he used her as a signal, and look-out ship. Sending his pilot on shore, he arranged with the Yankee master—one of your long, lean, slab-sided fellows, that looked like the planks he handled—a set of signals, by which the *Sumter* was to be circumvented.

The anchorage of St. Pierre is a wide, open bay, with an exit around half the points of the compass. The *Iroquois*, as she kept watch and ward over the *Sumter*, generally lay off the centre of this sheet of water. As the *Sumter* might run out either north of her, or south of her, it was highly important that the *Iroquois* should know, as promptly as possible, which of the passages the little craft intended to take. To this end, the signals were arranged. Certain lights were to be exhibited, in certain positions, on board the Yankee schooner, to indicate to her consort, that the *Sumter* was under way, and the course she was running. I knew nothing, positively, of this arrangement. I only knew that the pilot of the *Iroquois* had frequently been seen on board the Yankee. To the mind of a seaman, the rest followed, as a matter of course. I could not know what the precise signals were, but I knew what signals I should require to be made to me, if I were in Captain Palmer's place. As the sequel will prove, I judged correctly.

I now communicated my suspicions to the Governor, and requested him to have a guard stationed near the schooner, to prevent this contemplated breach of neutrality. But the Governor paid no more attention to this complaint, than to the others I had made. It was quite evident that I must expect to take care of myself, without the exercise of any *surveillance,* "by night or by day," by Monsieur Condé. This being the case, I bethought myself of turning the enemy's signals to my own account, and the reader will see, by and by, how this was accomplished.

In the meantime, the plot was thickening, and becoming very interesting, as well to the islanders, as to ourselves. Not only was the town agog, but the simple country people, having heard what was going on, and that a naval combat was expected, came in, in great numbers, to see the show. The crowd increased, daily, in the market-place, and it was wonderful to witness the patience of these people. They would come down to the beach, and gaze at us for hours, together, seeming never to grow weary of the sight. Two parties were formed, the *Sumter* party, and the *Iroquois* party; the former composed of the whites, with a small sprinkling of blacks; the latter of the blacks, with a small sprinkling of whites. The Governor, himself, came up from Fort de France, in a little sail-schooner of war, which he used as a yacht. The Mayor, and sundry councilmen, came off to see me, and talk over the crisis. The young men boarded me in scores, and volunteered to help me whip the *barbare.* I had no thought of fighting, but of running; but of course I did not tell *them* so—I should have lost the French nationality, they had conferred upon me.

The *Iroquois* had arrived, on the 14th of November. It was now the 23d, and I had waited all this time, for a dark night; the moon not only persisting in shining, but the stars looking, we thought, unusually bright. Venus was still three hours high, at sunset, and looked provokingly beautiful, and brilliant, shedding as much light as a miniature moon. To-night—the 23d—the moon would not rise until seven minutes past eleven, and this would be ample time, in which to escape, or be captured. I had some anxiety about the weather, however, independently of the phase of the moon, as in this climate of the gods, there is no such thing as a dark night, if the sky be clear. The morning of the 23d of November dawned provokingly clear. It clouded a little toward noon, but, long before sunset, the clouds had blown off, and the afternoon became as bright, and beautiful, as the most ardent lover of nature in her smiling moods, could desire. But time pressed, and it was absolutely necessary to be moving. Messengers had been sent hither, and thither, by the enemy, to hunt up a reinforcement of gunboats, and if several of these should arrive, escape would be almost out of the question. Fortune had favored us, thus far, but we must now help ourselves. The *Iroquois* was not only twice as heavy as the *Sumter*, in men, and metal, as the reader has seen, but she had as much as two or three knots, the hour, the speed of her. We must escape, if at all, unseen of the enemy, and as the latter drew close in with the harbor, every night, in fraud of the promise he had made, and in violation of the laws of war, this would be difficult to do. Running all these reasons rapidly through my mind, I resolved to make the attempt, without further delay.

CHAPTER VIII

"Stand By to Cut!"

I GAVE ORDERS TO THE FIRST LIEUTENANT, TO see that every person belonging to the ship was on board, at sundown, and directed him to make all the necessary preparations for getting his anchor, and putting the ship under steam, at eight P. M.—the hour of gun-fire; the gun at the garrison to be the signal for moving. The ship was put in her best sailing trim, by removing some barrels of wet provisions aft, on the quarter-deck; useless spars were sent down from aloft, and the sails all "mended," that is, snugly furled. Every man was assigned his station, and the crew were all to be at quarters, a few minutes before the appointed hour of moving. I well recollect the *tout ensemble* of that scene. The waters of the bay were of glassy smoothness. The sun had gone down in a sky so clear, that there was not a cloud to make a bank of violets, or a golden pyramid of. Twilight had come and gone; the insects were in full chorus—we were lying within a hundred yards of the shore—and night, friendly, and at the same time unfriendly, had thrown no more than a semi-transparent mantle over the face of nature.

The market-place, as though it had some secret sympathy with what was to happen, was more densely thronged than ever, the hum of voices being quite audible. The muffled windlass on board the *Sumter* was quietly heaving up her anchor. It is already up, and the "cat hooked," and the men "walking away with the cat." The engineer is standing, lever in hand, ready to start the engine, and a seaman, with an uplifted axe, is standing near the taffarel, to cut the stern fast. One minute more and the gun will fire! Every one is listening eagerly for the sound. The *Iroquois* is quite visible, through our glasses, watching for the *Sumter*, like the spider for the fly. A flash! and the almost simultaneous boom of the eight o'clock gun, and, without one word being uttered on board the *Sumter*, the axe descends upon the fast, the engineer's lever is turned, and the ship bounds forward, under a full head of steam.

A prolonged, and deafening cheer at once arose from the assembled multitude, in the market-place. Skilful and trusty helmsmen, under the direction of the "master," bring the *Sumter's* head around to the south, where they hold it, so steadily, that she does not swerve a hair's breadth. There is not a light visible on board. The lantern in the captain's cabin has a jacket on it, and even the binnacle is screened, so that no one but the old quartermaster at the "con" can see the light, or the compass. The French steamer-of-war, *Acheron*, lay almost directly in our course, and, as we bounded past her, nearly grazing her guns, officers and men rushed to the side, and in momentary forgetfulness of their neutrality, waved hats and hands at us. As the reader may suppose, I had stationed a quick-sighted and active young officer, to look out for the signals, which I knew the Yankee schooner was to make. This young officer now came running aft to me, and said, "I see them, sir! I see them! —look, sir, there are two red lights, one above the other, at the Yankee schooner's mast-head." Sure enough, there were the lights; and I knew as well as the exhibitor of them, what they meant to say to the *Iroquois*, viz.: "Look out for the Sumter, she is under way, standing south!"

I ran a few hundred yards farther, on my present course, and then stopped. The island of Martinique is mountainous, and near the south end of the town, where I now was, the mountains run abruptly into the sea, and cast quite a shadow upon the waters, for some distance out. I had the advantage of operating within this shadow. I now directed my glass toward the *Iroquois*. I have said that Captain Palmer was anxious to catch me, and judging by the speed which the *Iroquois* was now making, toward the south, in obedience to her signals, his anxiety had not been at all abated by his patient watching of nine days. I now did, what poor Reynard sometimes does, when he is hard pressed by the hounds—I doubled. Whilst the *Iroquois* was driving, like mad, under all steam, for the south, wondering, no doubt, at every step, what the d——l had become of the *Sumter*, this little craft was doing her level-best, for the north end of the island. It is safe to say, that, the next morning, the two vessels were one hundred and fifty miles apart! Poor Palmer! he, no doubt, looked haggard and careworn, when his steward handed him his dressing-gown, and called him for breakfast on the 24th of November; the yell of Actæon's hounds must have sounded awfully distinct in his ears. I was duly thankful to the slab-sided lumberman, and to Governor Condé—the one for violating, and the other for permitting the violation of the neutral waters of France—the signals were of vast service to me.

Various little *contre-temps* occurred on board the *Sumter,* on this night's run. We were obliged to stop some fifteen or twenty precious minutes, opposite the very town, as we were retracing our steps to the northward, to permit the engineer to cool the bearings of his shaft, which had become heated by a little eccentricity of movement. And poor D., a hitherto-favorite quartermaster, lost his *prestige,* entirely, with the crew, on this night. D. had been famous for his sharp sight. It was, indeed, wonderful. When nobody else in the ship could "make out" a distant sail, D. was always sent aloft, glass in hand, to tell us all about her. As a matter of course, when the question came to be discussed, as to who the look-out should be, on the occasion of running by the enemy, I thought of D. He was, accordingly, stationed on the forecastle, with the best night-glass in the ship. Poor D.! if he saw one *Iroquois,* that night, he must have seen fifty. Once, he reported her lying right "athwart our fore-foot," and I even stopped the engine, on his report, and went forward, myself, to look for her. She was nowhere to be seen. Now she was bearing down upon our bow, and now upon our quarter. I was obliged to degrade him, in the first ten minutes of the run; and, from that time, onward, he never heard the last of the *Iroquois.* The young foretop-men, in particular, whose duty it was to take the regular look-out aloft, and who had become jealous of his being sent up to their stations, so often, to make out sails, which they could give no account of, were never tired of poking fun at him, and asking him about the *Iroquois.*

The first half hour's run was a very anxious one for us, as the reader may suppose. We could not know, of course, at what moment the *Iroquois,* becoming sensible of her error, might retrace her steps. It was a marvel, indeed, that she had not seen us. Our chimney was vomiting forth dense volumes of black smoke, that ought to have betrayed us, even if our hull had been invisible. I was quite relieved, therefore, as I saw the lights of the town fading, gradually, in the distance, and no pursuer near; and when a friendly rain squall overtook us, and enveloping us in its folds, travelled along with us, for some distance, I felt assured that our run had been a success. Coming up with the south end of the island of Dominica, we hauled in for the coast, and ran along it, at a distance of four or five miles. It was now half-past eleven, and the moon had risen. The sea continued smooth, and nothing could exceed the beauty of that night-scene, as we ran along this picturesque coast. The chief feature of the landscape was its weird-like expression, and aspect of most profound repose. Mountain, hill, and valley lay slumbering in the moonlight; no living thing, except ourselves, and now and then, a coasting vessel close in with the land, that seemed also to be asleep, being seen. Even the town of Rousseau, whose white walls we could see shimmering in the moonlight, seemed more like a city of the dead, than of the living. Not a solitary light twinkled from a window. To add to the illusion, wreaths of mist lay upon the mountain-sides, and overhung the valleys, almost as white, and solemn looking as winding-sheets.

We came up with the north end of Dominica, at about two A. M., and a notable change now took place, in the weather. Dense, black clouds rolled up, from every direction, and amid the crashing, and rattling of thunder, and rapid, and blinding lightning, the rain began to fall in torrents. I desired to double the north end of the island, and to enable me to do this, I endeavored, in sea phrase, to "hold on to the land." The weather was so thick, and dark, at times, that we could scarcely see the length of the ship, and we were obliged often to slow down, and even stop the engine. For an hour or two, we literally groped our way, like a blind man; an occasional flash of lightning being our only guide. Presently the water began to whiten, and we were startled to find that we were running on shore, in Prince Rupert's Bay, instead of having doubled the end of the island, as we had supposed. We hauled out in a hurry. It was broad daylight, before we were through the passage [between Dominica and Guadeloupe], when we were struck by a strong northeaster, blowing almost a gale. I now drew aft the try-sail sheets, and heading the ship to the N. N. W., went below and turned in, after, as the reader has seen, an eventful night. The sailor has one advantage over the soldier. He has always a dry hammock, and a comfortable roof over his head; and the reader may imagine how I enjoyed both of these luxuries, as stripping off my wet clothing, I consigned my weary head to my pillow, and permitted myself to be sung to sleep by the lullaby chanted by the storm.

The day after our escape from Martinique was Sunday, and we made it, emphatically, a day of rest—even the Sunday muster being omitted, in consideration of the crew having been kept up nearly all the preceding night. I slept late, nothing having been seen to render it necessary to call me. When I came on deck, the weather still looked angry, with a dense bank of rain-clouds hanging over the islands we had left, and the stiff northeaster blowing as freshly as before. We were now running by the island of Deseada [Desirade], distant about ten miles. At noon we observed in latitude 16° 12', and, during the day, we showed the French colors to a French bark, running for Guadeloupe, and to a Swedish brig standing in for the islands. Being in the track of commerce, and the night being dark, we carried, for the first time, our side-lights, to guard against collision. It was a delightful sensation to breathe the free air of heaven, and to feel the roll of the sea once more; and as I sat that evening, in the midst of my officers, and smoked my accustomed cigar, I realized the sense of freedom, expressed by the poet, in the couplet,—

> "Far as the breeze can bear, the billow foam,
> Survey our empire, and behold our home!"

We had no occasion, here, to discuss jurisdictions, or talk about marine leagues; or be bothered by *Iroquois,* or bamboozled by French governors.

Monday, November 25th.—Morning clear, with trade-clouds and a fresh breeze. We are still holding on to our steam, and are pushing our way to the eastward; my intention being to cross the Atlantic, and see what can be accomplished in European waters. We may be able to exchange the *Sumter* for a better ship. At seven, this morning, we gave chase to a Yankee-looking hermaphrodite brig. We showed her the United States colors, and were disappointed to see her hoist the English red in reply. In the afternoon, a large ship was descried running down in our direction. When she approached sufficiently near, we hoisted again the United States colors, and hove her to with a gun. As she rounded to the wind, in obedience to the signal, the stars and stripes were run up to her peak. The wind was blowing quite fresh, but the master and his papers were soon brought on board, when it appeared that our prize was the ship *Montmorency,* of Bath, Maine, from Newport, in Wales, and bound to St. Thomas, with a cargo of coal, for the English mail-steamers rendezvousing at that island. Her cargo being properly documented, as English property, we could not destroy her, but put her under a ransom bond, for her supposed value [$20,000], and released her. We received on board from her, however, some cordage and paints; and Captain Brown was civil enough to send me on board, with his compliments, some bottles of port wine and a box of excellent cigars. The master and crew were paroled, not to serve against the Confederate States during the war, unless exchanged.

The morning of the 26th of November dawned clear, with the wind more moderate, and a smoother sea. A ship of war being seen to windward, running down in our direction, we beat to quarters, and hoisted the U. S. colors. She was a heavy ship, but being a sailing vessel, we had nothing to fear, even if she should prove to be an enemy. Indeed, it would have been only sport for us, to fall in with one of the enemy's old time sailing-frigates. Our agile little steamer, with her single long-range gun, could have knocked her into pie, as the printers say, before the majestic old thing could turn round. It was in the morning watch, when holystones and sand, and scrubbing-brushes and soap were the order of the hour, and we surprised the stranger, consequently, in her morning dishabille, for her rigging was filled with scrubbed hammocks, and a number of well-filled clothes-lines were stretched between her main and mizzen shrouds. She proved to be Spanish; and was steering apparently for the island of Cuba. We observed to-day in latitude 20° 7'; the longitude, as told by our faithful chronometer, being 57° 12'. . . .

Soon after passing the Spanish ship, sail ho! was cried from the mast-head, in a sharp, energetic voice, as though the look-out had, this time, scented real game. The chase was one of those well-known schooners, twice before described in these pages, as being unmistakable—hence the energy that had been thrown into the voice of the look-out. She soon came in sight from the deck, when we gave chase. In a couple of hours we had come up with, and hove her to, with a gun. She proved to be the *Arcade,* from Portland, Me., with a load of staves, bound to Guadeloupe, where she intended to exchange her staves for rum and sugar. The owner of the staves had not thought it worth while to certify that his property was neutral, and so we had no difficulty with the papers. We had not made much of a prize. The little craft was sailed too economically to afford us even a spare barrel of provisions. The number of mouths on board were few, and the rations had been carefully adjusted to the mouths. And so, having nothing to transfer to the *Sumter,* except the master and crew, we applied the torch to her in a very few minutes. The staves being well seasoned, she made a beautiful bonfire, and lighted us over the seas some hours after dark.

During the night, the wind lulled, and became variable, and we hauled down the fore and aft sails, and brought the ship's head to the north-east. . . .

November 27th.—Morning thick, with heavy clouds and rain, clearing as the day advanced. Afternoon clear, bright weather, with a deep blue sea, and the trade-wind blowing half a gale from the north-east. At six P.M., put all sail on the ship, and let the steam go down. We had already consumed half our fuel, and it became necessary to make the rest of our way to Europe under sail. Our boilers had been leaking for several days, and the engineer availed himself of the opportunity to repair them. The weather is sensibly changing in temperature. We are in latitude 20° 22', and the thermometer has gone down to 78°—for the first time, in five months. We have crossed, to-day, the track of the homeward-bound ships, both from the Cape of Good Hope, and Cape Horn, but have seen no sail. We cannot delay to cruise in this track, as we have barely water enough, on board, to last us across the Atlantic.

November 28th.—Weather changeable, and squally—wind frequently shifting during the day, giving indications of our approach to the northern limit of the trade-wind, crossing which we shall pass into the variables.

November 29th.—Thick, ugly weather—this term ugly being very expressive in the seaman's vocabulary. The wind is veering, as before, blowing half a gale, all the time, and a cold rain is pouring down, at intervals, causing the sailors to haul on their woollen jackets, and hunt up their long-neglected sou'westers. We observed in latitude 25° 51' to-day; the longitude being 57° 36'.

November 30th.—The morning has dawned bright, and beautiful, with a perfectly clear sky. The boisterous wind of yesterday has disappeared, and we have nearly a calm—the sea wearing its darkest tint of azure. We are, in fact, in the calm-belt of Cancer, and having no fuel to spare, we must be content to creep through it under sail, as best we may. A sail has been reported from aloft. It is a long way off, and we forbear to chase.

December 1st.—Another beautiful, bright, morning, with a glassy sea, and a calm. This being the first of the month, the sailors are drawing their clothing, and "small stores" from the paymaster, under the supervision of the officers of the different divisions. The paymaster's steward is the shopman, on the occasion, and he is "serving" a jacket to one, a shirt to another, and a pair of shoes to a third. His assortment is quite varied, for besides the requisite clothing, he has tobacco, and pepper, and mustard; needles, thimbles, tape, thread, and spool-cotton; ribbons, buttons, jack-knives, &c. Jack is not allowed to indulge in all these luxuries, *ad lib*. He is like a school-boy, under the care of his preceptor; he must have his wants approved by the officer of the division to which he belongs. To enable this officer to act understandingly, Jack spreads out his wardrobe before him, every month. If he is deficient a shirt, or a pair of trousers, he is permitted to draw them; if he has plenty, and still desires more, his extravagance is checked. These articles are all charged to him, at cost, with the addition of a small percentage, to save the Government from loss. When the monthly requisitions are all complete, they are taken to the Captain, for his approval, who occasionally runs his pencil through a *third*, or a *fourth* pound of tobacco, when an inveterate old chewer, or smoker is using the weed to excess; he rarely interferes in other respects. On the present occasion, woollen garments are in demand; Jack, with a prudent forethought, preparing himself for the approaching change in the climate. Much of the clothing, which the sailor wears, is made up with his own hands. He is entirely independent of the other sex, in this respect, and soon becomes very expert with the needle.

The 3d of December brought us another prize. The wind was light from the south-east, and the stranger was standing in our direction. This was fortunate, as we might hope to capture him by stratagem, without the use of steam. The *Sumter*, when not under steam, and with her smoke-stack lowered, might be taken for a clumsy-looking bark. Throwing a spare sail over the lowered smoke-stack, to prevent it from betraying us, we hoisted the French flag, and stood on our course, apparently unconscious of the approaching stranger. We were running free, with the starboard studding-sails set, and when the stranger, who, by this time, had hoisted the United States colors, crossed our bows, we suddenly took in all the studding-sails, braced sharp up, tacked, and fired a gun, at the same moment. The stranger at once hauled up his courses, and backed his main-topsail. He was already under our guns. The clumsy appearance of the *Sumter*, and the French flag had deceived him. The prize proved to be the *Vigilant*, a fine new ship, from Bath, Maine, bound to the guano island of Sombrero, in the West Indies; some New Yorkers having made a lodgment on this barren little island, and being then engaged in working it for certain phosphates of lime, which they called mineral guano. We captured a rifled 9-pounder gun, with a supply of fixed ammunition, on board the *Vigilant*, and some small arms. We fired the ship at three P.M., and made sail on our course. The most welcome part of this capture was a large batch of New York newspapers, as late as the 21st of November. The Yankees of that ilk had heard of the blockade of the "Pirate *Sumter*," by the *Iroquois*, but they had n't heard of Captain Palmer's rueful breakfast on the morning of the 24th of November.

December 4th.—Weather clear, and becoming cool—thermometer, 76°. We have run some 140 miles to the eastward, during the last twenty-four hours, under sail, and as we are dragging our propeller through the water, I need not tell the reader what a smacking breeze we have had. It is delightful to be making so much easting, under sail, after having been buffeted so spitefully, by the east wind, for the last five months, whenever we have turned our head in that direction. Ten of the crew of the *Vigilant* are blacks, and as our ship is leaking so badly that the constant pumping is fagging to the crew, I have set the blacks at the pumps, with their own consent. The fact is, some of these fellows, who are runaway slaves, have already recognized "master," and whenever I pass them, grin pleasantly, and show the whites of their eyes. They are agreeably disappointed, that they are not "drawn, hung, and quartered," and rather enjoy the change to the *Sumter*, where they have plenty of time to bask in the sun, and the greasiest of pork and beans without stint. In arranging the *Vigilant's* crew

"STAND BY TO CUT!"

into messes, a white bean and a black bean have been placed, side by side, at the mess-cloth, my first lieutenant naturally concluding, that the white sailors of the Yankee ship would like to be near their colored brethren. Cæsar and Pompey, having an eye to fun, enjoy this arrangement hugely, and my own crew are not a little amused, as the boatswain pipes to dinner, to see the gravity with which the darkies take their seats by the side of their white comrades. This was the only mark of "citizenship," however, which I bestowed upon these sons of Ham. I never regarded them as prisoners of war—always discharging them, when the other prisoners were discharged, without putting them under parole.

[There were several points of international law that came up during the *Iroquois* episode and they can best be taken up at this juncture. First as to the general question of a belligerent man-of-war's duration of stay in a neutral port and, analogously, the frequency of visit. It was not until the First World War that the regulations of such visits were strictly enforced. At the same time there can be no question but that the several neutrals were not justified in permitting the virtually unlimited visits of the *Sumter* (ten days, for instance, in St. Pierre and fourteen in Martinique altogether). Likewise it was not legal for the *Iroquois* to make so many separate entries into territorial waters at St. Pierre; for Semmes was correct in holding that the visits of her boats were the equivalent of visits of the *Iroquois* herself.

[On the other hand there is no general obligation upon a belligerent man-of-war to remain in port any *longer* than she desires, or even to drop anchor while in the harbor. Of course if the *Sumter* had stood out ahead of the *Iroquois* on one of the occasions when the latter was inside, then the French would have been obliged to prevent the *Iroquois* from following until twenty-four hours later. This event, however, did not come to pass. When the *Iroquois* entered the harbor at night, steamed around, and then departed, she probably violated harbor regulations but little else.

[Although in 1861 it was not considered particularly serious for a belligerent man-of-war to remain for an indefinite period in a neutral port under ordinary circumstances, the appearance of the *Iroquois* to blockade the *Sumter* made a great difference. It brought a very much stronger obligation upon the neutral authorities to cause the *Sumter* either to depart within a reasonable time or be interned. If the law had been as it is at present, she would probably have been allowed a period of twenty-four hours after she was fit to leave; this would make thirty-one hours after the *Iroquois'* appearance. Instead of this, the *Sumter* simply stayed on for nine additional days until she had a moonless night for her escape.

[The signalling from the harbor to the *Iroquois* was of course a breach of neutrality. This act, however, instead of assisting in the *Sumter's* capture, was the most important factor in her escape—thanks to the clever tactics of Semmes. As pointed out on an earlier occasion, no neutral should have supplied the *Sumter* with coal which was to be used for operations against the enemy.

[When the word of the *Sumter's* escape reached Washington, Secretary of the Navy Welles "hit the ceiling" and ordered Commander Palmer to be relieved of his command of the *Iroquois*. No one could justly be held at fault, however. On a dark night it is practically impossible without searchlights to spot a darkened ship under the land, at even an appreciable fraction of the distance separating the two vessels in this case. Without violating French neutrality the only chance the *Iroquois* had of sighting the *Sumter* was to get close enough to her either by design or by guesswork. When cooler counsel prevailed in the Navy Department—which was soon—Palmer was restored to his command; in fact, he was out for less than four months. Almost immediately he and his ship distinguished themselves under Farragut during the course of operations in the Mississippi River, especially before Vicksburg. Only three months after Palmer regained his ship he was promoted to captain and given command of the flagship *Hartford*. He became commodore before the end of the war and rear admiral afterwards. Torpedo-boat destroyer No. 161, sunk in World War II, was named for him.]

CHAPTER IX

The North Atlantic in December

DECEMBER 5th.—WEATHER THICK AND UGLY—the wind hauling to the north, and blowing very fresh for a while. Reefed the topsails. At noon, the weather was so thick, that no observations could be had for fixing the position of the ship—latitude, by dead reckoning, 30° 19′; longitude 53° 02′. During the afternoon and night, it blew a gale from N. E. to E. N. E. Furled the mainsail, and set the reefed trysail instead; and the wind still increasing, before morning we hauled up and furled the foresail. For the next two or three days, we had a series of easterly gales, compelling me to run somewhat farther north than I had intended. We carried very short sail, and most of the time we were shut down below—that is, such of the crew as were not on watch—with tarpaulin-covered hatches, and a cold, driving rain falling almost incessantly. What with the howling of the gale, as it tears through the rigging, the rolling and pitching of the ship, in the confused, irregular sea, and the jog, jog, jog of the pumps, through half the night, I have had but little rest.

December 8th.—At ten A.M. descried a sail from the deck, startlingly close to; so thick has been the weather. The stranger being a bark, taunt-rigged, with skysail poles, and under top-sails, we mistook him at first for a cruiser, and raised our smoke-stack, and started the fires in the furnaces. Having done this, we approached him somewhat cautiously, keeping the weather-guage of him, and showed him the United States colors. He soon hoisted the same. Getting a nearer view of him, we now discovered him to be a whaler. The engineer at once discontinued his "firing up," and the smoke-stack was again lowered, to its accustomed place. Upon being boarded, the bark proved to be the *Eben Dodge,* twelve days out, from New Bedford, and bound on a whaling voyage to the Pacific Ocean. She had experienced a heavy gale, had sprung some of her spars, and was leaking badly—hence the easy sail she had been under. Although the sea was still very rough, and the weather lowering, we got on board from the prize, some water, and provisions, clothing, and small stores. The supply of pea-jackets, whalers' boots, and flannel over-shirts, which our paymaster had been unable to procure in the West Indies, was particularly acceptable to us, battling, as we now were, with the gales of the North Atlantic, in the month of December. We brought away from her, also, two of her fine whale-boats, so valuable in rough weather; making room for them on deck, by the side of the *Sumter's* launch. The crew of the *Dodge,* consisting of twenty-two persons, made a considerable addition to our small community. We fired the prize at half-past six, P.M., as the shades of evening were closing in, and made sail on our course. The flames burned red and lurid in the murky atmosphere, like some Jack-o'-lantern; now appearing, and now disappearing, as the doomed ship rose upon the top, or descended into the abyss of the waves.

Having now forty-three prisoners on board, and there never being, at one time, so many of the *Sumter's* crew on watch, it became necessary for me to think of precautions. It would be easy for forty-three courageous men, to rise upon a smaller number, sleeping carelessly about the decks, and wrest from them the command of the ship. Hitherto I had given the prisoners the run of the ship, putting no more restrictions upon them, than upon my own men, but this could no longer be. I therefore directed my first lieutenant to put one-half of the prisoners in single irons—that is, with manacles on the wrists only—alternately, for twenty-four hours at a time. The prisoners, themselves, seeing the necessity of this precaution, submitted cheerfully to the restraint—for as such only they viewed it—and not as an indignity. . . .

December 10th.—The weather remains still unsettled. The wind, during the last five or six days, has gone twice around the compass, never stopping in the west, but lingering in the east. The barometer has been in a constant state of fluctuation, and there will doubtless, be a grand climax before the atmosphere regains its equilibrium. These easterly winds are retarding our passage very

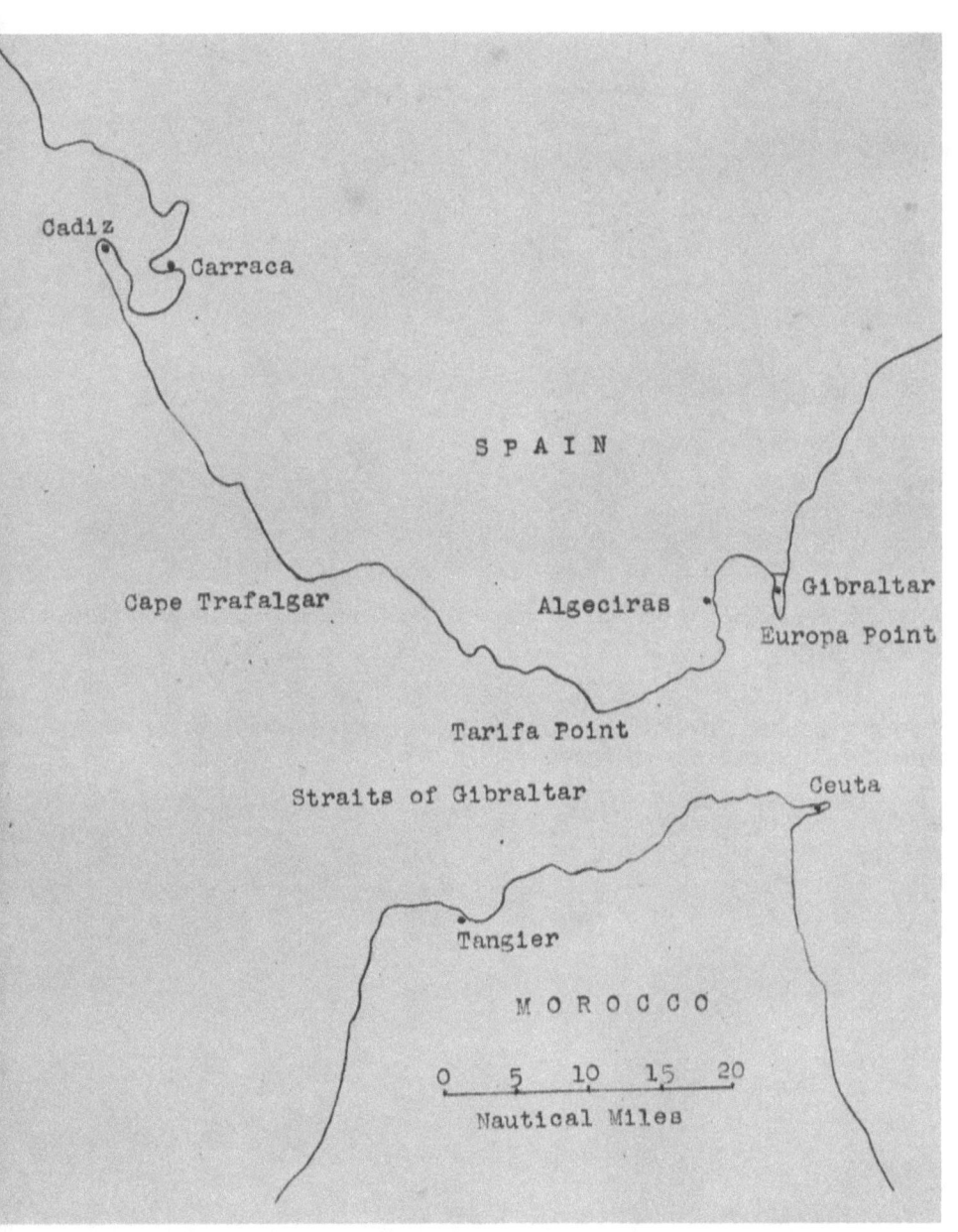

GIBRALTAR AND VICINITY

THE U.S. STEAM SLOOP-OF-WAR *Tuscarora*. She helped keep the *Sumter* bottled up in Gibraltar.

SEMMES'S NEMESIS, THE U.S.S. *Kearsage*. She helped blockade the *Sumter* in Gibraltar; she sank the *Alabama*.

much, and taxing our patience. Observed, to-day, in latitude 32° 39′; the longitude being 49° 57′.

The next day, the weather culminated, sure enough, in a gale. The barometer began to settle, in the morning watch, and dense black clouds, looking ragged and windy, soon obscured the sun, and spread an ominous pall over the entire heavens. I at once put the ship under easy sail; that is to say, clewed up everything but the topsails and trysails, and awaited the further progress of the storm. The wind was as yet light, but the barometer, which had stood at 29.70 at eight o'clock, had fallen to 29.59 by two P.M. The dense canopy of clouds now settled lower and lower, circumscribing more and more our horizon, and presently fitful gusts of wind would strike the sails, pressing the ship over a little. It was time to reef. All hands were turned up, and the close reefs were taken, both in topsails and trysails; the jib hauled down and stowed, and the top-gallant yards sent down from aloft. The squalls increasing in frequency and force, the gale became fully developed by three P.M. The wind, which we first took from about E. S. E., backed to the N. E., but did not remain long in that quarter, returning to east. It now began to blow furiously from this latter quarter, the squalls being accompanied by a driving, blinding rain; the barometer going down, ominously down, all the while.

As the night closed in, an awful scene presented itself. The aspect of the heavens was terrific. The black clouds overhead were advancing and retreating like squadrons of opposing armies, whilst loud peals of thunder, and blinding flashes of lightning that would now and then run down the conductor, and hiss as they leaped into the sea, added to the elemental strife. A streaming scud, which you could almost touch with your hand, was meanwhile hurrying past, screeching and screaming, like so many demons, as it rushed through the rigging. The sea was mountainous, and would now and then strike the little *Sumter* with such force as to make her tremble in every fibre of her frame. I had remained on deck during most of the first watch, looking anxiously on, to see what sort of weather we were going to make. The ship behaved nobly, but I had no confidence in her strength. Her upper works, in particular, were very defective. Her bends, above the main deck, were composed of light pine stanchions and inch plank, somewhat strengthened in the bows. Seeing the fury of the gale, and that the barometer was still settling, I went below about midnight, and turned in to get a little rest, with many misgivings. I had scarcely fallen into an uneasy slumber, when an old quartermaster, looking himself like the demon of the storm, with his dishevelled hair and beard dripping water, and his eyes blinking in the light of his lantern, shook my cot, and said, "We've stove in the starboard bow-port, sir, and the gun-deck is all afloat with water!" Here was what I had feared; unless we could keep the water out of the between-decks, all the upper works, and the masts along with them, would be gone in a trice. I hurried at once to the scene of disaster, but before I could reach it, my energetic and skilful first lieutenant had already, by the aid of some planks and spare spars, erected a barricade that would be likely to answer our purpose.

The gale lulled somewhat in an hour or two afterward, and I now got some sleep. I was on deck again, however, at daylight. The same thick gloom overspread the heavens, the scud was flying as furiously, and as low as before, and the gale was raging as fiercely as ever. But we had one great comfort, and that was *daylight*. We could see the ship and the heavens—there was nothing else visible—and this alone divested the gale of half its terrors. At last, at six A.M., the barometer reached its lowest point, 29.32, which, in the latitude we were in, was a very low barometer. Any one who has watched a barometer under similar circumstances, will understand the satisfaction with which I saw the little telltale begin to rise. It whispered to me as intelligibly as if it had been a living thing, "the gale is broken!" We had been lying to, all this time, under a close-reefed main-topsail. We now bore up under a reefed foresail, and kept the ship on her course, east by south. She scudded as beautifully as she had lain to, darting ahead like an arrow, on the tops of the huge waves that followed her like so many hungry wolves, and shaking the foam and spray from her bows, as if in disdain and contempt of the lately howling storm.

December 13th.—Weather clear, with passing clouds. Wind fresh from the south-west, but abating, with a rapidly rising barometer. The cyclone, for such evidently the late gale was, had a diameter of from three hundred and fifty to four hundred miles. We took it in its northern hemisphere—the gale travelling north. Hence it passed over us in nearly its entire diameter—the vortex at no great distance from us. Observed in latitude 33° 28'; the longitude being

47° 03'. Repairing damages. The ship leaks so badly as to require to be pumped out twice in each watch. During the heaviest of the gale, the masters and mates of the captured ships offered their services, like gallant men, to assist in taking care of the ship. We thanked them, but were sufficiently strong-handed ourselves.

December 14th.—We had an alarm of fire on the berth deck last night. The fire-bell, sounded suddenly in a sleeping city, has a startling effect upon the aroused sleepers, but he who has not heard it, can have no conception of the knell-like sound of the cry of fire! shouted from the lungs of an alarmed sailor on board a ship, hundreds of miles away from any land. It is the suddenness with which the idea of danger presents itself, quite as much as the extent of the danger, which intimidates. Hence the panics which often ensue, when a ship is discovered to be on fire. Ships of war, as a rule, are not the subjects of panics. Discipline keeps all the passions and emotions under control, as well those which arise from fear, as from lawlessness. We had no panic on board the *Sumter,* although appearances were sufficiently alarming for a few moments. A smoke was suddenly seen arising through one of the ventilators forward, in the dead hour of the night, when except the sentry's lantern and the lamp in the binnacle, there should be no other fire in the ship. The midshipman of the watch, upon rushing below, found one of the prisoners' mattresses on fire. The flames were soon smothered, and the whole danger was over before the ship's crew were fairly aroused. Some prisoner, in violation of orders, had lighted his pipe for a smoke, after hours, and probably gone to sleep with it in his mouth. The prisoner could not be identified, but there were two sentinels on post, and these in due time paid the penalty of their neglect.

The punishment administered to the two delinquent sentinels . . . had the most salutary effect. Seamen are very much like children, requiring the reins to be tightened upon them from time to time. I made it a rule on board the *Sumter,* that punishment should follow the offence, with *promptitude,* and *certainty,* rather than severity; and this excellent rule had already performed marvels, in the matter of disciplining my ship.

Sunday, December 15th.—A fine bright morning, with a moderate breeze from the north-west, and the weather just cool enough to be delightfully bracing. We mustered the crew this morning, and read the articles of war for the first time in three weeks, owing to the bad weather. I did not inspect the ship below, according to custom, the sea being still rough, and the water ankle-deep on the gun-deck in consequence. Our new prisoners always looked upon the muster ceremonies on board the *Sumter*, with curiosity, as though they were surprised to find so much order and discipline, and so much attention to dress and ceremony, on board the "pirate" of which they had read, and whose "cut" they had so often admired, in their truth-loving and truth-telling newspapers. The latitude, today, is 34°, and the longitude 42° 05'.

We were quite surprised to find so much bad weather in the parallel, on which we were crossing the Atlantic. I had purposely chosen this parallel, that my little cock-boat of a ship might not be knocked in pieces, by the storms of the North Atlantic, and yet the reader has seen how roughly we have been handled. Nor were the fates more propitious for the next few days. Gale followed gale, with angry skies, and cloud and rain; there sometimes being lightning around the entire horizon, with now rolling, now crashing thunder. I had intended when I left the West Indies to touch at Fayal, in the Azores, for coal and water, but I found these islands so guarded and defended, by the Genius of the storm, that it would require several days of patience and toil, to enable me to reach an anchorage in one of them. I therefore determined to pass them, and haul up for the southern coast of Spain, running finally into Cadiz.

Christmas day was passed by us on the lonely sea, in as doleful a manner as can well be conceived. The weather is thus described in my journal. "Thermometer 63°; barometer 29.80. Heavy rain squalls—weather dirty, with lightning all around the horizon, indicating a change of wind at any moment. Under short sail during the night." The only other record of the day was that we "spliced the main brace;" that is, gave Jack an extra glass of grog. Groups of idle sailors lay about the decks, "overhauling a range of their memories"; how they had spent the last Christmas-day, in some "Wapping," or "Wide Water street," with the brimming goblet in hand, and the merry music of the dance sounding in their ears. Nor were the memories of the officers idle. They clasped in fancy their loved ones, now sad and lonely, to their bosoms once more, and listened to the prattle of the little ones they had left behind. Not the least curious of the changes that had taken place since the last Christmas day, was the change in their own official positions.

They were, most of them, on that day, afloat under the "old flag." That flag now looked to them strange and foreign. They had some of their own countrymen on board; not, as of yore, as welcome visitors, but as prisoners. These, too, wore a changed aspect—enemy, instead of friend, being written upon their faces. . . .

On the next day, we witnessed a curious natural illusion. The look-out called land ho! from the mast-head. The officer of the watch saw the land at the same time from the deck, and sent a midshipman below to inform me that we had made "high land, right ahead." I came at once upon deck, and there, sure enough, was the land—a beautiful island, with its blue mountains, its plains, its wood-lands, its coast, all perfect. It was afternoon. The weather had been stormy, but had partially cleared. The sun was near his setting, and threw his departing rays full upon the newly discovered island, hanging over it, as a symbol that, for a time, there was to be a truce with the storm, a magnificent rainbow. So beautiful was the scene, and so perfect the illusion—there being no land within a couple of hundred miles of us—that all the crew had come on deck to witness it; and there was not one of them who would not have bet a month's pay that what he looked upon was a reality.

The chief engineer was standing by me looking upon the supposed landscape, with perfect rapture. Lowering the telescope through which I had been viewing it, I said to him, "You see, now, Mr. F., how often men are deceived. You would no doubt swear that that is land." "Why should I not, sir?" said he. "Simply," rejoined I, "because it is Cape Flyaway." He turned and looked at me with astonishment, as though I were quizzing him, and said, "You surely do not mean to say, Captain, that that is not land; it is not possible that one's senses can be so much deceived." "Like yourself, I should have sworn it was land, if I did not know, from the position of the ship, that there is no land within a couple of hundred miles of us." Reaching out his hand for my glass, I gave it to him, and as he viewed the island through it, I was much amused at his ejaculations of admiration, now at this beauty, and now at that. "Why," said he, "there is the very coast, sand beach and all, with beautiful bays and indentations, as though inviting the *Sumter* to run in and anchor." As the sun sank lower and lower, withdrawing now one ray, and now another, first the rainbow began to disappear, and then the lower strata of the island to grow a little gray, and then the upper, until, as the sun dipped, the whole gorgeous fabric, of mountain, woodland, plain, and coast, was converted into a leaden-colored cloud-bank. The engineer handing me my glass, said, "Captain, I will be a cautious witness hereafter, in a court of justice, when I am questioned as to a fact, which has only been revealed to me through a single sense." "I see," I replied, "that you are becoming a philosopher. Many metaphysicians have maintained that all nature is a mere phantasmagoria, so far as our senses are capable of informing us."

For the last two weeks, we had been crossing a desert tract of the ocean, where a sail is seldom seen. We now began to approach one of the beaten highways, over which a constant stream of travel is passing—the road leading from the various ports of Europe to the equator and the coast of Brazil, and thence east and west, as may be the destination of the wayfarer.

December 28th.—A fine, bright day, with the wind light from the south-west. At daylight, "Sail ho!" came ringing from the mast-head. The sail crossing our bows, we took in our studding-sails, hauled up south-east, to intercept her, and got up steam. Our latitude being 35° 17′, and longitude 20° 53′, we were within striking distance of Cadiz or Gibraltar, and could afford now to use a little steam. The chase did not reward us, however, as she proved to be English—being the ship *Richibucto,* from Liverpool, for Vera Cruz, laden with salt. We received from her some English newspapers, which gave us several items of interesting intelligence. All England was in mourning for the death of Prince Albert. The *Trent* affair was causing great excitement, and the Confederate States steamer *Nashville,* Captain Pegram, had arrived at Southampton, having burned a large Yankee ship, the *Harvey Birch.* This ship having been burned in the English Channel, much attention was attracted to the act; especially as the ship was tea-laden, and supposed to be worth near half a million of dollars.

The next day was rainy, with a light wind from the south-east. Only two sails were seen, and to neither of them did we give chase; but on the morning of the 30th of December, we fell in with a perfect stream of ships. "Sail ho!" was shouted at daylight from the mast-head, and repeated at short intervals, until as many as twenty-five were reported. We at once got up steam, and commenced chasing; but though we chased diligently, one ship after another, from eight o'clock in the morning until four in the afternoon, we did not overhaul a single ship of the enemy! We actually boarded sixteen sail, a number of others showing us their colors. The ships boarded were of the following nationalities:—Four Dutch, seven English, two French, one Swedish, one Prussian, one Hamburg. Here was quite a representation of the nations of Europe, and I amused myself taking the vote of these ships, according to our American fashion, upon the war. Their sentiments were elicited as follows:—I would first show them the United States colors, pretending to be a Federal cruiser; I would then haul down these colors, and show them the Confederate flag. The result was that but one ship—the Prussian—saluted the United States flag, and that all the other ships, with one or two exceptions, saluted the Confederate States flag. We were then beating the enemy, and the nations of the earth were worshipping success.

So large a fleet of ships—not being a convoy—so far out at sea, was quite a curiosity, and may serve to show the landsman how accurately we have mapped out, upon the ocean, the principal highways of commerce. There were no mile-posts on the road these ships were travelling, it is true, but the road was none the less "blazed" out, for all that—the blazes being on the wind and current charts. The night succeeding this busy day set in cloudy and ugly, with a fresh breeze blowing from the eastward; and so continuous was the stream of ships, all sailing in the contrary direction from ourselves, that we had serious apprehensions of being run over. To guard against this, we set our side-lights, and stationed extra lookouts. Several ships passed us during the night, hurrying forward on the wings of the wind, at a rapid rate, and sometimes coming so close, in the darkness, as almost to make one's hair stand on end. The next morning the weather became clear and beautiful, and the stream of ships had ceased.

The reader may be curious to know the explanation of this current of ships. It is simple enough. They were all Mediterranean ships. At the strait of Gibraltar there is a constant current setting into the Mediterranean. This current is of considerable strength, and the consequence is, that when the wind also sets into the strait—that is to say, when it is from the westward—it is impossible for a sailing-ship to get out of the strait into the Atlantic. She is obliged to come to anchor in the bay of Gibraltar, and wait for a change of wind. This is sometimes a long time in coming—the westerly winds continuing here, not unfrequently, two and three weeks at a time. As a matter of course, a large number of ships collect in the bay, waiting for an opportunity of exit. I have seen as many as a hundred sail at one time. In a few hours after a change of wind takes place, this immense fleet will all be under way, and such of them as are bound to the equator and the coast of Brazil, the United States, West Indies, and South America, will be found travelling the blazed road of which I have spoken; some taking the forks of the road, at their respective branching-off places, and others keeping the main track to the equator. Hence the exodus the reader has witnessed.

Perhaps the reader needs another explanation—how it was, that amid all that fleet of ships, there was not one Yankee. This explanation is almost as easy as the other. Commerce is a sensitive plant, and at the rude touch of war it had contracted its branches. The enemy was fast losing his Mediterranean trade, under the operation of high premiums for war risks.

We began now to observe a notable change in the weather, as affected by the winds. Along the entire length of the American coast, the clear winds are the west winds, the rain-winds being the east winds. Here the rule is reversed; the west winds bringing us rains, and the east winds clear weather. The reason is quite obvious. The east winds, sweeping over the continent of Europe, have nearly all of their moisture wrung out of them before they reach the sea; hence the dryness of these winds, when they salute the mariner cruising along the European coasts. . . . The change was very curious to us at first, until we became a little used to it.

Another change was quite remarkable, and that was the great difference in temperature which we experienced with reference to latitude. Here we were, in midwinter, or near it, off the south coast of Spain, in latitude 36°, nearly that of Cape Henry at the entrance of the Chesapeake Bay, and unless the weather was wet, we had not felt the necessity of a pea-jacket. . . .

[The effects of the Gulf Stream which crosses the North Atlantic and (in part) flows down the coast of Europe.]

December 31st.—The last day of the year, as though it would atone to us for some of the bad weather its previous days had given us, is charming. There is not a cloud, as big as a man's hat, anywhere to be seen, and the air is so elastic that it is a positive pleasure to breathe it. The temperature is just cool enough to be comfortable, though the wind is from the north. At daylight, a couple of sail were reported from aloft, but, as they were at a great distance, and out of our course, we did not chase. Indeed, we have become quite discouraged since our experience of yesterday. A third sail was seen at noon, also at a great distance. These are probably the laggards of the great Mediterranean wind-bound fleet. We observed, to-day, in latitude 35° 22'; the longitude being 16° 27'. It becoming quite calm at eight P. M., I put the ship under steam; being about 490 miles from Cadiz.

January 1st, 1862.—Nearly calm; wind light from the south-west, and sky partially overcast. The sea is smooth, and we are making nine knots, the hour. We made an excellent run during the past night, and are approaching the Spanish coast very rapidly. Nothing seen during the day. At nine P. M. a sail passed us, a gleam of whose light we caught for a moment in the darkness. The light being lost almost as soon as seen, we did not attempt to chase. Latitude 35° 53'; longitude 13° 14'.

On the next day we overhauled a French, and a Spanish ship. It had been my intention, when leaving Martinique, to cruise a few days off Cadiz, before entering the port, and for this purpose I had reserved a three days' supply of fuel; but, unfortunately, the day before our arrival we took another gale of wind, which shook us so severely, that the ship's leak increased very rapidly; the engineer reporting that it was as much as he could do to keep her free, with the bilge pumps, under short steam. The leak was evidently through the sleeve of the propeller, and was becoming alarming. I therefore abandoned the idea of cruising, and ran directly for the land. Night set in before anything could be seen, but having every confidence in my chronometers, I ran without any hesitation for the Light, although we had been forty-one days at sea, without testing our instruments by a sight of land. We made the light—a fine Fresnel, with a red flash—during the mid-watch, and soon afterward got soundings. We now slowed down the engine, and ran in by the lead, until we judged ourselves four or five miles distant from the light, when we hove to. The next morning revealed Cadiz, fraught with so many ancient, and modern memories, in all its glory, though the weather was gloomy and the clouds dripping rain.

"Fair Cadiz, rising o'er the dark blue sea!"

as Byron calls thee, thou art indeed lovely! with thy white Moresque-looking houses, and gayly curtained balconies, thy church-domes which carry us back in architecture a thousand years, and thy harbor thronged with shipping. Once the Gades of the Phœnician, now the Cadiz of the nineteenth century, thou art perhaps the only living city that can run thy record back so far into the past.

We fired a gun, and hoisted a jack for a pilot, and one boarding us soon afterward, we steamed into the harbor. The Confederate States' flag was flying from our peak, and we could see that there were many curious telescopes turned upon us, as we passed successively the forts and the different quays lined with shipping. As the harbor opened upon us, a magnificent spectacle presented itself. On our left was the somewhat distant coast of Andalusia, whose name is synonymous with all that is lovely in scenery, or beautiful in woman. One almost fancies as he looks upon it, that he hears the amorous tinkle of the guitar, and inhales the fragrance of the orange grove. Seville is its chief city, and who has not read the couplet,

> "Quien no ha visto Sevilla
> No ha visto maravilla,"

which may be rendered into the vernacular thus:

> "He who hath not Seville seen,
> Hath not seen wonders, I ween."

The landscape, still green in mid-winter, was dotted with villas and villages, all white, contrasting prettily with the groves in which they were embowered. Casting the eye forward, it rested upon the picturesque hills of the far-famed wine district of Xeres, with its vineyards, wine-presses, and pack-mules. Some famous old wine estates were pointed out to us by the pilot.

We ran through a fleet of shipping before reaching our anchorage off the main quay, the latter lined on both sides with market-boats; and as much more shipping lay beyond us. I was, indeed, quite surprised to find the harbor, which is spacious, so thronged. It spoke well for the reviving industry of Spain. With a little fancy one might imagine her still the mistress of the "Indies," and that these were her galleons come to pour the mineral treasures of half a world in her lap. All nations were represented, though the Spanish flag predominated. Wearing this flag there were many fine specimens of naval architecture—especially lines of steamships plying between Cadiz, the West Indies, and South America. A number of the merchant-ships of different nations hoisted their flags in honor of the *Sumter* as she passed; and one Yankee ship—there being three or four of them in the harbor—hoisted hers, as much as to say, "You see we are not afraid to show it."

CHAPTER X

Battling the Don

THE SPANISH OFFICIALS BEGAN TO ANNOY US even before we let go our anchor—a health officer boarding us, and telling us that he should have to quarantine us for three days, unless we could show him a clean bill of health. We told him that our health was clean enough, but that we had no bill to establish the fact, whereupon he went on shore to consult his superiors. I sent by him, the following communication to the United States Consul, whose name was Eggleston:—

> CONFEDERATE STATES STEAMER SUMTER,
> CADIZ, January 4, 1862.
>
> SIR:—I have the honor to inform you, that I have on board this ship forty-three prisoners of war—late the crews of a ship, a bark, and a schooner, property of citizens of the United States, burned by me on the high seas. These men having elected to be discharged on *parole*, I am ready to deliver them to you.

Mr. Eggleston, proving to be quite a diplomat, refused to give me my official title, in replying to my note; and of course, I could have no further communication with him. In the afternoon, the Health Officer again came off to inform us that the important questions, of the cleanness of our health, and the discharge of our prisoners, had been telegraphed to Madrid, and that we might soon expect a reply from her Majesty, the Queen.

The next morning I received, by the hands of the same officer, a peremptory order, from the Military Governor, to proceed to sea, within twenty-four hours! I sat down and wrote him the following reply:—

> CONFEDERATE STATES STEAMER SUMTER,
> CADIZ, January 5, 1862.
>
> SIR:—I have had the honor to receive through the health officer of the port, an order purporting to come from the Government of Spain, directing me to proceed to sea within twenty-four hours. I am greatly surprised at this unfriendly order. Although my Government has not yet been formally recognized by Spain, as a *de jure* government, it has been declared to be possessed of the rights of a belligerent, in the war in which it is engaged, and it is the duty of Spain to extend to my ship the same hospitality that she would extend to a ship of war of the opposite belligerent. It can make no difference that one of the belligerents is a *de jure* nation, and the other a *de facto* nation, since it is only war rights, or such as pertain to belligerents, which we are discussing.
>
> I am aware of the rule adopted by Spain, in common with the other great powers, prohibiting belligerents from bringing their prizes into her ports, but this rule I have not violated. I have entered the harbor of Cadiz, with my single ship, and I demand only the hospitality to which I am entitled by the laws of nations—the Confederate States being one of the *de facto* nations of the earth, by Spain's own acknowledgment, as before stated.
>
> I am sorry to be obliged to add, that my ship is in a crippled condition. She is damaged in her hull, is leaking badly, is unseaworthy, and will require to be docked and repaired before it will be possible for her to proceed to sea. I am therefore constrained, by the force of circumstances, most respectfully to decline obedience to the order which I have received, until the necessary repairs can be made.
>
> Further:—I have on board forty-three prisoners, confined within a small space greatly to their discomfort, and simple humanity would seem to dictate, that I should be permitted to hand them over to the care of their Consul on shore, without unnecessary delay.

Again, the telegraphic wires were put in operation, and my reply to the Military Commandant went up to Madrid. In a few hours a reply came down, giving me permission to land my prisoners, and to remain a sufficient time to put the necessary repairs upon my ship. In the meantime the most offensive espionage was exercised toward me. A guard-boat was anchored near by, which overhauled all shore-boats which passed between the *Sumter* and the shore; and on the evening of my arrival, a Spanish frigate came down from the dock-yard, and anchored near my ship. There are no private docks in Cadiz, and I was obliged, therefore, to go into one of the government docks for repairs. Charles Dickens has given us an amusing account of an English Circumlocution Office, but English red tape dwindles into insignificance by the side of Spanish red tape. Getting into the hands of the Spanish officials was like getting into a Chancery suit. I thought I should never get out. The Military Commandant referred me to the Captain of the Port, and the Captain of the Port referred me back to the Military Commandant; until finally they both together referred me to the Admiral of the Dock-Yard; to whom I should have been referred at first. In the meantime, engineers and sub-engineers, and other officials whose titles it were tedious to enumerate, came on board, to measure the length of the ship and the breadth of the ship, calculate her tonnage, inspect her boilers, examine into the quantity of water she made during the twenty-four hours, and to determine generally whether we were really in the condition we had represented ourselves to be in, or whether we were deceiving her Majesty and the Minister of the Universal Yankee Nation at Madrid, for some sinister purpose.

The permission came for me, at length, to go into dock, and landing our prisoners, we got up steam and proceeded to Carraca, where the docks lie, distant some eight miles east of the city. The Navy Yard at Carraca is an important building-yard; it lies at the head of the bay of Cadiz, and is approached by a long, narrow, and somewhat tortuous channel, well buoyed. The waters are deep and still, and the Yard is, in every other respect, admirably situated. It reminded us much, in its general aspect and surroundings, of the Norfolk Navy Yard, in Virginia. We were not long delayed in entering the dock. A ship which had occupied the basin assigned to us—there were several of them—was just being let out as we approached, and in the course of an hour afterward, the *Sumter* was high and dry; so rapidly had the operation been performed. We examined her bottom with much curiosity, after the thumping she had had on the bar at Maranham, and were gratified to find that she had received no material damage. A small portion of her copper had been rubbed off, and one of her planks indented, rather than fractured. She was as sound and tight as a bottle, in every part of her, except in her propeller sleeve. It was here where the leak had been, as we had conjectured.

To the delight both of the Spanish officials, who were exceedingly anxious to get rid of us, lest we should compromise them in some way with the Great Republic, of whom they seemed to be exceedingly afraid, and ourselves, we found that the needed repairs would be slight. The boilers were a good deal out of condition, it is true, but as they were capable of bearing a low pressure of steam, sufficient to take us to sea, the officials would not listen to my proposals to repair them. I had one or two interviews, whilst I lay here, with the Dock-Admiral, whom I found to be a very different man from the Military Commandant. He was a polite and refined gentleman, expressed much sympathy for our people, and regretted that his orders were such that he could not make my repairs more thorough. He expressed some surprise at the backdown of the Federal Government, in the *Trent* affair, the news of which had just arrived, and said that he had fully reckoned upon our having Great Britain as an ally in the war. "Great Britain seems, herself, to have been of this opinion," said he, "as she has withdrawn all her ships of war from the Mediterranean station, for service on the American coast, and sent ten thousand troops to Canada."

From the moment my ship entered within the precinct of the Spanish Navy Yard, the very d—l seemed to have broken loose among my crew. With rare exceptions, a common sailor has no sense of nationality. He commences his sea-going career at so tender an age, is so constantly at sea, and sails under so many different flags, that he becomes eminently a citizen of the world. Although I had sailed out of a Southern port, I had not half a dozen Southern-born men among the rank and file of my crew. They were mostly foreigners—English and Irish preponderating. I had two or three Yankees on board, who had pretended to be very good Southern men, but who, having failed to reap the rich harvest of prize-money, which they had proposed to themselves, were now about to develop their true characters. Some of my boats' crews had visited the shore on duty, and whilst their boats were lying at the pier waiting for the officers to transact their business, the tempter had come along. Sundry Jack-Tars, emissaries of the *diplomatic* Mr. Eggleston, the Federal Consul, had rolled along down the pier, hitching up their trousers, and replenishing their tobacco quids as they came along. "Cadiz is a nice place," said they to my boats' crews, "with plenty of grog, and lots of fun. We have gotten tired of our ships, and are living at free quarters at the Consul's. Come with us, and let us have a jolly good time together." And they did come, or rather go, for, on one single night, nine of my rascals deserted. This was whilst we were still in dock. Being let out of dock, we dropped down to the city, and being afloat again, we were enabled to prevent a general stampede, by the exercise of firmness and vigilance. I directed an officer to be sent in each boat, whenever one should have occasion to communicate with the shore, armed with a revolver, and with orders to shoot down any one who should attempt to desert. Two or three other sailors slipped away, notwithstanding these precautions, but there the matter ended. Hearing that my deserters were harbored by the United States Consul, I addressed the following letter on the subject to the Governor of the city:—

> CONFEDERATE STATES STEAMER SUMTER,
> CADIZ, January 16, 1862.

SIR:—I have the honor to inform you, that whilst my ship was in dock at Carraca, nine of my seamen deserted, and I am informed that they are sheltered and protected by the United States Consul. I respectfully request that you will cause these men to be delivered up to me; and to disembarrass this demand of any difficulty that may seem to attend it, permit me to make the following observations.

1st. In the first place, my Government has been acknowledged as a *de facto* government by Spain, and as such it is entitled to all the rights of a belligerent, in its war with the Government of the United States.

2d. All the rights and privileges, therefore, which would attach to the flag of the United States, should one of the ships of that country enter this harbor, equally attach to the flag of the Confederate States, mere ceremonial excepted.

3d. It has been and is the uniform custom of all nations to arrest, upon request, and to hand over to their proper officers, deserters from ships of war, and this without stopping to inquire into the nationality of the deserter.

4th. If this be the practice in peace, much more necessary does such a practice become in war, since otherwise the operations of war might be tolerated in a neutral territory, as will be seen from my next position.

5th. Without a violation of neutrality, an enemy's consul in a neutral territory cannot be permitted to entice away seamen, from a ship of the opposite belligerent, or to shelter or protect the same: for if he be permitted to do this, then his domicil becomes an enemy's camp in a neutral territory.

6th. With reference to the question in hand, I respectfully submit that the only facts, which your Excellency can take cognizance of, are that these deserters entered the waters of Spain under my flag, and that they formed a part of my crew. The inquiry cannot pass a step beyond, and Spain cannot undertake to decide, as between the United States Consul and myself, to which of us the deserters in question more properly belong. In other words, she has no right to look into any plea set up by a deserter, that he is a citizen of the United States, and not of the Confederate States.

7th. I might, perhaps, admit, that if a Spanish subject, serving under my flag, should escape to the shore, and should satisfy the authorities that he was held by force, either without contract, or in violation of contract, he might be set at liberty, but such is not the present case. The nationality of the deserters not being Spanish, Spain cannot, as I said before, inquire into it. To recapitulate: the case which I present is simply this. Several of the crew serving on board this ship, under voluntary contracts, have deserted, and taken refuge in the Consulate of the United States. To deprive me of the power, with the assistance of the police, to recapture them, would in effect convert the Consulate into a camp, and enable the Consul to exercise the rights of a belligerent in neutral territory. He might cripple me as effectually by this indirect means, as if he were to assault me by means of an armed expedition.

I took precisely what I expected by this remonstrance, that is to say, nothing. I was fighting here, as I had been in so many other places, against odds—the odds being the stationed agents, spies, and pimps of a recognized government. Our Southern movement, in the eyes of Spain, was a mere political revolution, and like all absolute governments, she had no sympathy with revolutionists. It was on this principle that the Czar of Russia had fraternized so warmly with the Federal President.

Another difficulty now awaited the *Sumter*. I had run the blockade of New Orleans, as the reader has seen, with a very slim exchequer; that exchequer was now exhausted, and we had no means with which to purchase coal. I had telegraphed to Mr. Yancey, in London, immediately upon my arrival, for funds, but none, as yet, had reached me, although I had been here two weeks. In the meantime, the authorities, under the perpetual goading of the United States Chargé in Madrid, Mr. Perry, and of Mr. Consul Eggleston, were becoming very restive, and were constantly sending me invitations to go to sea. Before I had turned out on the morning of the 17th of January, an aide-de-camp of the Governor came on board, to bring me a peremptory order from his chief, to depart *within six hours*. I went on shore, for the first time, to have an official interview with the blockhead. I found him, contrary to all Spanish rule, a large, thick-set, bull-necked fellow, with whom, I saw at the first glance, it would be of but little use to reason. I endeavored to make him understand the nature of the case; how it was that a steamer could no more go to sea without fuel, than a sailing-ship without a mast; but he was inexorable. He was, in short, one of those dunder-headed military men, who never look, or care to look, beyond the orders of their superiors. The most that he would undertake to do, was to telegraph to Madrid my statement, that I was out of fuel, but expected momentarily to be supplied with funds to purchase it. He added, however, "but if no reply comes *within the six hours*, you must go to sea." I had retained enough coal on board from my last cruise, to run me around to Gibraltar—a run of a few hours only—and I now resolved to have nothing more to do with Spain, or her surly officials.

I returned on board, without further delay, and gave orders to get up steam, and make all the other necessary preparations for sea. As we were weighing our anchor, an aide-de-camp of the Governor came off in great haste to say, that his Excellency had heard from Madrid in reply to his telegram, and that her Majesty had graciously given me permission to remain another twenty-four hours; but that at the end of that time I must depart without fail. The aide-de-camp added that his Excellency, seeing that we were getting up steam, had sent him off to communicate the intelligence to me verbally, in advance of the official communication of it by letter, which he was preparing. I directed the aide to say to his chief that he needn't bother himself with the preparation of any letter, as I should not avail myself of her Majesty's gracious permission—she having been a little too ungracious in meting out the hours to me. He departed, and we got under way. As we passed abreast of the Government House, a boat shoved off in a great hurry, and came pulling out to us, with a man standing up in the bow, shaking a letter at us with great vehemence. It was the letter the aide-de-camp had spoken of. We paid no attention whatever to the signal, and the boat finding, after some vigorous pulling, that she could not overtake us, turned back. In half an hour afterward, we were outside the Cadiz bar, and had discharged the pilot.

This was the second Spanish experiment we had made in the *Sumter*. I never afterward troubled her Majesty, either in her home ports, or those of any of her colonies. I had learned by experience that all the weak powers were timid, and henceforth, I rarely entered any but an English or a French port. We should have had, during all this controversy, a Commissioner at the Court of Madrid, one having been dispatched thither at the same time that Mr. Yancey was sent to London, and Mr. Mann to Brussels, but if there was one there, I did not receive a line from him. The Federal Chargé seemed to have had it all his own way. There is no proposition of international law clearer, than that a disabled belligerent cruiser—and a steamer without coal is disabled—cannot be expelled from a neutral port, and yet the *Sumter* was, in fact, expelled from Cadiz. As remarked some pages back, the Demos, and the Carpet-bagger will revenge us in good time.

We did enjoy some good things in the harbor of Cadiz, however. One was a superb dinner, given us at the principal hotel by an English admirer, and another was the market. The latter is unexcelled in any part of the world. Fine beef and mutton from Andalusia, fish from the sea, and fruits and wines from all parts of Spain, were present in profusion. Although we were in midwinter, there were a variety of vegetables, and luscious oranges and bananas that had ripened in the open air. . .

The afternoon was bright and beautiful as the *Sumter*, emerging from the harbor of Cadiz, felt once more the familiar heave of the sea. There was no sail in sight over the vast expanse of waters, except a few small coasting-craft, and yet what fleets had floated on the bosom of these romantic waters! The names of Nelson, Collingwood, Jervis, and others, came thronging upon the memory. Cape St. Vincent and Trafalgar were both in the vicinity. The sun, as he approached his setting, was lighting up a scene of beauty, peace, and tranquillity, and it was difficult to conjure those other scenes of the storm, and the flying ships, and the belching cannon, so inseparably connected with those great names.

It was too late to attempt the run to Gibraltar that night, with the hope of arriving at a reasonable hour, and so we "held on," in nautical phrase, to the light—that beautiful red flash which I have before described—until midnight, when we gave the ship her steam, and turned her head in the direction of the famous Strait, or Gut, as the sailors sometimes less euphoniously call it. The weather, in the meantime, had changed, the wind had died entirely away, and the sea was calm, but rifts of cloud were passing over the moon, indicating an upper current in the higher atmosphere, that might portend storm or rain on the morrow. We steamed along the bold Spanish coast, at a distance of only a few miles, and entered the Strait before daylight, passing the Tarifa light at about five A.M.

The Pillars of Hercules, that for so many centuries bounded the voyages of the ancient mariners, rose abruptly and majestically on either hand of us, softened and beautified by the moonlight. We had the Strait all to ourselves, there being no sail visible. The Genius of the ancient time seemed to hover over the scene, so solemn and mysterious did everything appear. But no! the Genius of the ancient time could not be there, for the quiet waters were broken by the prow of the *steamship,* from a hemisphere of which the Genius had not conceived. . . .

We made the light at Gibraltar just as the day was dawning, and, hurried on by the current, moved rapidly up the Strait. Several sail that were coming down the Mediterranean became plainly visible from the deck as the twilight developed into day. We could not think of running into Gibraltar before overhauling these sails; we might, perchance, find an enemy among them, and so we altered our course and gave chase; as so many barks, ancient and modern, heathen, Christian, and Moor had done before us, in this famous old Strait. The telescope soon revealed the secret of the nationality of two of the sails; they being, as plainly as symmetry and beauty of outline, the taper and grace of spars, and whiteness of canvas—produced upon our own cottonfields—could speak, American. To these, therefore, we directed our attention. It was a couple of hours before we came up with the first of these ships. She was standing over toward the African side of the Strait, though still distant from the land, some six or seven miles. We hoisted our own colors, and fired the usual gun.

She hauled up her courses, and backed her maintopsail at once, and in a moment more, we could see the brightest of stars and stripes fluttering in the breeze, and glittering, in very joyousness, as it were, in the rays of the morning's sun; for the captain of the prize had evidently treated himself to a new ensign. The cat ran close enough to parley with the mouse, before she put her paw upon it. The bark, for such the prize was, proved to be the *Neapolitan*, of Kingston, Mass., from Messina, in the island of Sicily, bound for Boston, with a cargo of fruit, dried and fresh, and *fifty tons of sulphur*. She had been freshly painted, with that old robber, the bald eagle, surrounded by stars, gilded on her stern; her decks looked white and sweet after the morning's ablution which she had just undergone; her sails were well hoisted, and her sheets well home; in short, she was a picture to look at, and the cat looked at her, as a cat only can look at a sleek mouse. And then only to think, that the sly little mouse, looking so pretty and so innocent, should have so much of that villainous material called sulphur in its little pouch!

The master stated in his deposition, that the entire cargo belonged to the British house of Baring Bros., it being consigned to an agent of theirs in Boston. The object of so wording the deposition was, of course, to save the cargo as neutral property, but as I happened to know that the Boston house of the Barings, instead of being an agent merely, was a partner of the London house, the master took nothing by his deposition. Besides, if there had been no doubt as to the British ownership, sulphur going to an enemy's country is contraband of war; and in this case the contraband of war was not only condemnable of itself, but it tainted all the rest of the cargo, which belonged to the same owner. The master, who was as strongly marked in his Puritan nationality, as the Israelite is in the seed of Abraham, feeling himself securely intrenched behind the Baring Bros., was a little surprised when I told him that I should burn his ship, and began to expostulate. But I had no time for parley, for there was another ship demanding my attention; and so, transferring the prisoners from the doomed ship to the *Sumter*, as speedily as possible, the *Neapolitan* was burned; burned in the sight of Europe and Africa, with the turbaned Moor looking upon the conflagration, on one hand, and the garrison of Gibraltar and the Spaniard on the other. Previously to applying the torch, we took a small liberty with some of the excellent fruit of the Barings, transferring a number of drums of figs, boxes of raisins and oranges, to the cooks and stewards of the different messes.

[Since the character of the cargo was in dispute—enemy or neutral—it was illegal to destroy this vessel. She should have been either released or sent in to a Confederate port for adjudication by a prize court.]

We now steamed off in pursuit of the other sail. This second sail proved also to be American, as we had supposed. She was the bark *Investigator,* of Searsport, Maine, from one of the small ports of Spain, bound for Newport, in Wales, with a cargo of iron ore. The cargo being properly documented as British property, we could not destroy her, but were compelled to release her under ransom bond. [As with the *Montmorency* mentioned on page 141, this bond provided that the ransom ($11,250 *in Confederate money!*) should be paid to the "President of the Confederate States, within thirty days after the close of the present war between the United States and the Confederate States of America." Consequently the contract became void before the payment fell due.] The capturing and disposing of these two ships had occupied us several hours, during which the in-draught of the Strait had set us some miles to the eastward of the Rock. We now, at half-past two P. M., turned our head in the direction of Gibraltar, and gave the ship all steam. By this time the portent of last night had been verified, and we had an overcast sky, with a strong northwester blowing in our teeth. With the wind and current both ahead, we had quite a struggle to gain the anchorage.

It was half-past seven P. M., or some time after dark, that we finally passed under the shadow of the historical rock, with the brilliant light on Europa Point throwing its beams upon our deck; and it was a few minutes past eight o'clock, or evening gun-fire, when we ran up to the man-of-war anchorage, and came to. We had no occasion to tell the people of Gibraltar who we were. They were familiar with our Cadiz troubles, and had been expecting us for some days; and accordingly, when the signal-man on the top of the Rock announced the appearance of a Confederate States' steamer in the Strait, every one knew that it was the *Sumter*. And when, a short time afterward, it was announced that the little steamer was in chase of a Yankee, the excitement became intense.

Half the town rushed to Europa Point and the signal-station, to watch the chase and the capture; and when the flames were seen ascending from the doomed *Neapolitan,* sketch-books and pencils were produced, and all the artists in the crowd went busily to work to sketch the extraordinary spectacle; extraordinary in any age, but still more extraordinary in this. . . .

In a few minutes after anchoring, we were boarded by a boat from the English frigate, which had the guard for the day. The officer made us the usual "tender of service" from the Port Admiral. We sent a boat ourselves to report our arrival on board the health ship, and to inquire if there would be any quarantine; and after a *long* day of excitement and fatigue,—for I had not turned in since I left the Cadiz light, the night before—I sought my berth, and slept soundly, neither dreaming of Moor or Christian, Yankee or Confederate. John spread me the next morning a sumptuous breakfast, and brought me off glowing accounts of the Gibraltar market, filled with all the delicacies both of Spain and Morocco. The prize which we had liberated on ransom-bond, followed us in, and was anchored not far from us. There was another large American ship at anchor.

At an early hour a number of English officers, of the garrison and navy, and citizens called on board to see us; and at ten o'clock I went on board the frigate whose boat had boarded us the previous night, to return the commanding naval officer's visit. He was not living on board, but at his quarters on shore, whither I proceeded at two P. M. Landing at the Navy Yard, an orderly conducted me thence to his neat little cottage, perched half way up the rock, and embowered by shade trees, in the most charming little nook possible. I found Captain—now Rear-Admiral—Sir Frederic Warden a very clever specimen of an English naval officer; and we had a pleasant conversation of half an hour together. Having lost one of my anchors, I asked the loan of one from him until I could supply myself in the market. He replied that he had every disposition to oblige me, but that he must first submit the question to the "law officers of the Crown." I said to him playfully, "these 'law officers of the Crown' of yours must be sturdy fellows, for they have some heavy burdens to carry; when I was at Trinidad the Governor put a whole cargo of coal on their shoulders, and now you propose to saddle them with an anchor!" He said pleasantly, in return, "I have not the least doubt of the propriety of your request, but we must walk according to rule, you know." The next morning, bright and early, a boat came alongside, bringing me an anchor.

From Captain Warden's, I proceeded to the residence of the Governor and Military Commander of the Rock, Sir William J. Codrington, K. C. B. His house was in the centre of the town, and I had a very pleasant walk through shaded avenues and streets, thronged with a gayly dressed population, every third man of which was a soldier, to reach it. The same orderly still accompanied me. I was in uniform, and all the sentinels saluted me as I passed; and I may as well mention here, that during the whole of my stay at this military and naval station, my officers and myself received all the honors and courtesies due to our rank. No distinction whatever was drawn, that I am aware of, between the *Sumter,* and any of the enemy's ships of war that visited the station, except in the matter of the national salute. Our flag not being yet recognized, except for belligerent purposes, this honor was withheld. We dined at the officers' messes, and they dined on board our ship; the club and reading-rooms were thrown open to us, and both military and citizens were particular in inviting us to partake of all the festivities that took place during our stay.

My conductor, the orderly, stopped before a large stone mansion on the principal street, where there was a sentinel walking in front of the door, and in a few minutes I was led to a suite of large, airy, well-furnished rooms on the second floor, to await his Excellency. It was Sunday, and he had just returned from church. He entered, however, almost immediately. I had seen him a hundred times, in the portraits of half the English generals I had ever looked upon, so peculiarly was he *English* and *military.* He was a polite gentleman of the old school, though not a very old man, his age being not more than about fifty-five. Governor Codrington was a son of the Admiral of the same name, who, as the commander-in-chief of the combined English, French, and Russian fleets, had gained so signal a victory over the Turkish fleet, in the Mediterranean, in 1827, which resulted in the independence of Greece, and the transfer of Prince Otho of Bavaria to the throne of that country. His rank was that of a lieutenant-general in the British army. I reported my arrival to his Excellency, and stated that my object in visiting Gibraltar was to repair, and coal my ship, and that I should expect to have the same facilities extended to me, that he would extend to an enemy's cruiser under similar circumstances. He assented at once to my proposition, saying that her Majesty was exceedingly anxious to preserve a strict neutrality in our unhappy war, without leaning to the one side or the other. "There is one thing, however," continued he, "that I must exact of you during your stay, and that is, that you will not make Gibraltar, a station, from which to watch for the approach of your enemy, and sally out in pursuit of him." I replied, "Certainly not; no belligerent has the right to make this use of the territory of a neutral. Your own distinguished admiralty judge, Sir William Scott, settled this point half a century and more ago, and his decisions are implicitly followed in the American States."

The Governor gave me permission to land my prisoners, and they were paroled and sent on shore the same afternoon. We could do nothing in the way of preparing the *Sumter* for another cruise, until our funds should arrive, and these did not reach us until the 3d of February, when Mr. Mason, who had by this time relieved Mr. Yancey, as our Commissioner at the Court of London, telegraphed me that I could draw on the house of Frazer, Trenholm & Co., of Liverpool, for the sum I needed. In the mean time, we had made ourselves very much at home at Gibraltar, quite an intimacy springing up between the naval and military officers and ourselves; whereas, as far as we could learn, the Yankee officers of the several Federal ships of war, which by this time had arrived, were kept at arm's-length, no other than the customary official courtesies being extended to them. We certainly did not meet any of them at the "club," or other public places. . . .

On the day after my visit to the Governor, Colonel Freemantle, of the Coldstream Guards, the Governor's aide-de-camp and military secretary, came off to call on me on behalf of the Governor, and to read to me a memorandum, which the latter had made of my conversation with him. There were but two points in this memorandum:—"First: It is agreed that the *Sumter* shall have free access to the work-shops and markets, to make necessary repairs and supply herself with necessary articles, contraband of war excepted. Secondly: The *Sumter* shall not make Gibraltar a *station,* from which to sally out from the Strait, for the purposes of war." I assented to the correctness of the conversation as recorded, and there the official portion of the interview ended. I could not but be amused here, as I had been at other places, at the exceeding scrupulousness of the authorities, lest they should compromise themselves in some way with the belligerents.

I found Colonel Freemantle to be an ardent Confederate, expressing himself without any reserve, and lauding in the highest terms our people and cause. He had many questions to ask me, which I took great pleasure in answering, and our interview ended by a very cordial invitation from him to visit, in his company, the curiosities of the Rock. This is the same Colonel Freemantle, who afterward visited our Southern States during the war, and made the acquaintance of some of our principal military men; writing and publishing a very interesting account of his tour. I met him afterward in London, more of a Confederate than ever. Freemantle was not an exception. The army and navy of Great Britain were with us, almost to a man, and many a hearty denunciation have I heard from British military and naval lips, of the coldness and selfishness of the Palmerston-Russell government.

CHAPTER XI

"The Rock"

GIBRALTAR, BEING A STATION FOR SEVERAL steam-lines, was quite a thoroughfare of travel. The mixed character of its resident population, too, was quite curious. All the nations of the earth seemed to have assembled upon the Rock, for the purposes of traffic, and as each nationality preserved its costume and its language, the quay, market-place, streets and shops presented a picture witnessed in few, if in any other towns of the globe. The attractions for traffic were twofold: first, Gibraltar was a free port, and, secondly, there were seven thousand troops stationed there. The consequence was, that Christian, Moor, and Turk, Jew and Gentile, had assembled here from all the four quarters of the earth, bringing with them their respective commodities. The London tailor had his shop alongside that of the Moor or Turk, and if, after having been measured for a coat, to be made of cloth a few days only from a Manchester loom, you desired Moorish slippers, or otto of roses, or Turkish embroidery, you had only to step into the next door.

Even the shopmen and products of the far East were there; a few days of travel only sufficing to bring from India, China, and Japan, the turbaned and sandalled Hindoo, the close-shaved and long-queued Chinaman, and the small-statured, deep-brown Japanese, with their curious stuffs and wares, wrought with as much ingenuity as taste. The market was indeed a curiosity. Its beef and mutton, both of which are very fine, are brought from the opposite Morocco coast, to and from which small steamers ply regularly. But it is the fruits and vegetables that more especially astonish the beholder. Here the horn of plenty seems literally to have been emptied. The south of Spain, and Morocco, both fine agricultural countries, have one of those genial climates which enables them to produce all the known fruits and vegetables of the earth. Whatever you desire, that you can have, whether it be the apple, the pear, or the cherry of the North, or the orange, the banana, or the date of the South. The Spaniards and Moors are the chief market people.

Nor must we forget the fishermen, with their picturesque boats, rigged with their long, graceful latteen yards and pointed sails, that come in laden with the contributions of the sea from the shores of half a dozen kingdoms. Fleets of these little craft crowd the quay day and night, and there is a perfect Babel of voices in their vicinity, as the chaffering goes on for the disposal of their precious freight, much of it still "alive and kicking." By the way, one of the curiosities of this quay, whilst the *Sumter* lay in Gibraltar, was the frequent proximity of the Confederate and the Federal flag. When landing I often ran my boat into the quay-steps, alongside of a boat from a Federal ship of war; the *Kearsarge* and the *Tuscarora* taking turns in watching my movements—one of them being generally anchored in the Bay of Gibraltar, and the other in the Bay of Algeziras, a Spanish anchorage opposite. No breach of the peace ever occurred; the sailors of the two services seemed rather inclined to fraternize. They would have fought each other like devils outside of the marine league, but the neutral port was a powerful sedative, and made them temporarily friends. They talked, and laughed and smoked, and peeled oranges together, as though there was no war going on. But the sailor is a cosmopolite, as remarked a few pages back, and these boats' crews could probably have been exchanged, without much detriment to each other's flag.

Sunday, January 26th.—A charming, balmy day, after the several days of storm and rain that we have had. At ten A. M., I went on shore to the Catholic church. The military attendance, especially of the rank and file, was very large. I should judge that, at least, two thirds of the troops stationed here are Irish, and there is no distinction, that I can discover, made between creeds. Each soldier attends whatever church he pleases. It is but a few years back, that no officer could serve in the British army without subscribing to the Thirty-Nine Articles—the creed of the "Established Church." After church, I took a stroll "up the Rock," and was astonished to find so much arable soil on its surface. The Rock runs north and south. Its western face is an inclined plane, lying at an angle of about thirty degrees with the sea-level. Ascending gradually from the water, it rises to the height of fifteen hundred feet. From this height, a plummet-line let down from its eastern face would reach the sea without obstruction, so perpendicular is the Rock in this direction. This face is of solid rock.

On the western face, up which I was now walking, is situated near the base, and extending up about half a mile, the town. The town is walled, and after you have passed through a massive gateway in the southern wall, you are in the country. As you approach the Rock from the sea, it matters not from what direction, you get the idea that it is nothing but a barren rock. I now found it diversified with fields, full of clover and fragrant grasses, long, well-shaded avenues, of sufficiently gentle ascent for carriage-drives, beautifully laid-out pleasure-grounds, and well-cultivated gardens. The parade-ground is a level space just outside the southern wall, of sufficient capacity for the manœuvre and review of five thousand men; and rising just south of this is the Alameda, consisting of a series of parterres of flowers, with shade-trees and shrubbery, among which wind a number of serpentine walks. Here seats are arranged for visitors, from which the exercise of the troops in the parade-ground below may be conveniently witnessed. A colossal statue of General Elliot, who defended the Rock in the famous siege that was laid to it in the middle of the last century by the Spaniards, is here erected.

The review of the troops, which takes place, I believe, monthly, is *par excellence,* the grand spectacle of Gibraltar. I had the good fortune to witness one of these reviews, and the spectacle dwells vividly, still, in my imagination. Drill of the soldiers, singly, and in squads, is the chief labor of the garrison. Skilful drill-sergeants, for the most part young, active, intelligent men, having the port and bearing of gentlemen, are constantly at work, morning and afternoon, breaking in the raw material as it arrives, and rendering it fit to be moulded into the common mass. Company officers move their companies, to and fro, unceasingly, lest the men should forget what the drill-sergeant has taught them. Battalion and regimental drills occur less frequently.

These are the labors of the garrison; now comes the pastime, viz., the monthly drill, when the Governor turns out, and inspects the troops. All is agog, on the Rock of Gibraltar, on reveiw days. There is no end to the pipe-claying, and brushing, and burnishing, in the different barracks, on the morning of this day. The officers get out their new uniforms, and horses are groomed with more than ordinary care. The citizens turn out, as well as the military, and all the beauty and fashion of the town are collected on the Alameda. On the occasion of the review which I witnessed, the troops—nearly all young, fine-looking men—presented, indeed, a splendid appearance. All the corps of the British army were there, represented save only the cavalry; and they were moved hither and thither, at will; long lines of them now being tied into what seemed the most inextricable knots, and now untied again, with an ease, grace, and skill, which called forth my constant admiration.

But it was not so much the movements of the military that attracted my attention, as the *tout ensemble* of the crowd. The eye wandered over almost all the nationalities of the earth, in their holiday costumes. The red fez cap of the Greek, the white turban of the Moor and Turk, and the hat of the Christian, all waved in a common sea of male humanity, and, when the eye turned to the female portion of the crowd, there was confusion worse confounded, for the fashions of Paris and London, Athens and Constantinople, the isles and the continents, all were there! What with the waving plumes of the generals, the galloping hither and thither of aides and orderlies, the flashing of the polished barrel of the rifle in the sun, the music of the splendid bands, and the swaying and surging of the civic multitude which I have attempted to describe, the scene was fairly beyond description. A man might dream of it, but could not describe it.

The stream of visitors to the *Sumter* continued for some days after our arrival. Almost every steamer from England brought more or less tourists and curiosity-hunters, and these did us the honor to visit us, and frequently to say kind words of sympathy and encouragement. Among others, the Duke of Beaufort and Sir John Inglis visited us, and examined our ship with much curiosity. The latter, who had earned for himself the title of the "hero of Lucknow," in that most memorable and barbarous of all sieges, was on his way to the Ionian Islands, of which he had recently been appointed Governor.

January 23d.—Weather clear and pleasant. We received a visit from Captain Warden to-day, in return for the visit I had made him upon my arrival. He came off in full uniform, to show us that his visit was meant to be official, as well as personal. Nothing would have pleased the gallant captain better, than to have been able to salute the Confederate States' flag, and welcome our new republic among the family of nations. We discussed a point of international law while he was on board. He desired, he said, to call my attention to the well-known rule that, in case of the meeting of two opposite belligerents in the same neutral port, twenty-four hours must intervene between their departure. I assented readily to this rule. It had been acted upon, I told him, by the Governor of Martinique, when I was in that island—the enemy's sloop *Iroquois* having been compelled to cruise in the offing for fear of its application to her. I remarked, however, that it was useless for us to discuss the rule here, as the enemy's ships had adroitly taken measures to evade it. "How is that?" he inquired. "Why, simply," I replied, "by stationing one of his ships in Gibraltar, and another in Algeziras. If I go to sea from Gibraltar, the Algeziras ship follows me, and if I go to sea from Algeziras, the Gibraltar ship follows me." "True," rejoined the captain, "I did not think of that." "I cannot say," continued I, "that I complain of this. It is one of those chances in war which perhaps nine men in ten would take advantage of; and then these Federal captains cannot afford to be over-scrupulous; they have an angry mob at their heels, shouting, in their fury and ignorance, 'Pirate! pirate!' " . . .

January 30th.—A fine, clear day, with the wind from the eastward. Having received a note last evening, from Colonel Freemantle, informing me that horses would be in readiness for us, this morning, at the Government House, to visit the fortifications, I went on shore the first thing after breakfast, and finding the Colonel in readiness, we mounted, and accompanied by an orderly to take care of our horses, rode at a brisk pace out of the western gate, and commenced our tour of inspection. Arriving at the entrance of the famous "galleries" situated about half-way up the Rock, we dismounted, and dived into the bowels of mother Earth.

The Spaniards have been celebrated above all other people for fortifications. They have left monuments of their patience, diligence, and skill all over the world, wherever they have obtained a foothold. . . .

The famous underground "galleries" of the Rock of Gibraltar, are huge tunnels, blasted and bored, foot by foot, in the living rock, sufficiently wide and deep to admit of the placing, and working of heavy artillery. They are from one third of a mile, to half a mile in length, and there are three tiers of them, rising one above the other; the embrasures or port-holes of which resemble, when viewed from a distance, those of an old-time two-decker. Besides these galleries for the artillery, there have also been excavated in the solid rock, ample magazines, and store and provision rooms, and tanks for the reception of water. These receptacles are kept constantly well supplied with munitions, both *de guerre,* and *de bouche,* so that if the garrison should be driven from the fortifications below, it could retreat to this citadel, close the massive doors behind them, and withstand a siege.

We passed through all the galleries, ascending from one to the other, through a long, rough-hewn stairway—the Colonel frequently stopping, and explaining to me the history of some particular nook or battlement—until we finally emerged into the open air through a port-hole, or doorway at the very top of the Rock, and stood upon a narrow footway or platform, looking down a sheer precipice of fifteen hundred feet, upon the sea breaking in miniature waves at the base of the Rock. There was no rail to guard one from the precipice below, and I could but wonder at the *nonchalance* with which the Colonel stepped out upon this narrow ledge, and walked some yards to get a view of the distant coast of Spain, expecting me to follow him. I did follow him, but I planted my feet very firmly and carefully, feeling all the while some such emptiness in the region of the "bread-basket," as Marryatt describes Peter Simple to have experienced when the first shot whistled past that young gentleman in his first naval engagement.

The object of the Colonel, in this flank movement, was to show me a famous height some distance inland, called the "Queen of Spain's Chair," ...

Descending back through the galleries, to where we had left our horses, we remounted, and following a zigzag path, filled with loose stones, and running occasionally along the edges of precipices, down which we should have been instantly dashed in pieces, if our sure-footed animals had stumbled, we reached the signal-station. On the very apex of the rock, nature seemed to have prepared a little *plateau,* of a few yards square, as if for the very purpose for which it was occupied—that of over-looking the approaches from every direction, to the famous Rock. A neat little box of a house, with a signal-mast and yard, and a small plot of ground, about as large as a pocket-handkerchief, used as a garden, occupied the whole space. Europe, and Africa, the Mediterranean, and the Atlantic were all visible from this eyry. The day was clear, and we could see to great distances. There were ships in the east coming down the Mediterranean, and ships in the west coming through the famous Strait; they all looked like mere specks. Fleets that might shake nations with their thunder, would be here mere cock-boats. The country is mountainous on both sides of the Strait, and these mountains now lay sleeping in the sunshine, covered with a thin, gauzy veil, blue and mysterious, and wearing that air of enchantment which distance always lends to bold scenery.

"We had a fine view of your ship, the other day," said the signal-man to me, "when you were chasing the Yankee. The latter was hereaway, when you set fire to her"—pointing in the direction. "Are there many Yankee ships passing the Rock now?" I inquired. "No. Very few since the war commenced." "It would not pay me, then, to cruise in these seas?" "Scarcely."

As we turned to go to our horses, we were attracted by the appearance of three large apes, that had come out of their lodging-place in the Rock, to sun themselves. These apes are one of the curiosities of the Rock, and many journeys have been made in vain to the signal-station, to see them. The Colonel had never seen them before, himself, and the signal-man congratulated us both on our good fortune. "Those are three old widows," said he, "the only near neighbors I have, and we are very friendly; but as you are strangers, you must not move if you would have a good look at them, or they will run away." . . .

We passed down the mountain-side to the south end of the Rock, where we exchanged salutations with the General and Mrs. Codrington, who had come out to superintend some repairs upon a country house which they had at this end; and reaching the town, I began to congratulate myself that my long and fatiguing visit of inspection was drawing to a close. Not so, however. These Englishmen are a sort of cross between the Centaur and the North American Indian. They can ride you, or walk you to death, whichever you please; and so Freemantle said to me, "Now, Captain, we will just take a little gallop out past the 'neutral ground,' and then I think I will have shown you all the curiosities." The "neutral ground" was about three miles distant, and "a gallop" out and back, would be six miles! Imagine a sailor who had not been on horseback before, for six months; who had been riding for half a day one of those accursed English horses, with their long stride, and swinging trot, throwing a man up, and catching him again, as if he were a trap-ball; who was galled, and sore, and jaded, having such a proposition made to him! It was worse than taking me out on that narrow ledge of rock fifteen hundred feet above the sea, to look at the Queen of Spain's Chair. But I could not retreat. How could an American, who had been talking of his big country, its long rivers, the immense distances traversed by its railroads and steamboats, and the capacity for endurance of its people in the present war, knock under to an Englishman, and a Coldstream Guardsman at that, on this very question of endurance? And so we rode to the "neutral ground."

This is a narrow strip of territory, accurately set off by metes and bounds, on the isthmus that separates the Rock from the Spanish territory. As its name implies, neither party claims jurisdiction over it. On one side are posted the English sentinels, and on the other, the Spanish; and the *all's-well!* of the one mingles strangely, at night, with the *alerta!* of the other. We frequently heard them both on board the *Sumter,* when the night was still. I got back to my ship just in time for a six o'clock dinner, astonished John by drinking an extra glass of sherry, and could hardly walk for a week afterward.

A day or two after my visit to the Rock, I received a visit from a Spanish naval lieutenant, sent over, as he stated, by the Admiral from Algeziras, to remonstrate with me against the burning of the ship *Neapolitan within Spanish jurisdiction.* The reader who has read the description of the burning of that ship, will be as much astonished as I was at this visit. The Spanish Government owns the fortress of Ceuta, on the African shore opposite Gibraltar, and by virtue of this ownership claims, as it would appear, jurisdiction for a marine league at sea, in the neighborhood of the fortress. It was claimed that the *Neapolitan* had been captured within this league. The lieutenant having thus stated his case, I demanded to know on what testimony the Admiral relied, to establish the fact of the burning within the league. He replied that the United States Consul at Gibraltar had made the statement to the Admiral. Here was the "cat out of the bag" again; another United States Consul had turned up, with his intrigues and false statements. The nice little piece of diplomacy had probably been helped on, too, by the commanders of the Federal ships of war, that had made Algeziras a rendezvous, since I had been anchored in the Bay of Gibraltar. When the Spanish officer had done stating his case, I said to him:—"I do not recognize the right of your Admiral to raise any question with me, as to my capture of the *Neapolitan*. The capture of that ship is an accomplished fact, and if any injury has been done thereby to Spain, the Spanish Government can complain of it to the Government of the Confederate States. It has passed beyond the stage, when the Admiral and I could manage it, and has become an affair entirely between our two Governments."

This was all the official answer I had to make, and the lieutenant, whose bearing was that of an intelligent gentleman, assented to the correctness of my position. I then said to him:—"But aside from the official aspect of the case, I desire to show you, that your Admiral has had his credulity played upon by his informant, the Consul, and whatever other parties may have approached him on this subject. They have made false statements to him. It is not only well known to hundreds of citizens of the Rock, who were eye-witnesses of the burning of the *Neapolitan*, that that vessel was burned at a distance of from six to seven miles from the African coast, but I have the testimony of the master of the captured vessel himself, to the same effect." I then sent for my clerk, whom I directed to produce and read the deposition of the master, which, according to custom, we had taken immediately upon effecting the capture. In that deposition, after having been duly sworn, the master had stated that the capture was made about five miles from Europa Point, the southern extremity of the Rock of Gibraltar. The Strait is about fourteen miles wide at this point, which would put the ship, when captured, nine miles from Ceuta! The lieutenant, at the conclusion of the reading, raised both hands, and with an expressive smile, ejaculated, *"Es possible?"* . . .

The *Sumter's* boilers were very much out of condition when she arrived at Gibraltar, and we had hoped, from the fact that

Gibraltar was a touching-point for several lines of steamers, that we should find here, machine and boiler shops sufficiently extensive to enable us to have a new set of boilers made. We were disappointed in this; and so were compelled to patch up the old boilers as best we could, hoping that when our funds should arrive, we might be enabled to coal, and run around to London or Liverpool, where we would find all the facilities we could desire. My funds arrived, as before stated, on the 3d of February, and I at once set about supplying myself with coal. I sent my first lieutenant and paymaster on shore, and afterward my engineer, to purchase it, authorizing them to pay more than the market-price, if it should be necessary. The reader will judge of my surprise when these officers returned, and informed me that they found the market closed against them, and that it was impossible to purchase a pound of coal in any direction!

It has been seen, in the course of these pages, how often I have had occasion to complain of the conduct of the Federal Consuls, and one can scarcely conceive the trouble and annoyance which these well-drilled officials of Mr. Seward gave me. I could not, of course, have complained, if their bearing toward me had been simply that of open enemies. This was to be expected. But they descended to bribery, trickery, and fraud, and to all the other arts of petty intrigue, so unworthy of an honorable enemy. Our Southern people can scarcely conceive how little our non-commercial Southern States were known, in the marts of traffic and trade of the world. Beyond a few of our principal ports, whence our staple of cotton was shipped to Europe, our nomenclature even was unknown to the mass of mere traders. The Yankee Consul and the Yankee shipmaster were everywhere. Yankee ships carried out cargoes of cotton, and Yankee ships brought back the goods which were purchased with the proceeds. All the American trade with Europe was Yankee trade—a ship here and there excepted. Commercial men, everywhere, were thus more or less connected with the enemy; and trade being the breath of their nostrils, it is not wonderful that I found them inimical to me. With rare exceptions, they had no trade to lose with the South, and much to lose with the North; and this was the string played upon by the Federal Consuls. If a neutral merchant showed any inclination to supply the *Sumter* with anything she needed, a runner was forthwith sent round to him by the Federal Consul, to threaten him with the loss of his American—*i. e.* Yankee—trade, unless he desisted.

Such was the game now being played in Gibraltar, to prevent the *Sumter* from coaling. The same Federal Consul, who, as the reader has seen a few pages back, stated in an official letter to the Spanish Admiral, that the *Neapolitan* had been captured within the marine league of the Spanish-African coast, whilst the captain of the same ship had sworn positively that she was distant from it, nine miles, was now bribing and threatening the coal-dealers of Gibraltar, to prevent them from supplying me with coal. Whilst I was pondering my dilemma, I was agreeably surprised, one morning, to receive a visit from an English shipmaster, whose ship had just arrived with some coal on board. He was willing, he said, to supply me, naming his price, which I at once agreed to give him. I congratulated myself that I had at last found an independent Englishman, who had no fear of the loss of Yankee trade, and expressed as much to him. "If there is anything," said he, "of which I am proud, it is just *that thing,* that I am an independent man." It was arranged that I should get up steam, and go alongside of him the next day. In the meantime, however, "a change came o'er the spirit" of the Englishman's dream. He visited the shore. What took place there, we do not know; but the next morning, whilst I was weighing my anchor to go alongside of him, according to agreement, a boat came from the ship of my "independent" friend to say, that I could not have the coal, unless I would pay him double the price agreed upon! He, too, had fallen into the hands of the enemy. The steam was blown off, and the anchor not weighed.

Finding that I could do nothing with the merchants, I had recourse to the Government. There was some coal in the Dock-Yard, and I addressed the following note to my friend, Captain Warden, to see if he would not supply me:—

CONFEDERATE STATES STEAMER SUMTER,
February 10, 1862.

SIR:—I have the honor to inform you, that I have made every effort to procure a supply of coal, without success. The British and other merchants of Gibraltar, instigated I learn by the United States Consul, have entered into the unneutral combination of declining to supply the *Sumter* with coal on any terms. Under these circumstances I trust the Government of her Majesty will find no difficulty in supplying me. By the recent letter of Earl Russell—31st of January, 1862—it is not inconsistent with neutrality, for a belligerent to supply himself with coal in a British port. In other words, this article has been pronounced, like provisions, innoxious; and this being the case, it can make no difference whether it be supplied by the Government or an individual (the Government being reimbursed the expense), and this even though the market were open to me. Much more then may the Government supply me with an innocent article, the market not being open to me. Suppose I had come into port destitute of provisions, and the same illegal combination had shut me out from the market, would the British Government permit my crew to starve? Or suppose I had been a sailing-ship, and had come in dismasted from the effects of a recent gale, and the dock-yard of her Majesty was the only place where I could be refitted, would you deny me a mast? The laws of nations are positive on this last point, and it would be your duty to allow me to refit in the public dock. And if you would not, under the circumstances stated, deny me a mast, on what principle will you deny me coal—the latter being as necessary to a steamer as a mast to a sailing-ship, and both being alike innoxious?

The true criterion is, not whether the Government or an individual may supply the article, but whether the article itself be noxious or innoxious. The Government may not supply me with powder—why? Not because I may have recourse to the market, but because the article itself is interdicted. A case in point occurred when I was in Cadiz recently. My ship was admitted into a Government dock, and there repaired. The reasons were, first, the repairs, themselves, were such as were authorized by the laws of nations; and secondly, there were no private docks in Cadiz. So here, the article is innocent, and there is none in the market—or rather none accessible to me, which is the same thing. Why, then, may not the Government supply me? In conclusion, I respectfully request that you will supply me with 150 tons of coal, for which I will pay the cash; or, if you prefer it, I will deposit the money with an agent, who can have no difficulty, I suppose, in purchasing the same quantity of the material from some of the coal-hulks, and returning it to her Majesty's dock-yard."

This application was telegraphed to the Secretary for Foreign Affairs, in London, and after the lapse of a week—for it took the "law-officers of the Crown" a week, it seems, to decide the question —was denied. On the same day on which I wrote the above letter, I performed the very pleasant duty of paying to the Spanish Consul at Gibraltar, on account of the authorities at Cadiz, the amount of the bill which the dock-yard officers at Caracca had rendered me, for docking my ship. The dock-yard Admiral had behaved very handsomely about it. I was entirely destitute of funds. He docked my ship, with a knowledge of this fact, and was kind enough to say that I might pay at my convenience. I take pleasure in recording this conduct on the part of a Spanish gentleman, who held a high position in the Spanish Navy, as a set-off to the coarse and unfriendly conduct of the Military Governor of Cadiz, of whom I have before spoken.

Failing with the British Government, as I had done with the merchants of Gibraltar, to obtain a supply of coal, I next dispatched my paymaster for Cadiz, with instructions to purchase in that port, and ship the article around to me. A Mr. Tunstall, who had been the United States Consul at Cadiz, before the war, was then in Gibraltar, and at his request, I sent him along with the paymaster. They embarked on board a small French steamer plying between some of the Mediterranean ports, and Cadiz. Tangier, a small Moorish town on the opposite side of the Strait of Gibraltar, lies in the route, and the steamer stopped there for a few hours to land and receive passengers, and to put off, and take on freight. Messrs. Myers and Tunstall, during this delay, went up into the town, to take a walk, and as they were returning, were set upon by a guard of Moorish soldiers, and made prisoners! Upon demanding an explanation, they were informed that they had been arrested upon a requisition of the United States Consul, resident in that town.

By special treaties between the Christian powers, and the Moorish and other non-Christian powers on the borders of the Mediterranean, it is provided that the consuls of the different Christian powers shall have jurisdiction, both civil and criminal, over their respective citizens. It was under such a treaty between the United States and Morocco, that the United States Consul had demanded the arrest of Messrs. Myers and Tunstall, as citizens of the United States, alleging that they had committed high crimes against the said States, on the high seas! The ignorant Moorish officials knew nothing, and cared nothing, about the laws of nations; nor did they puzzle their small brains with what was going on, on the American continent. All they knew was, that one "Christian dog," had demanded other "Christian dogs," as his prisoners, and troops were sent to the Consul, to enable him to make the arrest as a matter of course. . . .

[There were tremendous quantities of ink spilt and hair torn in several countries over this unique incident. When all was said and done, Semmes had no success in obtaining the release of Myers and Tunstall. Briefly the facts were as follows: Myers was of course a commissioned officer of a State whose belligerency was recognized. Tunstall, however, had no legal status other than that of a United States citizen. He had been U. S. Consul at Cadiz until the preceding summer at which time he had been relieved of his position because of alleged infidelity to the Government; he had not been home since. The seizure of the two men was effected by the Consul through his Consulate guard, the members of which were Moors. The act was of course illegal, at least in the case of Myers. However, in view of the treaty of extraterritoriality between the United States and Morocco, the Moorish Government was not at fault in regard to the seizures. Nor could it scarcely be blamed for its ignorance as to the course of action it should take subsequently; the case was highly anomalous especially for a country in the status of Morocco.

[No other neutral interceded. The prisoners were taken from Tangier to Algeciras (Spain) in the U. S. S. *Ino*. There the commanding officer of the U. S. S. *Tuscarora* was the senior U. S. naval officer present. Being under the impression (mistakenly) that the prisoners could not be held on a U. S. ship in a neutral port he sent an order to the captain of the *Ino*. In it he said that the alternatives were to put to sea immediately or set the prisoners free ashore. In view of the impossibility of immediate departure owing to bad weather (the *Ino* being a sailing ship) the despatch in effect ordered the release of the prisoners. The commanding officer of the *Ino* "positively declined" to give the men up and stated that he would put to sea immediately. This he was not able to do, being held up till the next day. Falling in shortly thereafter with a homeward bound merchant vessel he transferred his two charges to her. They were carried to Boston where they were paroled as though prisoners of war.

[The *Ino* was a clipper ship and, just prior to this incident, had crossed from Boston to Cadiz in the remarkable time of twelve days, possibly the fastest transatlantic crossing ever made by a sailing vessel. Her obstinate skipper was none other than the famous clipper ship driver, Josiah P. Cressy, who had been master of the even more famous *Flying Cloud* on each of her two sensational record runs from New York to San Francisco of less than ninety days.]

CHAPTER XII

The Sand is Running Out

THE *SUMTER* WAS NOW BLOCKADED BY THREE ships of the enemy, and it being impossible for me to coal, I resolved to lay her up, and proceed to London, and consult with my Government as to my future course. I might possibly have had coal shipped to me from London, or some other English port, but this would have involved expense and delay, and it was exceedingly doubtful besides, whether I could elude the vigilance of so many blockading ships, in a slow ship, with crippled boilers. In her best days, the *Sumter* had been a very inefficient ship, being always anchored, as it were, in the deep sea, by her propeller, whenever she was out of coal. A fast ship, propelled entirely by sail-power, would have been better.

When I look back now, I am astonished to find what a struggle it cost me to get my own consent to lay up this old ship. As inexplicable as the feeling is, I had really become attached to her, and felt as if I would be parting forever with a valued friend. She had run me safely through two vigilant blockades, had weathered many storms, and rolled me to sleep in many calms. Her cabin was my bed-room and my study, both in one, her quarter-deck was my promenade, and her masts, spars, and sails, my playthings. I had handled her in all kinds of weather, watching her every motion in difficult situations, as a man watches the yielding and cracking ice over which he is making a perilous passage. She had fine qualities as a sea-boat, being as buoyant, active, and dry as a duck, in the heaviest gales, and these are the qualities which a seaman most admires.

And then, there are other chords of feeling touched in the

sailor's heart, at the end of a cruise, besides the parting with his ship. The commander of a ship is more or less in the position of a father of a family. He necessarily forms an attachment for those who have served under him, and especially for such as have developed honorable qualities, and high abilities, and I had a number on board the *Sumter* who had developed both. I only regretted that they had not a wider field for the exercise of their abilities. I had officers serving with me, as lieutenants, who were equal to any naval command, whatever. But, unfortunately for them, our poor, hard-pressed Confederate States had no navy worth speaking of; and owing to the timidity, caution, and fear of neutrals, found it impossible to improvise one. And then, when men have been drenched, and wind-beaten in the same storm, have stood on the deck of the same frail little ship, with only a plank between them and eternity, and watched her battling with the elements, which threaten every moment to overwhelm her, there is a feeling of brotherhood that springs up between them, that it is difficult for a landsman to conceive.

There was another, and if possible, stronger chord which bound us together. In the olden time, when the Christian warrior went forth to battle with the Saracen, for the cross, each knight was the sworn brother of the other. They not only slept in the same tents, endured the same hardships, and encountered the same risks, but their faith bound them together with hooks of steel. Without irreverence be it spoken, we of the Southern States had, too, our faith. . . .

Besides my officers, I had many worthy men among my crew, who had stood by me in every emergency, and who looked forward with sorrowful countenances, to the approaching separation. The reader has been introduced to my Malayan steward, John, on several occasions. John's black, lustrous eyes filled with ill-concealed tears, more than once, during the last days of the *Sumter*, as he smoothed the pillow of my cot with a hand as tender as that of a woman, or handed me the choicest dishes at meals.

I had governed my crew with a rigid hand, never overlooking an offence, but I had, at the same time, always been mindful of justice, and I was gratified to find, both on the part of officers and men, an apparent forgetfulness of the little jars and discords which always grow out of the effort to enforce discipline, it matters not how suavely and justly the effort may be made.

Being more or less cut off from communication with the Navy Department, I deemed it but respectful and proper to consult with our Commissioner in London, Mr. Mason, and to obtain his consent before finally laying up the *Sumter*. Mr. Mason agreed with me entirely in my views, and telegraphed me to this effect on the 7th of April. The next few days were busy days on board the *Sumter*. Upon the capture of Paymaster Myers, I had appointed Lieutenant J. M. Stribling Acting Paymaster, and I now set this officer at work, closing the accounts of the ship and paying off the officers and men. [Because of wholesale desertions at Cadiz and Gibraltar, only 46 enlisted men were left in the ship's company as of March 30.] The officers were formally detached from the command, as fast as paid off, and they embarked for London, on their way to another ship, or to the Confederate States, as circumstances might determine; and the men, with snug little sums in their pockets, were landed, and as is usually the case with sailors, soon dispersed to the four quarters of the globe; each carrying with him the material for yarn-spinning for the balance of his life.

By the 11th of April we had completed all our preparations for turning over the ship to the midshipman who was to have charge of her, and in two or three days afterward, accompanied by Mr. Kell, my first lieutenant, and several other of my officers, I embarked on board the mail-steamer for Southampton. The following is an extract from the last letter that was written to the Secretary of the Navy from on board the *Sumter*:—

"I now have the honor to report to you, that I have discharged and paid off, in full, all the crew, numbering fifty, with the exception of the ten men detailed to remain by the ship, as servants, and to form a boat's crew for the officer left in charge. I have placed Midshipman R. F. Armstrong, assisted by Acting Master's Mate I. T. Hester, in charge of the ship, with provisions and funds for ten or twelve months, and I have directed all the other officers to return to the Confederate States, and report themselves to the Department. I will myself proceed to London, and after conferring with Mr. Mason, make the best of my way home. I trust the Department will see, in what I have done, an anxious desire to advance the best interests of our country, and that it will justify the responsibility, which, in the best exercise of my judgment, I felt it my duty to assume, in the difficult circumstances by which I was surrounded and embarrassed. Enclosed is a copy of my order to

THE SAND IS RUNNING OUT 193

Midshipman Armstrong, and a list of the officers and men left on board the ship."

A brief summary of the services of the *Sumter*, and of what became of her, may not be uninteresting to the reader, who has followed her thus far, in her wanderings. She cruised six months, leaving out the time during which she was blockaded in Gibraltar. She captured seventeen [eighteen] ships, as follows: the *Golden Rocket, Cuba, Machias, Ben. Dunning, Albert Adams, Naiad, Louisa Kilham, West Wind, Abby Bradford, Joseph Maxwell, Joseph Parke, D. Trowbridge, Montmorency, Arcade, Vigilant, Eben Dodge, Neapolitan,* and *Investigator.* It is impossible to estimate the damage done to the enemy's commerce. The property actually destroyed formed a very small proportion of it. [Eleven of the eighteen ships got free. See Appendix B, page 209.] The fact alone of the *Sumter* being upon the seas, during these six months, gave such an alarm to neutral and belligerent shippers, that the enemy's carrying-trade began to be paralyzed, and already his ships were being laid up, or sold under neutral flags—some of these sales being *bona fide,* and others fraudulent. In addition to this, the enemy kept five or six of his best ships of war constantly in pursuit of her, which necessarily weakened his blockade, for which, at this time, he was much pressed for ships. The expense to my Government of running the ship was next to nothing, being only $28,000, or about the price of one of the least valuable of her prizes.

[Thus ends the last direct quotation from Semmes's *Memoirs.*

[Perhaps the most flagrant infraction of international law by any party during the *Sumter's* whole career was the failure of the British authorities to intern the ship and her crew at Gibraltar. Nothing was done even after Semmes turned the vessel over to a midshipman and a few shipkeepers nearly three months after arrival. So the Federal ships had to continue their blockade.

[Six months later, on October 13, 1862, Master's Mate Hester, second in command, murdered Acting Midshipman William Anderson, his commanding officer; the most acceptable reason seems to be that Anderson had caught him stealing. The other Confederates present being unable to handle the situation, Hester was taken into custody by the British authorities ashore. Since no one was left higher than a sergeant of marines, Lieutenant Kell was sent back to the ship to take command. Even so, it was clearly quite impracticable for the Confederates either to take charge of the prisoner or to hold a court martial on him. In spite of all this, the *Sumter* and her crew still were not interned. The British agreed to transport Hester in a man-of-war all the way to the Southern States for trial, provided the Union should agree to let their ship through the blockade. When this vessel reached Bermuda the sought-for permission was refused. About that time some other British officials decided that their country had already rendered far more than the proper amount of assistance in the case; they washed their hands of the whole matter by turning Hester loose in Bermuda!

[The murder had determined the Confederates to get rid of the *Sumter* and she was sold at auction to British owners two months after the tragedy. So, instead of being interned, she hoisted the British merchant flag. Under all the circumstances, the sale was wholly invalid in so far as the *Sumter's* liability to capture was concerned. She was still *at least* as good prize as any Confederate merchantman might be. So the Union ships continued to maintain their watch. More than a year had dragged by since the *Sumter's* arrival. Finally on February 6, 1863, she escaped to sea on a pitch dark night in a howling gale. There was an even smaller chance of sighting and stopping her on this occasion than there had been at St. Pierre, Martinique.

[Now rechristened *Gibraltar,* Semmes's old ship made her way to Liverpool where she was refitted to carry cargo. She slipped once through the Union blockade of the Southern States in July, 1863, and escaped out again in December. The former *Sumter* foundered in the North Sea shortly after the close of the war.]

CHAPTER XIII

The Alabama *and After*

THE STAR OF COMMANDER SEMMES WAS STILL IN the ascendant. He was promoted to captain for his work in the *Sumter*. The remainder of his naval career is another full story and a thrilling one. He sailed from Gibraltar to London in a British merchantman and thence shortly to Nassau in the Bahamas. There he found orders directing him to take command of a new man-of-war, "No. 290," then completing in England for service under the Stars and Bars. And she, of course, was no less than the famous *Alabama*. Her cruise is another volume and only the highlights will be glimpsed in this one.

First, a few words about the *Alabama* before Semmes took her over. It has been mentioned that she was built in England. Under all the circumstances, and on all counts, it was a wholly unneutral act on the part of Great Britain to permit her construction and departure. Without going into the details of this situation, the authorities were finally goaded to action by the U. S. representatives and would have succeeded in preventing the completed ship from getting away if they had acted a few hours earlier than they did. The "290," however, staged a fictitious "trial trip" (on which incidentally she logged the excellent speed of 12.8 knots), and got to sea about one jump ahead of her obstructors.

This extended and extensive negligence on the part of the British government, together with the destruction of U. S. shipping which resulted, gave rise to the famous *"Alabama* Claims." When finally adjudicated in 1872, Great Britain had to pay the then staggering sum of $15,500,000 gold, plus interest, for the United

States ships and cargoes destroyed by the C. S. S. *Alabama, Florida,* and *Shenandoah*. The decision of the tribunal in the case of the *Alabama* was unanimous; the share chargeable to her was over six and a half million. The *Shenandoah* carried on her destruction —among the whalers in the North Pacific—for two months after the end of the war, no word of peace reaching her earlier. The fate of the *Florida* will be mentioned later. Of course the six and a half million, or even the fifteen and a half million, covered a very small part of the damage done to American sea trade. The mere threat of the *Alabama* and her lesser consorts, along with some other concurrent factors, drove America from her lofty maritime position, which she did not regain until the days of World War II.

No more of the *Alabama's* story will be given in reverse order; but it is desirable to appreciate at the start the significance of her operations before reading the next few pages which cover the high spots of her cruise. Captain Semmes, travelling via Liverpool, caught up with his new command in the Azores; there, after manning and fitting out from a supply ship, and shaking down, she commenced operations. Kell was again his executive officer and Freeman his engineer officer. The *Alabama* captured and burned her first prize on September 5, 1862, sixteen days after Semmes took over. This and eight of the next nine ships destroyed were members of the whaling fleet which then operated in the vicinity of the Azores. Two weeks were required for this work, and the whaling business in that part of the ocean was just about finished.

After the whaling fleet game was played out, the *Alabama* stretched across the ocean to and beyond the Grand Banks of Newfoundland and placed herself across the stream of transatlantic traffic. There she not only caught a dozen more ships, all sailing vessels as usual, but created the greatest consternation in Union shipping circles while her operations carried her within two hundred miles of New York City.

Next, dropping down to Fort de France, Martinique, to coal, Semmes had a very eventful 36 hours. On his first evening in port he had on his hands an alcohol-induced near-mutiny, which he quelled effectively. The next morning the powerful U. S. S. *San Jacinto* appeared off the entrance of the harbor prepared to bottle up or destroy the *Alabama*. This is the ship that had been Charles Wilkes's command earlier when he took the Confederate Commissioners Mason and Slidell out of the British merchant steamer *Trent* and almost precipitated a war between the United States and Great Britain. The present blockade might have had thrilling developments. But the very night following the Yankee's arrival was pitch black, and the *Alabama* simply steamed out to sea without either antagonist sighting the other. This was Semmes's second experience of the sort in Martinique waters; it will be remembered that he escaped previously from St. Pierre with the *Sumter* when the *Iroquois* was lying in wait for him. It was the fate of the *San Jacinto* to strike on a reef an hour and a half after the New Year of 1865 was ushered in, and she became a wreck.

There followed for the *Alabama* some wanderings in the Caribbean during which the pickings were lean. The voyage was marked by coaling ship from a tender and overhauling in out-of-the-way islands; Semmes's primary aim at that time was to fall upon a Union transport fleet expected shortly off Galveston, Texas. At the critical moment a squadron of men-of-war was sighted instead. The sighting, late in the day, was mutual. The U. S. S. *Hatteras*, an iron side-wheel gunboat, came down to investigate the stranger and was sunk very expeditiously by the *Alabama* in a short-range night action. The latter ship was the more powerful but accomplished her task so thoroughly that she incurred no damage to herself. For future reference it will interest the reader to bear in mind that the defeated vessel was commanded by Lieutenant Commander Homer C. Blake.

The next ports for the *Alabama* were, successively, Port Royal, Jamaica, where Semmes landed his prisoners; Santo Domingo City, now Ciudad Trujillo, Santo Domingo; the Brazilian island of Fernando de Noronha; and Bahia, Brazil. Almost a ship a week was the average bag in this span of five months. Most of them were burned; a few were ransomed, usually to take care of prisoners or neutral cargo.

At Bahia the *Alabama* came up with the *Georgia,* another Confederate raider. The simultaneous presence in port of two belligerent men-of-war was just about four times as upsetting to the local officials as was the presence of a single ship. The Union authorities were constantly urging the Brazilians to stiffen their enforcement of neutrality regulations. No flare-up occurred this time but it was in this very port of Bahia that a rather unique and famous incident came to pass later out of a somewhat similar situation. The C. S. S. *Florida,* one of the *"Alabama* Claims" sisters, entered the harbor there one day where an "Old Navy" ship, the heavy *Wachusett,* already lay at anchor. The over-zealous Union commander got under way, two nights later, and cut her out—i. e., he placed his ship alongside the *Florida,* captured her unawares, and brought her home. This of course was wholly illegal and a great offense against Brazil. The Washington government apologized profusely and made all due amends possible. The latter were to have included the restoration of the *Florida* to Brazilian authorities in the port of Bahia itself. However, before the return voyage started, the *Florida* sank at her moorings, probably sunk on purpose, of course, though this was never learned.

From Bahia the *Alabama* sailed to Cape Town, South Africa, and neighboring anchorages where she refitted. Semmes was en route to the East Indies. United States shipping had been scared so completely off of the Atlantic that he hoped to find better hunting far from home. Before leaving the South Atlantic he manned, armed and commissioned one of his captures, renamed her fittingly the *Tuscaloosa,* and sent her out to raid on her own. The *Tuscaloosa* captured (and ransomed) only two prizes during her brief career. However, this operation points up the vast possibilities within Semmes's grasp had it been possible to load down the *Alabama* with a huge complement of men and a large number of guns for such a purpose. Only the size of such a supply would have limited the complete chaos into which the *Alabama* could have thrown Northern shipping. Each prize fitted out could in turn fit out prizes of her own until the victims of raiders stemming from the *Alabama* could have snowballed to vast proportions. The requirements for such a project, however, were simply beyond the capacity of the Confederate Navy Department. Not only were officers lacking; native enlisted men had not even been available for the *Alabama* herself.

The East Indies venture netted Semmes only seven ships, but here again this figure is no measure of the effectiveness of his campaign. As soon as his presence even in the same part of the world was known, almost all Union ships holed up in port and dared not venture out for weeks and months. He spent three days at Singapore but made no stop at any other consequential port. The *Alabama* was in the Indian Ocean and the Far East for nearly six months. Thus her fare was only a ship a month instead of a ship

THE ALABAMA AND AFTER

a week, and Semmes was discouraged. He could not know until after the war how much his venture had achieved.

By the time Semmes reached Cape Town again on his way back, the engineering plant of the *Alabama* was wearing out, and he decided to strike out for Europe. Only two ships were captured during the following 78-day passage. News of the general trend of the war was discouraging. Semmes's all-round discouragement may be guessed by the fact that he devotes a scant three pages of his *Memoirs* to all these 78 days. He made port in the English Channel harbor of Cherbourg, France. Very soon, however, the stronger U. S. S. *Kearsarge* appeared and took up her position just outside the 3-mile limit. Semmes shortly afterwards took the *Alabama* out to engage her—June 19, 1864. It is not practicable to consider here either the hypotheses involved in his decision or the several phases of the battle which ensued. Suffice it to say that the *Kearsarge* succeeded in sinking her antagonist while remaining practically unscathed herself. Semmes and others were picked up by an English private yacht and thus escaped capture until the fighting was over, a year later.

Altogether, during her career of almost two years, the *Alabama* captured and burned 52 merchant ships; captured and ransomed 10; captured and sold 1; captured and commissioned 1, which, in turn, captured and ransomed 2; sank one U. S. man-of-war—a total of 67. The *Alabama* examined no less than 232 neutral vessels, at least to the point of identification, which is an indication of the energy and effectiveness with which Semmes carried out his operations. One more interesting and important point should be noted and that is the fact that not a single ship was sent in to a home port for adjudication by a prize court. As a result the ship's company failed to receive a penny of prize money. This was a blow to the foreign enlisted men who undoubtedly cherished this hope of reward as one of the legitimate reasons for shipping in the *Alabama*.

It cannot be repeated too often that the ships actually captured and destroyed comprised only a part of the damage inflicted by the Confederate raiders on enemy commerce.

After the battle with the *Kearsarge,* there was much lionization of Semmes. Next, a well-earned rest; this included a vacation on the Continent, after which he returned to England. And then followed the long trek home: three successive ships from Southampton to St. Thomas, Danish West Indies, thence to Havana, Cuba, and from there to Bagdad, Mexico, at the mouth of the Rio Grande. From Bagdad to Mobile by stagecoach, horseback, carriage, and even rowboat. After only a few days with his family, Semmes set out for Richmond. He finally reached the capital and reported for duty seven months after the loss of the *Alabama.* Three months had elapsed from the time he had left England until he set out from Mobile. It required two months to proceed from Bagdad to Richmond. Two weeks of this were needed to work his way through the Union lines from Mobile to Richmond.

In Richmond Semmes spent a night with Lee. The situation as observed by Semmes on his travels through the Confederacy led him to agree with Lee that the people had given up and that accordingly it was "all over." This was near the end of January, 1865.

Semmes was made a rear admiral and took over command of the James River fleet below Richmond, consisting of three ironclads and five small wooden gunboats. The situation was static in that each side was strong enough to prevent the other from moving on the river in the desired direction. The Confederate fleet had the assistance of shore batteries, and the blockading Union squadron had placed obstructions in the river. Also the actual or potential presence of mines deterred both forces. It was a demoralizing situation for Semmes, as his crews were deserting in large numbers. He could not take them to sea and whip them into shape.

Strangely enough Semmes found his old executive officer, J. M. Kell, in command of one of the ironclads when he took over the flotilla. Failing health, however, soon forced Kell's detachment. Even more strange is the fact that the strongest blockading vessel, the double-turreted monitor *Onondaga,* was commanded by none other than H. C. Blake, the unfortunate commander of the U. S. S. *Hatteras* when she was sunk by the *Alabama.* It was, of course, an exchange of prisoners following his capture and parole that had released Blake for further duty.

Approximately once a week Semmes visited the Secretary of the Navy in Richmond. Time dragged on till early April when the breaking of Lee's Petersburg lines forced the evacuation of Richmond. On very short notice and coming as a startling surprise, Semmes received orders from the Navy Department to blow up his ships, withdraw up the river with his crews, and form the 500 men into a body of troops to be incorporated into Lee's retreating army. In the flurry, however, he had never heard a word from Lee himself. Semmes blew up his ironclads and steamed up the river carrying in the gunboats the crews of all the ships. They were delayed a vital hour by a closed drawbridge and reached Manchester, across the river from Richmond, with no time to spare.

Then follows a unique, anomolous and fascinating story which unfortunately cannot be given here at length. Semmes found Richmond burning, troops and civilian refugees streaming from the city, and then piling up on the Manchester side with no rail or other transportation available. Finally the bridges were burned, the last army units having gotten across the river barely ahead of the approaching Federals. Now, what to do about "joining Lee's army in the field" as ordered? Semmes found a string of railway coaches, filled with civilians, and no engine. He cleared out the occupants, discovered a locomotive, and raised steam in it. Getting under way, Railway Superintendent Semmes found that the first slight grade, only a few hundred yards out, was too much for the engine; so another one was found, fired up, and hooked on. All of this took time but at last they were under steam, Danville bound. An amusing incident came to pass after the train had covered some distance: a number of railroad personnel appeared on the scene and attempted to take over their normal functions. Semmes brushed them aside. A high official of the railroad protested Semmes's actions to Jefferson Davis! The little caravan rolled through Burkesville Junction just an hour and a half before Sheridan got there and tore up the rails. It was that close.

The amphibious force reached Danville and reported for duty to President Davis and Secretary Mallory. The sailors were organized as a brigade of artillery and Semmes was made an acting brigadier general. They stood by at Danville for ten days; shortly after Lee's surrender (April 9), they were ordered to Greensboro, N. C., by General Joseph E. Johnston who was holding out there against Sherman. Semmes's "army" began to melt away rapidly after Appomattox. Even many of the officers deserted; but who can blame them? They simply started home when they knew the fighting was over. The brigade thinned to 250 men. On May 1 the final surrender articles were signed.

Peace!—Or was it? In a group including one of his sons, Semmes found his way home to Mobile after a journey entailing weeks of time. Following the many weary war years he was ready to devote himself once more to his beloved law. Now, when all had surrendered at Greensboro, the job had been done on a mass scale; the Confederate unit commanders as a rule filled in the names of their officers and men on forms already signed by the Federal commissioners. These forms granted immunity from molestation in return for a pledge not to take up arms again. Semmes knew that there were many in the Union who were "out to get him" for his effective sea raids. Accordingly he took pains to fill out his surrender blank quite formally. He inserted his name, Navy *and* Army ranks, etc., then signed his name in the presence of the Federal commissioner who next signed it in his turn. Thus Semmes was fully covered. His immunity could not be clouded later by anyone bringing the accusation that he had slipped through during the rush. But—on December 15 he was arrested! He was taken to Washington, the purpose being to put him on trial for his "war crimes." Try as his enemies would, however, they could discover nothing that would bear up under scrutiny—that would stand up in a court if Semmes were haled before it. Months dragged by with Semmes confined but not too unpleasantly quartered. At last it was concluded that he had been guilty of no reprehensible acts in or out of the war, and he was released on April 7, 1866, without any trial even being held.

It was not until December, 1868, that all civil rights were restored to Semmes, and to many others at the same time. In this interval the requirements were such that his law practice was virtually barred because of his former membership in the Confederate armed forces. He was not allowed to fill a judgeship to which he was elected a month after his release from arrest.

A few months later he was offered the chair of Moral Philosophy and English Literature at Louisiana State Seminary at Alexandria, Louisiana. In fact its president wanted Semmes to take *his* job but the latter graciously declined. He took the professorship offered, the salary being $3,000 a year, and entered upon his duties on New Year's Day, 1867. Thus he took part in the reëstablishment of the institution. It developed into the present Louisiana State University at Baton Rouge. Its head, before the Civil War, had been none other than General Sherman!

Semmes was eminently fitted for his position but there was the unfortunate angle that he was much older than his colleagues. This, combined with his absence from home, made for a lonely existence and undoubtedly had a bearing upon his short tenure of the position. For, after only three months at Alexandria, he went to Memphis to become editor of that city's *Daily Bulletin*. From a complication of circumstances he left this job in six months even though it paid $5,000 a year. He thought then, and more than once thereafter, of returning to the Seminary, but he never went back.

Semmes spent the following year or two lecturing on his war experiences and writing his *Memoirs* from which we have just read many extracts. His talks brought in $1,000 a month for a time. The *Memoirs* were published in 1869, and later were designated by Kaiser Wilhelm II as required reading for his admirals. At long last, commencing about four years after the end of the war, he devoted his time exclusively to the practice of law in Mobile. A son, Oliver, was a partner until called to the bench in 1874.

Appreciative fellow citizens presented Semmes with a home in Mobile, located at 802 Government Street. A widowed daughter lived in Mobile as well as his son Oliver. The father had two other sons and two other daughters also. There were many grandchildren; and there were many visits to the new home by those of the second and third generation who lived in other states. The old gentleman was a quiet, kindly but austere father and grandfather. He was broad in most of his views but missed the correct answer in that he opposed coöperation between whites and blacks. Unlike parts of his *Memoirs,* deleted herein, he was not bitter in either speech or action toward the North or toward any other highly controversial object of passion then current. And he was tolerant in religion, taking no exception when two of his sons became Episcopalians.

Ever since the war, Semmes's health had not been good. His cruises had taken a toll. In his later years he was not sickly but neither was he robust. As the year 1877 opened, he began to suffer from a chronic intestinal condition. He had a summer home at Pointclear, Alabama, on the east side of Mobile Bay. There he was vacationing when his final illness came upon him. After a brief and comparatively painless spell he passed away on August 30, being then nearly 68 years of age.

His body lay in state; flags were flown at half-mast; guns sounded on the day of the funeral. On that day a severe storm raged, a fitting epitaph. In 1900 a monument was erected to his memory at the intersection of Government and Royal Streets. On the day of its dedication, again the storm raged.

The name of Raphael Semmes stands on the pages of history as the first great commerce raider of the days of steam.

APPENDICES

INDEX

APPENDIX A

Chronology, C. S. S. Sumter

April 17, 1861	Steamer *Habana* ordered purchased at New Orleans.
April 18, 1861	Name changed to *Sumter* and Semmes ordered to command.
April 22, 1861	Semmes took command.
June 3, 1861	*Sumter* placed in commission.
June 18, 1861	Left New Orleans, headed down river.
June 19, 1861	Arrived at anchorage between Forts Jackson and St. Philip.
June 21, 1861	Steamed down Mississippi River to the Head of the Passes.
June 30, 1861	Escaped from river via Pass à L'Outre.
July 6, 1861	Arrived Cienfuegos, Cuba.
July 7, 1861	Left Cienfuegos.
July 16, 1861	Arrived St. Anne's, Curaçoa.
July 24, 1861	Left St. Anne's.
July 26, 1861	Arrived Puerto Cabello, Venezuela.
July 27, 1861	Left Puerto Cabello.
July 30, 1861	Arrived Port of Spain, Trinidad.

August 5, 1861	Left Port of Spain.
August 15, 1861	Arrived Cayenne, French Guiana.
August 16, 1861	Left Cayenne.
August 19, 1861	Arrived Paramaribo, Dutch Guiana.
August 30, 1861	Left Paramaribo.
September 6, 1861	Arrived Maranaham, Brazil.
September 15, 1861	Left Maranaham.
November 9, 1861	Arrived Fort de France, Martinique.
November 13, 1861	Left Fort de France and arrived St. Pierre, Martinique.
November 23, 1861	Escaped from St. Pierre.
January 4, 1862	Arrived Cadiz, Spain.
January 17, 1862	Left Cadiz.
January 18, 1862	Arrived Gibraltar.
April 11, 1862	Semmes turned *Sumter* over to a midshipman and skeleton crew.
October 13, 1862	Midshipman Anderson, commanding *Sumter*, murdered by second in command. Lieut. Kell ordered back to ship to take charge.
December 9, 1862	*Sumter* sold to English commercial firm, and name changed to *Gibraltar*.
February 6, 1863	Escaped from Gibraltar; proceeded to Liverpool.
July, 1863	Reached the Confederacy as a blockade runner.
December, 1863	Escaped to sea and returned to England.

(Shortly after the war the former *Sumter* foundered in the North Sea.)

APPENDIX B

Northern Vessels Captured by The C. S. S. Sumter

(none set free)

Ships Burned (7)

Date	Name	Class	Position
July 3, 1861	Golden Rocket	Clipper ship	10 miles WSW Isle of Pines
Sept. 25, "	Joseph Parke	Brigantine	450 miles NE Amazon River
Oct. 27, "	Daniel Trowbridge	Schooner	300 miles E Guadeloupe
Nov. 26, "	Arcade	Schooner	400 miles ExN Virgin Islands
Dec. 3, "	Vigilant	Ship	350 miles ESE Bermuda
Dec. 8, "	Eben Dodge	Bark	500 miles ExS Bermuda
Jan. 18, 1862	Neapolitan	Bark	Straits of Gibraltar

Ships Captured But Not Held Successfully (11)

Date	Name	Class	Position
July 4, 1861	Cuba	Brigantine	30 miles SE Isle of Pines
" 4, "	Machias	"	" " " " " "
" 5, "	Ben Dunning	"	Off Cienfuegos, Cuba
" 5, "	Albert Adams	"	" " "
" 6, "	Naiad	"	" " "
" 6, "	Louisa Kilham	Bark	" " "
" 6, "	West Wind	Bark	
" 25, "	Abby Bradford	Schooner	30 miles off LaGuayra, Venezuela
" 27, "	Joseph Maxwell	Bark	10 miles off Puerto Cabello, Venezuela
Nov. 25, "	Montmorenci	Ship	200 miles NE Guadeloupe
Jan. 18, 1862	Investigator	Bark	Straits of Gibraltar

Seven of these ships were returned to their owners by neutral authorities. As to the other four, the crew of the *Cuba* recaptured her from a prize crew; the *Abby Bradford* was recaptured by a U. S. naval vessel (D.D. Porter's *Powhatan*); the *Montmorenci* and *Investigator* were released on ransom bonds which became void upon the extinction of the Confederacy.

APPENDIX C

Neutral Vessels Overhauled by The C. S. S. Sumter
(all set free)

Date	Name	Class	Nationality	Position
1861				
July 3		Brig	Spanish	Near Isle of Pines
" 8		Brigantine	Spanish	Between Cienfuegos and the Cayman Islands
" 28		Schooner	Venezuelan	Between Puerto Cabello and Tortuga Island
Aug. 7		Brigantine	Dutch	100 miles off British Guiana
" 19	Vulture	Side wheel man-of-war	French	Mouth of Surinam River
Oct. 5	Spartan	Brig	British	400 miles northeast of Cayenne
" 24	Noir Mouché	Brig	French	300 miles east of Martinique
" 25		Ship	Prussian	300 " " " Guadeloupe
" 27		Brigantine	British	300 " " " "
" 30	Una	Brig	Danish	100 " " " "
Nov. 2	Falcon	Brigantine	British	250 " " " "
" 2		Brigantine	British	250 " " " "
" 3		Man-of-war steamer	British	200 " " " "
" 5	Rothsay	Brigantine	British	100 " " " "
" 5	Pauvre Orphelin	Brigantine	French	100 " " " "
" 5	Plover	Ship	British	100 " " " "
" 7	Weymouth	Schooner	British	40 " " " "
" 7		Bark	British	2 miles west of Dominica
" 7	Fleur de Bois	Brig	French	5 " " " "
" 8		Brigantine	British	40 " " " "
" 24		Bark	French	15 " east of Guadeloupe
" 24		Brig	Swedish	15 " " " "
" 25		Hermaphrodite brig	British	200 " northeast of "
" 26		Man-of-war bark	Spanish	400 miles east by north of Virgin Islands

210

APPENDICES

" 26		Brig	Spanish	400 miles east by north of Virgin Islands
" 26		Schooner	British	400 miles east by north of Virgin Islands
Dec. 22		Bark	French	200 miles southwest of Azores
" 28	*Richibucto*	Bark	British	200 miles southeast of Azores
Dec. 30		Bark	Dutch	400 miles west of Gibraltar
" 30		Ship	"	" " " " "
" 30		"	"	" " " " "
" 30		"	"	" " " " "
" 30		"	"	" " " " "
" 30		Bark	British	" " " " "
" 30		"	"	" " " " "
" 30		Brig	"	" " " " "
" 30		"	"	" " " " "
" 30		"	"	" " " " "
" 30		"	"	" " " " "
" 30		"	"	" " " " "
" 30		Ship	French	" " " " "
" 30		Brig	"	" " " " "
" 30		"	Swedish	" " " " "
" 30		Bark	Prussian	" " " " "
" 30		Brig	Hamburg	" " " " "
1862 Jan. 2		"	French	150 miles west of Gibraltar
" 3		"	Spanish	80 " " " "

(In compiling a list such as this one there are necessarily a few cases where it is doubtful whether the vessels should be included or omitted.)

INDEX

(Prepared at the University of North Carolina Press and not read by the author.)

Abby Bradford, captured by the *Sumter*, 64 ff.; captured by the *Powhatan*, 71; mentioned, 82, 193
Abeille, 94
Acheron, protects French neutrality, 130 ff. *passim*
Alabama, Semmes takes command of, 195; career of under Semmes, 196-200; sunk by the *Kearsarge*, 199; mentioned, 40, 178
"*Alabama* Claims," 195-96, 197
Albany, 33
Albert Adams, captured by the *Sumter*, 42-43, 46, 50, 70, 193
Algeziras, 179
Anderson, William, murdered by Hester, 193-94
Arcade, captured and burned by the *Sumter*, 141-42, 193
Armstrong, Richard F., midshipman on the *Sumter*, 19, 192, 193
Asterion, 111
Asteroid. See *Asterion*

Bahia, Brazil, the *Alabama* stops at, 197-98
Barbadoes, 36, 55
Beaufort, Duke of, visits the *Sumter*, 178
Beaufort, W. P., sailmaker on the *Sumter*, 19
Belligerent rights, of the Confederacy, vi, 46, 58, 80, 103-4, 161, 172
Ben. Dunning, captured by the *Sumter*, 42-43, 46, 50, 70, 193
Blake, Lt. Commander Homer C., commands the *Hatteras*, 197, 200
Bocas del Drago, 79
Bram's Point, the *Sumter* anchors at, 90 ff.

Brand, Captain, 17
Brandywine, 4
Brooklyn, blockades the *Sumter*, 15 ff. *passim*; pursues the *Sumter*, 26 ff., 70
Brooks, William P., engineer on the *Sumter*, 19
Bum-boats, 60
Byron, George Gordon, quoted, 77, 106, 157

Cadiz, the *Sumter* stops at, 157 ff.
Cadmus, 82-84, 103
"Cape Flyaway," 153-54
Cape Garupi. See Garupi, Cape
Cape Orange. See Orange, Cape
Cape St. Roque. See St. Roque, Cape
Cape San Antonio. See San Antonio, Cape
Carraca, the *Sumter* stops at, 162 ff.
Castro, President Julián, asks the *Sumter* to join him in a revolution, 61-62
Cayman Islands, 54
Cayenne, the *Sumter* stops at, 88 ff.
Chapman, Robert T., lieutenant on the *Sumter*, 19; description of, 34-35; confers with the governor of Curaçoa, 57-59; mentioned, 11, 14, 48, 49, 122, 123
Cienfuegos, the *Sumter* stops at, 43 ff; mentioned, 41, 42, 70, 72, 73
Coal, as contraband of war, 51 n, 81, 104; Semmes' difficulty in obtaining, 81, 87, 104, 106, 123, 165-66, 184 ff.
Code, between Semmes and Secretary of Navy, 18
Codrington, Sir William J., Semmes visits, 172-73; mentioned, 181
Codrington, Mrs., 181
Commerce, U. S., with Cuba, 51; with South America, 68; with Brazil, 106; effect of *Sumter* upon, 110-11, 118, 120, 193; affected by Civil War, 156; com-

213

pared to commerce of Southern states, 184-85; effect of *Alabama* upon, 195 ff.
Commerce destruction, Semmes champions, 8, 9; and the *Sumter*, 17-18, 36, 110-11, 118, 120, 193; and the *Alabama*, 195 ff.
Condé, Governor Maussion de, promises a supply of coal to the *Sumter*, 121, 123; sends *Acheron* to protect neutrality of France, 130 ff. *passim*
Confederacy, not recognized as *de jure* government, vi, 80, 82, 161, 165, 172; Semmes purchases munitions for, 8-9; foreign sympathy for, 49, 105, 112-13, 119, 125, 155, 163, 174
Confederate Navy. See Navy, Confederate.
Conner, Commodore, 6
Consort, 5
Constellation, Semmes ships on, 4
Consuls, Federal, at Cienfuegos, Cuba, 51; at St. Anne's, Curaçoa, 57; power of abroad, 68, 89, 187 ff; at Puerto Cabello, Venezuela, 68 ff. *passim*; at Cayenne, French Guiana, 89; at Maranham, Brazil, 103; at St. Pierre, Martinique, 123; at Cadiz, 160 ff. *passim*; at Gibraltar, 183 ff. *passim*; role of in seizure of Myers and Tunstall, 187 ff.
Contraband of war, coal as, 51 n, 81, 104; cargo of *Neapolitan* as, 169-70
Cressy, Josiah P., 189
Crew of the *Sumter*, enlistment of, 13; character of, 17; size of, 18-19; health of, 23, 63, 118; keep pets, 60, 84; desertions among, 64, 163-64, 192; Semmes describes daily life of, 85-86, 91, 95, 143; discipline of, 90-91, 151, 191; misdemeanors of, 123-24; nationality of, 163, 176; Semmes' attachment to, 191
Crol, Governor, 58 ff. *passim*
Crusader, pursues the *Sumter*, 95
Cuba, captured by the *Sumter*, 40-41, 70; recaptured by her own crew, 41; mentioned, 46, 50, 52-53, 69, 193
Cuddy, Thomas C., gunner on the *Sumter*, 19
Cummings, Simeon W., engineer on the *Sumter*, 19
Curaçoa Island, the *Sumter* stops at, 56 ff., 70; mentioned, 55
Currents. See Tides and currents.

Daniel Trowbridge, captured by the *Sumter*, 116, 193; burned, 117
Davis, Jefferson, and Semmes, 8; mentioned, 35, 83, 103, 201
Desirade, 140
Dias, Señor Don Mariano, appointed prize agent by Semmes, 50-51; mentioned, 73
Dictionaries, used in sending code messages, 18
Dominica, 139
Duchatel, Captain, commands the *Acheron*, 130 ff. *passim*
Duncan, Major, 17, 20

Eben Dodge, captured and burned by the *Sumter*, 147-48, 193
Eggleston, Ebenezer S., U. S. Consul in Cadiz, 160-61, 163, 166
Electra, 7
Elliot, General, 177
Empire Parish, brings provisions to the *Sumter*, 25
Erie, 4
Europa Point, 170, 171
Evans, General, 35
Evans, William E., lieutenant on the *Sumter*, 19; description of, 35; mentioned, 89, 110
Extraterritoriality, treaty of between U. S. and Morocco, 187-88

Falcon, 118
Fleur de Bois, 119
Flirt, 7
Florida, captured by the *Wachusett*, 197-98; mentioned, 196
Flying Cloud, 189
Food supplies aboard the *Sumter*, fish as, 114, 115; captured from enemy vessels, 116-17, 170
Fort de France, the *Sumter* anchors at, 121 ff. *passim*; mentioned, 196
Fort Jackson. See Jackson, Fort
Fort St. Philip. See St. Philip, Fort
Fort Sumter. See Sumter, Fort
France, relations of with the *Sumter*, 79 ff. *passim*; neutrality of, 121; the *Iroquois* violates neutral waters of, 130 ff. *passim*
Frayles Islands, 76
Frazer, Trenholm & Co., 173

INDEX

Freeman, Miles J., engineer on the *Sumter*, 19; mentioned, 35
Freemantle, Colonel, visits the *Sumter*, 173-74; rides with Semmes, 179-82
Fuel. *See* Coal

Galt, Dr. Francis L., surgeon on the *Sumter*, 19; description of, 35
Garupi, Cape, 98
Georgia, 197
Gibraltar. *See Sumter*
Gibraltar, the *Sumter* arrives at, 168 ff.; the *Sumter's* stay at, 175 ff.
Golden Rocket, pursued and captured by the *Sumter*, 37-38, 70; burned, 38-39; mentioned, 193
Great Britain, relations of with the *Sumter*, 79 ff. *passim;* neutrality of, 82
Great Comet of 1861, 30-31
"Great Constable," 88
Guerin, Mr., visits the *Sumter*, 122; visited by Semmes, 125
Gulf of Paria. *See* Paria, Gulf of
Gwathmey, Lieutenant, 22

Habana. *See Sumter*
Harvey Birch, burned by the Nashville, 154
Hatteras, sunk by the *Alabama*, 197; mentioned, 200
Hester, I. T., murders William Anderson, 193-94; mentioned, 192
Hicks, William A., midshipman on the *Sumter*, 19; letter from Semmes to, 72-73
Hillyar, Captain, visits the *Sumter*, 83-84; mentioned, 103
Holden, Midshipman John F., death of, 15
Holden, W. B., 15
Holland, relations of with the *Sumter*, 79 ff. *passim*
Hollins, Commodore George N., 23
Howell, B., 1st lieutenant of Marines on the *Sumter*, 19; mentioned, 35
Hudgins, Albert G., midshipman on the *Sumter*, 19; letter from Semmes to, 52-53
Huevo Passage, 79-80
Huger, Lieutenant, 22

Inglis, Sir John, visits the *Sumter*, 178

Ino, 188
International law, force of in time of war, v; Semmes' knowledge and observance of, v, vi, 50, 62, 71, 72, 74, 83, 161, 164-65, 167, 173, 179, 186; and neutrals supplying belligerents with coal, 51 n; and the *Sumter-Iroquois* episode, 130 ff. *passim*, 145-46; and belligerent ships in neutral ports, 179, 186; British infraction of at Gibraltar, 193. *See also* Neutrality
Investigator, captured by the *Sumter*, 170, 193
Iroquois, at St. Thomas Island, 128; arrives at Martinique, 129; blockades the *Sumter*, 130 ff.; and international law, 145-46; mentioned, 179
Isle of Pines, 37, 70
Itacolomi, Mount, 98, 99
Ivy, 20

Jackson, 22
Jackson, Fort, 17
Jamaica, 54
Jason, 24
John, steward on the *Sumter*, 114, 115, 117, 128, 171, 191
Johnston, General Joseph E., 201
Joseph Maxwell, captured by the *Sumter*, 71 ff.; mentioned, 80, 193
Joseph Parke, captured and burned by the *Sumter*, 109-10, 193

Kearsarge, sinks the *Alabama*, 199; mentioned, 40, 176
Kell, John McIntosh, lieutenant on the *Sumter*, 19; description of, 33-34; accompanies Semmes to England, 192; mentioned, 193, 200
Keystone State, searches for the *Sumter*, 95; pursues the *Sumter*, 118

Laguayra, 64 ff. *passim*
La Mouche Noire, 115
Lavater and Spurzheim, rules of, 36
Law, Semmes' study of, 3, 7; Semmes' practice of, 33, 202, 203. *See also* International law
Law of Nations. *See* International law
Lee, General Robert E., visited by Semmes, 200
Leeds and Co., 16

Le Pauvre Orphelin, 119
Lexington, 3, 79
Louisa Kilham, captured by the *Sumter*, 44-45, 46, 50, 70, 193

Machias, captured by the *Sumter*, 40-41, 46, 50, 70, 193
McRae, 22
Mallory, Stephen R., Secretary of the Confederate States Navy, 9; Semmes requests funds of, 14; sends sailing orders to the *Sumter*, 17; letter from Semmes to, 69-71; visited by Semmes, 200, 201; mentioned, 13, 21, 22, 23, 36, 73
Manassas, 22
Manassas, battle of, 35
Mann, A. Dudley, 167
Maranham, the *Sumter* stops at, 99 ff.
Marine life, described by Semmes, 75-76, 88
Maroni River, 90
Martinique, the *Sumter* stops at, 119 ff.; mentioned, 145
Mason, James Murray, Semmes secures permission from to "lay up" the *Sumter*, 192; and the *Trent* affair, 196; mentioned, 173
Mecasky, Benjamin P., boatswain on the *Sumter*, 19
Memoirs of Service Afloat, by Semmes, 199, 203
Mercure, 128
Mexican War, Semmes' service in, 4-5, 6-7
Minnesota, blockades the *Sumter*, 16
Mirage. See "Cape Flyaway"
Mississippi River, as anchorage for *Sumter*, 17 ff. *passim*; mentioned, 69, 70, 93
Moise, Judge, 69
Montmorency, captured by the *Sumter*, 140-41; mentioned, 170, 193
Mont Pelée. See Pelée, Mont
Moore, Governor Thomas O., 19
Munitions, Semmes' purchase of for the Confederacy, 8-9; aboard the *Sumter*, 12 ff. *passim*, 31, 59; and fortification of Gibraltar, 180
Myers, Henry, paymaster on the *Sumter*, 19; description of, 35; captured by Moorish soldiers, 187-88, 192; mentioned, 71, 72, 80, 81, 89, 122, 123, 127

Naiad, captured by the *Sumter*, 44-45, 46, 50, 70, 193
Nashville, burns the *Harvey Birch*, 154
Navy, Confederate, commerce destruction as strongest weapon of, 8; weakness of, 191; and James River fleet, 200-1
Navy, U. S., Semmes resigns from, 8; and blockade of Mississippi, 15 ff. *passim*; and blockade of Southern ports, 47
Neapolitan, captured and burned by the *Sumter*, 169-70, 182-83, 185, 193
Neutrality, principles of, vi-vii, 51 n; British, 41, 58, 80, 172 ff.; Spanish, 46 ff., 58, 161 ff. *passim*, 182-83; Dutch, 57 ff., 93; French, 38, 41, 121 ff. *passim*, 128 ff. *passim*; Venezuelan, 66 ff.; Brazilian, 103-4, 197-98; and the *Sumter-Iroquois* episode, 128 ff. *passim*, 145-46; and the "*Alabama* Claims," 195-96. See also International law
New Orleans, as the *Sumter's* home port, 11 ff. *passim*, 69, 70
Newspapers, received aboard the *Sumter*, 63, 84, 94, 95, 118, 154
Niagara, blockades the *Sumter*, 16; pursues the *Sumter*, 95
Norfolk Navy Yard, 13

O'Brien, Matthew, engineer on the *Sumter*, 19
Onondaga, 200
Orange, Cape, 97
Orinoco River, waters of, 84
Oruba Island, 56

Palmer, Captain James S., commands the *Iroquois*, 128 ff. *passim*, 144, 146
Paramaribo, the *Sumter* stops at, 93 ff.
Paria, Gulf of, the *Sumter* enters, 79
Pass à L'Outre, 15, 20 ff. *passim*, 70
Pegram, Captain, commands the *Nashville*, 154
Pei Ho River, 34
Pelée, Mont, 121, 126
Perry, Commodore Oliver Hazard, death of, 79; mentioned, 4
Perry, Horatio J., 166
Pillars of Hercules, 168
Pilots' Association, 20
Pines, Isle of, 37
Pinto, Captain, 102 ff. *passim*
Plover, 119

Poinsett, Semmes receives command of, 4-5
Porpoise, 5
Porter, Lt. David Dixon, commands the *Powhatan*, 23, 118
Port of Spain, the *Sumter* anchors at, 80; departure of the *Sumter* from, 84
Port Orange, 90
Porto, Senhor, 102 ff. *passim*
Powhatan, blockades the *Sumter*, 20 ff. *passim*; captures the *Abby Bradford*, 71; pursues the *Sumter*, 118
Prince Rupert's Bay, 139
Prisoners of war, treatment of aboard the *Sumter*, 37, 40, 123, 144-45, 148; discharged from *Sumter*, 80, 123, 160, 161, 162; discharged from *Alabama*, 197; Myers and Tunstall seized as, 187-88
Puerto Cabello, the *Sumter* stops at, 64 ff.; the *Sumter* leaves, 74

"Queen of Spain's Chair," 180-82

Remize Islands, 88
Richibucto, 154
Richmond, 22
Robinson, William, carpenter on the *Sumter*, 19
Rock, the. *See* Gibraltar
Rothsay, 118
Rousseau, Commodore Lawrence, 11, 25, 69
Roy, Mr., assists Semmes in fitting out the *Sumter*, 13
Ruhl, Eugene, letter from Semmes to, 69

St. Anne, 57 ff. *passim*
St. Philip, Fort, 17
St. Pierre, the *Sumter* coals at, 126 ff.; mentioned, 122, 123, 145
St. Roque, Cape, 36, 55, 106
St. Thomas Island, neutrality of, 128
"Salut" Islands, 89-90
San Antonio, Cape, 36, 70
San Jacinto, blockades the *Alabama*, 196-97
San Joao Island, 98
Scott, General Winfield, 6
Semmes, Oliver, 203
Semmes, Raphael, birth and early life of, 3; naval career of, 3 ff.; studies law, 3, 7; marries Anne Elizabeth Spencer, 4; receives command of the *Poinsett*, 4-5; takes command of the *Somers*, 5-6; and the Mexican War, 5-7; serves as Light-House Inspector, 7-8; becomes a commander in the Confederate Navy, 8; activities of during the Civil War, 8 ff.; takes command of the *Sumter*, 9-10; and the *Sumter*, 11 ff.; fits out the *Sumter* for sailing, 12 ff.; puts to sea in the *Sumter*, 26 ff.; on marine life, 75-76, 88; on tides and currents, 108, 155-56; describes Cadiz, 157-58; "lays up" the *Sumter*, 190 ff.; promoted to captain, 195; takes command of the *Alabama*, 195; writes *Memoirs*, 199, 203; made rear admiral and put in charge of James River fleet, 200 f.; haled into court for "war crimes," 202; becomes professor at Louisiana State Seminary, 202-3; becomes editor of *Daily Bulletin*, 203; illness and death of, 203-4
Seward, Wm. H., U. S. Secretary of State, 57, 103, 184
Shenandoah, 196
Sheridan, General Richard B., 201
Sherman, General William T., 201
Ship, use of term, vii
Ship Island, 24, 30
Shubrick, Rear-Admiral, 79
Shufeldt, Consul, 95
Silver Mountains, 88
Sinclair, Commander Terry, 13
Slidell, John, and the *Trent* affair, 196; mentioned, 19
Smith, W. Breedlove, captain's clerk on the *Sumter*, 19
Somers, Semmes takes command of, 5-6
Spain, excludes Semmes' prizes from her ports, 48-49; neutrality of, 73, 163 ff. *passim*, 182-83
Spanish Main, the *Sumter* sails along, 54 ff.
Spartan, chased by the *Sumter*, 111-13; mentioned, 117
Spencer, Anne Elizabeth, marries Semmes, 4
Spurzheim and Lavater, rules of, 36
Star of the West, crew of the *Sumter* on, 13, 15
Storms. *See* Weather conditions
Stribling, John M., lieutenant on the *Sumter*, 19; description of, 35; pro-

moted to paymaster, 192; mentioned, 20, 21

Sumter, Semmes' description of, 9-10, 11; formerly the *Habana*, 10; fitted out for voyage, 12-13; munitions aboard, 12 ff. *passim*, 31, 59; commissioned, 16; speed of, 16, 28; fuel capacity of, 16-17; and commerce destruction, 17-18, 36, 110-11, 118, 120, 193; officers of, 19, 33 ff., 191; escapes from Pass à L'Outre, 26 ff.; prizes of, 37 ff. *passim*, 43 ff., 46, 65, 70, 71, 109-10, 116-17, 140 ff., 168 ff., 193; *incognito*, 43-44, 61, 92, 111 ff., 119, 140, 141, 143-44, 147; neutral vessels overhauled by, 92-93, 111 ff., 115 ff. *passim*, 154-55, 157; escapes the *Iroquois* at Martinique, 136 ff.; damaged by storm, 149-50; fire aboard, 151; repaired at Cadiz, 162-63; Semmes' love for, 190; Semmes leaves, 192; lost at sea, 194; sold at auction and rechristened *Gibraltar*, 194. *See also* Crew of the Sumter

Sumter, Fort, attack on, 8, 9

Surinam River, 90, 91, 93

Tattnall, Commodore, 34

Tides and currents, affect voyage of Sumter, 76, 87, 107 ff., 155-56. *See also* Weather conditions

Trade. *See* Commerce

Tredegar Iron Works, 8

Trent, 154, 163, 196-97

Trinidad, the Sumter stops at, 79 ff.; Semmes describes coast of, 84

Tunstall, Mr., captured by Moorish soldiers, 187-88

Tuscaloosa, 198

Tuscarora, 176, 188

Una, 117

U. S. Navy. *See* Navy, U. S.

Vigilant, captured and burned by the Sumter, 144, 193; crew of, 144-45

Vulture, and the Sumter, 91-94

Wachusett, captures the *Florida*, 198

Warden, Sir Frederic, visits the Sumter, 179; letter from Semmes to, 185-86; mentioned, 171

Warren, 5

Weather conditions, effects of upon voyage of Sumter, 54 ff., 76 ff., 113-14, 139, 142, 149 ff., and *passim*. *See also* Tides and currents

Welles, Gideon, U. S. Secretary of the Navy, 146

West Wind, captured by the Sumter, 44-45, 46, 50, 70, 193

Wetson, J., 105, 106

Weymouth, 119

Wilkes, Captain Charles, and the *Trent* affair, 196-97

Wilson, Joseph D., midshipman on the Sumter, 19

Yancey, Wm. Lowndes, 165, 167, 173

www.ingramcontent.com/pod-product-compliance
Lightning Source LLC
Chambersburg PA
CBHW021402290426
44108CB00010B/343